**OCTOBER 25th, 1944, 6:44 a.m. . . .**

There on the horizon, twenty-two miles off to the southwest and bearing north, were masts . . . Ensign Zeola and Ensign Tetz were in the wardroom when the alarm sounded.

Seaman Quinn was in the spud locker peeling potatoes. Seaman Heinl had a spoonful of beans poised about two inches from his mouth when the bell began to ring. Lieutenant Pyzdrowski was in his stateroom.

Pysdrowski walked casually out to the catwalk, where he met Zeola and Tetz. The three looked out across the water, and there they saw the tall black tripod masts of the Japanese battleships. Zeola blew out his breath. "Kee-rist," he said, "look at those pagodas . . ."

# THE MEN OF THE GAMBIER BAY

INTRODUCTION BY ADMIRAL THOMAS H. MOORER, USN (RET.)

AVON
PUBLISHERS OF BARD, CAMELOT, DISCUS AND FLARE BOOKS

Grateful acknowledgment is made to Little, Brown and Company for permission to reprint the map drawn by Sam Bryant for *American Caesar* Copyright © 1978 by William Manchester; and to Chappell and Company, Inc., owner of publication & allied rights throughout the world, for permission to use the three lines appearing on p. v taken from the last scene of *Camelot* Copyright © 1960 by Alan Jay Lerner & Frederick Loewe. International copyright secured.



AVON BOOKS
A division of
The Hearst Corporation
959 Eighth Avenue
New York, New York 10019


Published by arrangement with Paul S. Eriksson, Publisher
Library of Congress Catalog Card Number: 79-15792
ISBN: 0-380-55806-8



The Paul S. Ericksson, Publisher edition contains the following Library of Congress Cataloging in Publication Data:

Hoyt, Edwin Palmer.
The Men of the Gambier Bay.
Bibliography: p. 265
Includes index.
1. Gambier Bay (Ship) 2. Philippine Sea, Battles of the, 1944. I. Title.
D774.G23H69 940.54'26

First Avon Printing, August, 1981



Printed in the U.S.A.

10 9 8 7 6 5 4 3 2 1

"Ask ev'ry person if he's heard the story;
And tell it strong and clear if he has not:
That once there was a fleeting wisp of glory . . ."

—*Camelot*

# Contents

# Introduction

They were quite small, and very slow, and lightly armed, with but a limited number of aircraft that crowded their flight decks above and hangar decks below. And the crews who manned them, for the most part, were as new to the business of war as were the ships which had been created at an incredibly rapid rate since the attack on Pearl Harbor.

But the ships, and the crews—both unlikely candidates for glory—met and melded into remarkably effective fighting units in a classic combination of men and machines. These were the "jeep carriers," the "baby flattops" (affectionate names given to the doughty escort carriers—the CVEs), and the men who made them come alive succeeded in re-writing the book on sea-based aviation to launch a new legend in valor.

From a dozen shipyards the little carriers came, to be manned by young Americans with old ideas of doing whatever was necessary to get the job done. And, as the record now clearly shows, from Casablanca to the Carolines, from the Aleutians to the Admiralties, from Tarawa to Tacloban, they did what they came to do. The task was great, the cost was great, and the price was paid in men and ships.

This is the story of how the men of one of those ships, the USS *Gambier Bay* (CVE-73), learned the unfamiliar ways of war in order to accomplish their task and, in learning, came to know too the ultimate pride of service as they fought her, fiercely, to a climax the like of which few have experienced and survived.

For the men of the *Gambier Bay*—and in truth they

*were* the *Gambier Bay*—the story is of their ship, from the building of her hull in the Kaiser shipyard in Vancouver, through the building of her character as a finely-honed crew-and-ship team. Ship, men, airplanes—the story moves across the Pacific, island-by-island, combat-by-combat, toward the final hour of her sinking under the massive firepower of the Japanese Fleet in Leyte Gulf.

As one of those who participated in the events of the Pacific War, I count the exploits of the *Gambier Bay* and her sister ships as indispensable to our final victory, and I count myself privileged to have served with the likes of the navy men of the *Gambier Bay*.

And, as others now read and become aware of the magnificent contribution of such men and such ships, I am certain there will be for them, too, a renewed sense of pride which every American can share, in their men and in their ships, then, now, and in the future.

THOMAS H. MOORER
*Admiral, U.S. Navy (Retired)*

## CHAPTER ONE

# The War

On December 6, 1941, Americans were living their lives as usual, for the most part. To be sure, the war in Europe had brought new tensions. Over a year earlier, President Roosevelt had declared a state of national emergency. Many young men had been called by the draft, and others had enlisted in the service. In the eastern half of the country in particular, most people knew someone who had gone to Canada to enlist and "get in the fight" or someone who was talking about doing so. But on the whole, the concerns of Americans on this day were those of a nation that hoped not to be involved in war.

In Manila, President Manuel Quezon of the Philippine commonwealth government indicated his hope that persons who did not have to remain in that capital city would not. This statement was widely interpreted by the press to mean a call to American civilians to leave the islands. Indeed, many had done so already as tensions grew between the western powers and Japan, but a ship was supposed to be leaving in two days for San Francisco. Hundreds were trying to get aboard her.

Singapore that day was put on a war footing, and all servicemen were called to their duty stations. In Honolulu, columnist James H. Chun of the *Star-Bulletin* wrote that the United States and Japan were just then closer to war than at any time since Commodore Matthew C. Perry had opened the Japanese islands to foreign trade nearly a hundred years before. If only the negotiations in progress in Washington could stave off disaster, said Mr. Chun, the tension would certainly ease.

But most people in Honolulu were more concerned with the expected shortage of Christmas trees for the season, and with the social activities looming in the holidays. The navy contingent had a round of parties coming up. The Honolulu Community Theater had just closed a presentation of *Mr. and Mrs. North* which had been hailed as an enormous success. Rear Adm. Raymond Spruance and his family were busy settling in at their new house at 4586 Aukai Street in the fashionable Kahala district. To be sure, the Pacific had been alive with rumors for weeks and a fleet of B-17 bombers had been dispatched from California to shore up the air defenses of Hawaii and the Pacific Fleet. A message had also come from a British agent in Manila that the Japanese were massing in Indochina and were ready to move in force in the Pacific. But in Los Angeles the big news that Saturday was that the arch-rivals of the south, University of California at Los Angeles and the University of Southern California, had fought all afternoon beneath the sun in the Rose Bowl and emerged with a 7-7 tie. In San Francisco, the big news was that Maxim Litvinov, the new Soviet ambassador to the United States, had just arrived by air from Siberia. The Russians, who had been regarded with deep suspicion since the Bolshevik revolution of 1918, were considered to be heroic fighters for freedom, since Hitler had invaded the USSR six months earlier. In Washington, much of the talk was about America's defense posture. One retired admiral, speaking candidly, said the United States was already involved in war in Europe, which was true. American ships were even then fighting German U-boats, but most Americans did not know this, and President Roosevelt was careful that they did not know how heavily he had committed the nation to a war that most Americans wanted to avoid. Navy Secretary Knox released his annual report on December 6, announcing proudly that the U.S. Navy had never been stronger, with 325 new ships and 2,059 new aircraft delivered. Off in Kansas City, Sen. Harry S. Truman was talking about government waste, not war. In Pittsburgh, newspaper readers were enwrapped in the story of the Mantle Club, supposedly a social club of national scope, which had turned out to be a first-class swindle designed to mulct the public of millions of dollars for uniforms and other "club" regalia. Nineteen indictments were handed down on December 5 in Pittsburgh. From the Middle West came reports of new ways of raising money for defense bonds: bond parties, at which everyone subscribed before they started dancing. In upstate New York, much of the talk was about strikes. The Chevrolet plant in Buffalo was about to be struck, and labor difficulties seemed to be bothering most heavy industry. Down in Georgia, when writer Vereen Bell picked up the newspaper, the big story was from Atlanta, where the Southeast Pipeline Company had just completed a new line running from Chattanooga to Port St. Joe, Florida, that was expected to solve the shortage of natural gas.

Down in Jacksonville, Louise Sherrod was much more interested in a news story from Miami Beach. Pictures of Sgt. William Buckley of the Army Air Corps and his wife Lila Jean were all over the newspapers. Sergeant Buckley and Jean were something like hero and heroine—symbols of the times. The sergeant had wanted desperately to become a pilot, but air corps regulations stipulated that only single men were taken for flight duty. Seeing the sergeant's distress, Lila Jean had divorced him, he had gone to flight school, passed his tests, become an airman, and then was allowed to get married. Then he and Lila Jean had gotten married again. This subject was of more than a little interest to Louise Sherrod, for it had not been so very long before that she had broken with her own aviator.

There were echoes of warlike behavior about. In New York, a crowd downtown watched in horror that day as an Army Air Corps fighter exploded over the city. But even bigger news to many was the inauguration of a Pan American Airways clipper service to Africa. The Gallup poll was not concerned that day with how Americans felt about Germany, Japan, or the possibility of war. The burning issue was the American attitude toward vitamins. And the *New York Times* turned its attention in its lead editorial to the pressing problems of the Hundred Neediest Persons Fund. As the day ended, and Americans retired to their beds, they looked forward to a quiet pre-Christmas Sunday in which they would digest the Sunday newspapers, read the ads for next week's Christmas shopping, and then turn on the radio toward evening to hear Eddie Cantor and Charlie McCarthy and Jack Benny. America was at peace, even if it was an uneasy peace.

Then, as the sun moved across the sky from the east, came the morning of December 7. At seven o'clock the cities and towns of the eastern seaboard began to come awake. When it was seven o'clock in southern Illinois, it was eight o'clock in Jacksonville, and all was well. When it was seven o'clock in San Francisco, it was ten o'clock in Jacksonville, and all was well. When it was seven o'clock in Honolulu, it was noon in Jacksonville, and suddenly all was not well at all.

Lt. Cdr. Richard Ballinger, the thirty-six-year-old duty officer of the Hawaiian Patrol Wing at Pearl Harbor, was taking his morning shower in the Bachelor Officers' Quarters when his assistant came bursting in to announce that one of the wing's seaplanes was attacking an unknown submarine at the entrance to Pearl Harbor. It was no drill: The message had come in the war code, which was not to be used for exercises. Ballinger hastened from the shower and glanced at his wristwatch. It was seven o'clock.

The Hawaiian Patrol Wing had been expecting something of this sort for weeks as rumors flew around Pearl Harbor that the Japanese were up to no good. Ballinger dressed and hurried to a telephone to call the staff operations officer who lived in Honolulu. The operations officer was up and alert. He had just taken a call from the CINCPAC duty officer who told him that a destroyer also reported attacking a submarine at the entrance to Pearl Harbor.

Were there two submarines? Lieutenant Commander Ballinger was ordered to send out the standby patrol squadron, which consisted of six seaplanes. He made the necessary call, and then went to the operations office of the commander-in-chief of the Pacific Fleet for further orders. As he waited inside the building, he heard the engine sounds of many aircraft. The big fleet carrier USS *Enterprise* was at sea with Task Force 8 under Vice Adm. William F. Halsey and was expected back at Pearl on Monday. Lieutenant Commander Ballinger did not look out the window; he assumed that Halsey had sent the planes ahead for some reason.

Then Lieutenant Commander Ballinger heard the unmistakable sound of a plane in a steep dive, and he went outside to look up. He saw many airplanes with bombs suspended from their wings, and, as he watched, one of them released its bombs. The patrol wing squadron was preparing to launch, and these bombs hit the first plane as it was on the ramp ready to roll into the water.

"My God, what is that guy doing?" Ballinger yelled. Just then, the seaplane blew up, and the one behind it was set afire. In seconds, the hangar was ablaze, all six planes were wrecked, and then the fire spread to the next hangar, which housed the wing's reserves. Bombs were dropping fast. Ballinger looked over at Battleship Row and saw battleships listing and the *Arizona* sinking. Until this point he had not been conscious of the character of the airplanes above, but now he saw the Rising Sun fireballs on the wings of a diving plane, and he realized that they were Japanese and that the war indeed had begun.

Ballinger waited no longer at OPS but headed for the wing's hangars and took charge. Then he took a detail of medics to the living quarters in the compound to check on the families of his men.

In a few minutes it was all over. The proud battleships of Battleship Row, symbols of the might of the Pacific Fleet, lay scattered and askew. The *Arizona* had sunk at her mooring, carrying down hundreds of young Americans to a watery death. Hundreds of others had been killed or wounded aboard other ships and on the ground by the surprise Japanese attack.

As the bombs and torpedoes began to explode, and the American military moved into tardy action, the radio waves began to hum across the Pacific. "Pearl Harbor has been bombed by the Japanese," said the message. In minutes radio stations all across America were interrupting broadcasts to bring the dreadful, sobering news to the nation, millions of whom still believed the United States could somehow manage to remain aloof from the war that was ravaging the world. Not all, of course. Not all.

One of those who knew certainly that war was coming was Capt. Hugh H. Goodwin, a Naval Academy graduate with years of service in China and the Philippines during the 1920s. He knew the Japanese, he had studied war plans against them at the Naval War College, and he was not surprised when the news came to Washington that December day. Captain Goodwin was just then preparing to go to Argentina. The Argentine government had asked the United States to help establish a naval war college for the training of cadets. Goodwin was one of two senior officers who had already been assigned to the job. He tried, that December, to get out of it and to get a ship, but there was no hope. He had his job and he had to do it. The best he could achieve was a promise from friends in Washington that after a year they would help him get his ship and get into the Pacific. For now, it was away to Buenos Aires, about as far from the war as one could get.

When the news of the Japanese attack struck Thomasville, Georgia, one young man who heard was Vereen Bell. The son of Georgia Supreme Court Justice R. C. Bell, he was just then basking in the success of his first novel, *Swamp Water*, which had been made into a motion picture, with the premier performance held in Waycross. He was writing for *Outdoor Life* magazine and working on his second novel, which *Collier's* magazine had already agreed to serialize. Already he was rich beyond his earliest dreams and the future was bright. He was a national celebrity; *Life* magazine sent an expedition into the Okefenokee Swamp, and Bell had been their guide. He was even an international celebrity: In London *The Times* Literary Supplement praised *Swamp Water* as the leading American novel of the year. War was the furthest thing from Vereen Bell's mind that December day, until the broadcasts came.

That day, after Sunday dinner, a sixteen-year-old high school boy named Tony Potochniak left the family house in Binghamton, New York, and went over to see Joseph Wychules, his pal. They disappeared into the Wychules' basement, where Joseph had a darkroom, and spent the afternoon developing and printing pictures. Potochniak did not learn about the Japanese attack until they came up from the basement that evening. Next day at school, all the kids were talking about it, and when a lot of them began to say they were going to enlist, Tony Potochniak got the war bug. But it did him no good; he would not be seventeen until June 1942, and his father would not sign the papers to let him enlist even then.

Rannie L. Odum, a boy from southern Illinois, was about as discouraged as one man could get on the morning of December 7, 1941. He had been trying to get into the navy for years. His dream was triggered by the 1933 movie *Hell Divers*, in which Clark Gable played an intrepid naval carrier pilot who was engaged in stirring adventures and got the girl, Jean Harlow, in the end.

From the beginning, however, Rannie's efforts to follow Clark Gable had been dogged by misfortune. His older brother Pete had secured an appointment to the Naval Academy, and his letters from Annapolis were the delight of the younger brother. But Pete washed out after his plebe year, and Rannie didn't even get that far. His first rigorous physical examination revealed the fact that his feet were as flat as a steam iron.

Odum's subsequent experiences are a revelation as to the state of American preparedness for the war. After enrolling in the University of Illinois, he had studied civil engineering and also earned his pilot's license in the Civilian Pilot Training Program at Urbana. Later he was persuaded by a naval aviation recruiting team to apply for training under a new program to become a naval aerological officer. When he arrived in New York, however, he and fifty other young men were told the program had been canceled for lack of funds. They could go home or stay on without pay. The U.S. Weather Bureau had been asked to take them as temporary employees, but this had to be fought through the bureaucracy, and would take time.

What to do? The decision was not too difficult for Rannie Odum and some of the others. They had spent their last cash, and did not have the fare home. They stayed. The civilians lent them money for meals, and they stayed without registering (or paying) in a university dormitory.

Early in December, Odum and five others in the program pooled their cash—$26—and bought a 1926 Chevrolet sedan. They were on a tour of New England when they pulled into a Vermont crossroads store around noon on December 7. They were eating lunch there when the news was announced on the radio that the Japanese had bombed Pearl Harbor. The middle-aged lady behind the counter looked sadly at the six young men. "Boys," she said, "our country is caught up in another terrible foreign war. Thousands of young men will be hurt and killed."

They all sat silent, listening to the radio. Then one of Odum's friends piped up: "Where is Pearl Harbor?"

Rannie Odum completed the aerological course a month after the Pearl Harbor attack and went home to Illinois to wait for orders. Finally they came: Take another navy physical examination. He was flunked by two navy doctors, but when he told his story to their boss, a commander, that doctor, who knew the ropes, wrote on the examination form: "Feet: first degree flat, not disqualifying." It was an enormous lie by naval standards, but at the moment entirely satisfactory to all concerned. Ens. R. L. Odum USNR AV(S) #131255 was in the navy and was ordered to the U.S. Naval Air Station at Miami.

When the devastating attack struck Pearl Harbor, Aviation Cadet William Roger McClendon was at Corpus Christi Naval Air Station, struggling with the intricacies of aerial navigation, elementary meteorology, aeronautical science, and the art of keeping an airplane off the ground except when one wanted to get there. He had left his studies at North Texas State University during his senior year to enter pilot training. On Saturday afternoon, Cadet McClendon had been downtown in Corpus Christi, ordering a new suit at one of the men's clothing stores. Then came Sunday and the news of the Japanese attack at Pearl Harbor. On Monday, Cadet McClendon canceled the order for his new suit. He wouldn't be needing it right away.

In Jacksonville, Florida, Louise Sherrod heard the news of the bombing when she idly switched on the radio. She was at home, and bored, because a few months earlier she had broken off a romance with Ens. Henry Burt Bassett, USNR. Restlessly, she moved around the house, trying to get her thoughts together. She waited for more information about the bombings, but there was no information. The cloak of secrecy had been brought down to mask the terrible extent of the damage, which had immobilized the American battleship fleet. Louise Sherrod decided to go to the movies to take her mind off the terrible news. Halfway through the show, the picture was interrupted by an announcement: "All service men report at once to your stations." When fully half the audience stood up, Louise Sherrod suddenly realized that the bombing of Pearl Harbor had put an end to a period of her life. She thought of Ens. Henry Burt Bassett, to whom she had not written once since their quarrel. How could a girl sacrifice her pride, she had said. But on Pearl Harbor day pride no longer mattered. She went home and wrote Burt a postcard which said, "I still love you." By return mail he wrote, asking her to marry him.

On the afternoon of December 7, 1941, AM1c Walter Flanders and his wife Mae decided to go to the Gator Bowl at Jacksonville to watch a football game. Flanders was an "airdale," a trained flight deck plane handler who had learned his specialty aboard the old carrier *Saratoga*. He was stationed at the naval station at Jacksonville, and the air station football team that day was playing the Norfolk Naval Air Station team. Midway in the game the announcer on the public address system broke into the play to report the bombing of Pearl Harbor. Flanders sat stunned for a moment, then the vision of Battleship Row at Pearl Harbor came into his mind. He turned to his wife. "Mae, I think we'd better get home. The base will be calling." She nodded. They left then, and went home to await the word. The war had come to AM1c Flanders.

In Manila, Adm. "Tommy" Hart had the word about the bombing within minutes after the occurrence. He knew then that his position was hopeless. The largest ship attached to the Asiatic Fleet was a cruiser. The single carrier, USS *Langley,* was virtually useless as a fighting ship, outmoded and slow, and more useful as a plane ferry than anything else. Hart and General MacArthur both knew that the U.S. Navy had nothing in Far Eastern waters capable of stopping the Japanese. As for slowing them even, the single hope was the submarine force, and the submarines were mostly the old S-boat class, again outmoded and short of range. The Asiatic Fleet, like all the American defenses, was crippled from the outset by all those years of congressional neglect. No one even knew at this point the most disastrous failure of all: Because Congress would not countenance "waste," the American naval forces were not allowed to fire live torpedoes in practice. Thus, no one knew that the American torpedoes were next to useless, for they ran erratically, and their warheads often failed to explode because of a faulty firing mechanism. In the Philippine campaign to come, American submarine commanders would fire and fire again at certain targets, and nothing would happen. At least this ignominy was concealed from the American fighters in the beginning. What they did not know would not hurt them, but it would also teach some valuable lessons for the future.

Admiral Hart decided under the circumstances, with the Japanese beginning to land on Luzon Island and large naval forces offshore, to dispatch the major elements of his fleet to the south to fight again, where it might count.

Seaman Hugh Bell was sound asleep in his bunk aboard the oiler USS *Trinity* in Manila Bay when the alarm sounded at 0430. On December 7, Japan had declared war on the United States, and he was told: Man your battle station.

All that night in the blackness Bell stood at his station at the five-inch gun, and nothing happened. The first air raid alarm sounded at 1220. All hands manned their guns, watching the planes that circled above them. Then came the all clear. They were U.S. Army planes. Nothing more of excitement happened. At 1600, the *Trinity* got under way; she was sent to sea with the old carrier *Langley* and a force that included the oiler *Pecos* and two destroyers. At 1800, the ship was blacked out, and they traveled all night through the darkness. At dawn they were alert again; the call to General Quarters came at 0845. Someone thought he had sighted a submarine. It was a false alarm. That day the cruisers *Huston* and *Boise* joined up. Bell did not know it, but he was part of Task Force 5, commanded by Adm. William A. Glassford, and on Admiral Hart's orders, the force was heading for Balikpapan in the Dutch East Indies, which the allies planned to use as a base for a last-ditch stand against the Japanese naval units moving south.

The days went by. The *Houston*'s scout planes droned lazily over the task force, watching. On December 10, at 1430, the *Langley* opened up on the water with every gun she could bring to bear; someone thought he had seen a submarine again. Nothing appeared. All was serene, and they steamed southward, until 1120 on December 12, when the klaxons and the speaker announced an air raid. The *Langley*, off *Trinity*'s beam, began to fire. *Trinity* began firing her guns, and they fired for a full minute before the captain ordered cease fire.

"Boys," he said, "you've been shooting at the planet Venus. . . ."

But there were aircraft about. At 1400, a PBY flew over, and they saw the American markings as the plane turned north toward Manila. At 1700, a Dutch patrol bomber appeared and circled the convoy. From that time on there was a constant succession of aircraft until they tied up at the pier in Balikpapan on December 15. The war had begun for Seaman Bell.

Henry A. Pyzdrowski, the son of a Pittsburgh church builder, had just completed his solo flight as a Civilian Pilot Training Program cadet that day, at Butler Airport thirty miles north of Pittsburgh. It was the custom for the instructors and other student pilots to await the landing of the soloist and, when he climbed out of the cockpit of his airplane, to drench him with a bucket of water. Pilot

Pyzdrowski landed and taxied up to the building. He stopped the engine and got out of the airplane—and nobody was there to give him the customary greeting. Puzzled and chagrined, Pyzdrowski went into the flight office. Half a dozen students and instructors were there but no one looked up. Their attention was riveted on the radio. Pyzdrowski moved forward.

"What's going on?" he asked.

"Shhh," said one of the others. "Listen. The Japanese have just bombed Pearl Harbor. . . ."

Silently, Pyzdrowski joined the group. Then he drove home, thinking about his pilot's lisense, which he ought to have in six months. His whole purpose in seeking a pilot's license was to further his chances of becoming a naval aviator, which he intended to do as soon as he had completed this, his sophomore year in college. It was a shock then, a few days later, when the CPTP officials announced the cancellation of all training licenses. But this was only temporary; a federal investigator came to screen Pyzdrowski and ascertain his reason for seeking a license. When he said he wanted to be a navy pilot, his student certificate was reinstated, and he went on with the program.

These stories, and stories like them, come from the war accounts of men who would later come together on one ship, the USS *Gambier Bay*, or in naval parlance, CVE-73. Young men who had never seen a ship or the sea, others who had already spent years in the navy, men who joined up to become pilots, and Naval Academy graduates who went where duty called—all these would join aboard the escort carrier to do their duty where God and the navy took them.

## CHAPTER TWO

# The Ship

The Pearl Harbor attack had proved to the American naval high command a contention that the naval aviators had been making unsuccessfully for years: The aircraft carrier and not the capital warship with heavy guns was the major naval weapon of the future. Yet the lesson was not immediately learned, because most of the senior naval "aviators" were not aviators at all, but battleship men who had gotten their wings so they could command carriers in days when the real aviators were too junior to hold such commands. Admiral King was one such man. He believed he knew a good deal more about the utilization of carriers than was actually the case; and since almost immediately King became commander-in-chief of the American naval forces, his ideas became effective orders. Carriers were employed singly, not in groups, each carrier to be the central ship in a large task force, surrounded by cruisers and destroyers. Battleships were not included in the U.S. force (as they were in the Japanese) because the American battleships could not keep up with the cruisers and carriers. The employment of the carriers, too, was cautious, but there was reason for caution. America had only a handful of carriers, and once the *Enterprise, Saratoga, Lexington, Yorktown, Hornet,* and *Wasp* were committed to the Pacific, the *Ranger* was all that was left for Atlantic waters. In the very first weeks of war the naval high command learned many lessons; not least of these was that more carriers were desperately needed. The U.S. Navy had shamefully neglected the lessons taught by the British for two years, and when war began, the senior American officer in charge of antisubmarine warfare was a chief petty officer! Neglect and a refusal to face facts left America's East Coast on December 8 with fewer than 100 naval craft capable of going to sea even to look for submarines. The same neglect had prevented development of naval air.

The auxiliary carrier program was, in the beginning, a ragtag and bobtailed operation. The first such ship, the *Long Island,* was built by converting the merchant ship *Mormacmail,* which took 77 days. This carrier had no "island," which put it in the "blind" class with the *Langley.* The lesson was soon learned, however, and other small carriers were built to different plans. The panic button was pushed, and quickly a handful of "jeep carriers" were produced: USS *Sangamon,* USS *Suwanee,* USS *Chenango,* and USS *Santee.* They were built on the hulls of oilers, and they were still really oilers in performance; *Sangamon* had a flank speed of 18.5 knots, theoretically, but that could be achieved only with the wind at the back of the carrier, "and going downhill," as one crew member put it, hardly the manner in which carriers launched planes.

Henry Kaiser, the operator of an enormous engineering combine, had contracted early in the defense effort to build ships for the American effort and to replace the thousands of tons of shipping then being destroyed by German U-boats in the Atlantic. Shipyards at Vancouver, Washington, Swan Island in the Willamette River at Portland, and in Richmond, California, were turning out Liberty ships, sometimes at the rate of one a day.

Early in 1942, seeing the need for a better standard small carrier, Kaiser approached the navy with plans for a "baby flattop." The principal employment was to escort ships and thus solve the problem of the dreadful gap in the middle of the Atlantic, where no air cover could reach from America or England, and where the merchant ships and their fragile and few destroyers and destroyer escorts and corvettes must run the gauntlet of German U-boat wolfpacks. Kaiser wanted to build thirty such vessels. The navy still had not quite gotten the idea about aircraft carriers and said no. Thereupon, Kaiser went to Adm. Emory S. Land, head of the United States Maritime Commission, and Land went to the White House. In some ways, Pres. Franklin D. Roosevelt was his own best admiral, and he became enthusiastic about the proposal. For one thing, he knew very well from his exchanges with Prime Minister Winston Churchill that the U-boats operating off the U.S. coast in the first six months of 1942 had done more damage than the Japanese did at Pearl Harbor, by far.

And so a contract was arranged. Kaiser would build fifty escort carriers on Maritime Commission P-1 hulls. The contract was signed in June 1942, and called for the first small carrier to be delivered in six months. Kaiser didn't make it. After all, this was his first effort in building a naval warship, and it seemed remarkable that, starting from scratch, naval architect George Sharpe and the Kaiser Yard at Swan Island were able to move as rapidly as they did. It was nine months, not six, but by then the first of the new class of CVE-55 ships was completed. On April 5, 1943, Mrs. Franklin D. Roosevelt came to the yard and christened the first of the new series of ships: *Casablanca*.

Capt. Hugh Goodwin, down in Buenos Aires, had kept up his barrage of communications to Washington, and at the end of his year he was brought back. As promised, he was offered the command of the USS *Casablanca* and went to the West Coast to commission the ship. But there were delays, one after another, in her shakedown period, and finally the navy ordered Goodwin back to Washington. He was assigned to planning and later became deputy chief of naval operations for air.

Meanwhile, the small carriers were coming off the ways of the Kaiser shipyard, where what industrial writers often called "a miracle of production" was taking place. In this case, the hyperbole was certainly justified: In 1942 at Richmond, California, Kaiser built the Liberty ship *Robert E. Peary* in seven days, fourteen hours and twenty-nine minutes. To build the CVEs and the cargo ships in the Northwest, Kaiser assembled thousands of workers, many of them recruited from Minneapolis and points east. In 110 days the Kaiser organization built Vanport City in swampland between Portland and Vancouver, Washington, and created Oregon's second largest city. At the peak it contained 10,400 housing units, hospitals, schools, and shops. The ships were built by entirely new methods, welded rather than riveted, and prefabricated, cut up again if necessary into movable sections, and mounted in position by huge cranes. The yards worked three shifts, twenty-four hours a day, one shift's welders competing against the next on a hull to see who could lay down the most feet of welding in a day. That sort of competition kept an excitement bubbling in the yard and a care for the quality of the ship they were sending forth to go to sea.

The ships kept coming off the ways. They were anything but elegant ships, these *Casablanca*-class carriers. By late 1942, when the CVE program was moving ahead, the number of shipyards in America had jumped from about a dozen to 300, all building various craft for the war effort. All of these vessels competed for certain materials. The *Bogue*-class carriers, built in Tacoma, were the first to get started and were given a common combination of diesel and steam machinery. The *Commencement Bay* class, also built at Tacoma, were promised standard geared turbines. The *Casablanca* class were the Cinderellas, sometimes called the "Woolworth carriers," and because they were last in line, to them was relegated the Skinner Uniflow reciprocating steam engine. In peacetime no naval constructor in his right mind would have chosen the Skinner for any ship; the engines were cranky, hard to manage, and very expensive to operate: It was hard to maintain an adequate supply of clean boiler feed water. The condensate often contained lubricating oil, carried with the expended steam. The engineers put loofa sponges in the hot wells and diatomaceous earth filters in the condensate lines, but not at first. All this had to be learned, and the Skinner could be an engineer's nightmare. But there it was, that was the allocation, it was all that was available, and whoever was going to be in charge had to make the best of it.

The *Casablanca* had been built in 241 days. With each new hull the shipbuilders worked against their own time, and when Hull No. 319 was laid down in the summer of 1943, they had learned a good deal about speeding up the processes. No. 319 was built in 171 days and launched on November 22, 1943, christened by Mrs. H. C. Zitzewitz, wife of a commander who was on duty at the shipyard. Why the wife of a mere commander? For one reason, so many ships were being built in Kaiser yards that virtually every woman of prominence in the area had "christened her ship" by the winter of 1943. The yards were hard put to find sponsors. "Jeep carriers" were coming along so fast the market was extremely small. Nevertheless, she was launched and christened, and the name chosen for Hull No. 319 was the USS *Gambier Bay.* It came from an obscure haven in Alaskan waters that had been named by Capt. George Vancouver, the English explorer of the 18th century, for James Gambier, a British naval officer who enjoyed a distinguished career and finally became a peer and Admiral of the Fleet. The *Gambier Bay* was the nineteenth *Casablanca*-class carrier launched that year. The shipyard workers had promised President Roosevelt eighteen carriers by the end of 1943, and the *Gambier Bay* was their bonus for the war effort.

Once launched, *Gambier Bay* was sent down river and into the Columbia. She was sailed to Astoria, at the mouth of the Columbia, for outfitting and commissioning. She was 512 feet long (flight deck 80′ × 480′), 108 feet of beam, and she displaced 7,800 tons. She carried one five-inch gun on the fantail, eight twin 40-mm and twenty 20-mm antiaircraft guns in cuplike mountings above the hangar deck. "Baby flattop" was one name for her class. Her real weapons were the thirty aircraft that she would carry into battle; but for these ships there was very little consideration of "battle" in the usual naval sense. The navy wanted them for escort duty; their normal prey would be submarines, so the five-inch gun seemed quite adequate. It could destroy the conning tower of a surfaced submarine, and even hole the pressure hull. Like her sister ships, the *Gambier Bay* was designed with frugality and hurry in mind.

The whole concept had been to take what was basically a merchant ship hull and make a carrier from it with minimum change for the shipbuilder. The main deck of the ship, had she been a merchantman, became the hangar deck. The flight deck was put atop, and a second deck was constructed below to accommodate the crew. Storerooms, magazines, and gasoline stowage were also on the second deck. The accommodations were spartan: steel bulkheads, bunks, and navy gray paint. Protection against bombs and gunfire came in the form of splinter shields for control and gun stations. The only practical means of protecting against torpedoes was a series of transverse bulkheads to subdivide the ship into compartments. There was nothing extra; there was a war to be won, and she was designed to play her part in it and for that purpose only.

By the time the *Gambier Bay* was launched, some of

those who would sail in her were already wondering just how well she actually was designed for that role. On November 24, during the American assault on the Gilbert Islands, the escort carrier *Liscome Bay* was torpedoed by a Japanese submarine and sank in fifteen minutes, taking down Rear Adm. H. M. Mullinix, Capt. I. D. Wiltsie, fifty-one other officers, and 591 enlisted men. The *Liscome Bay* was a Kaiser ship, Hull No. 302, launched on April 19, that year, but not actually taken over by the navy until August 7. Her life, then, had actually been just over three months.

The sinking of the *Liscome Bay* was reported from the Gilberts by Correspondent Robert Sherrod of *Life* magazine and other reporters, and Louise Sherrod Bassett shivered a little at her brother's story. For, by this time, she and Ensign Bassett had married, and she knew he was going to be assigned to an escort carrier. In the ready cynicism of servicemen, the Kaiser carriers were dubbed "Kaiser coffins," and many of those scheduled to serve in them came west with more than a little nervousness of spirit. Their minds were hardly eased by the joshing of the "old salts." What did CVE mean, they would ask the boots? And when the youngsters stumbled, they would answer their own question:

C = Combustible,
V = Vulnerable,
E = Expendable
CVE = USS *Gambier Bay*

The little game never failed to give the youngsters a jolt. But the absolute truth of the statement was not to be known even to the old salts until one day in October. Then everyone aboard the *Gambier Bay* would remember the formula.

## CHAPTER THREE

# The Captain

Flying his desk in Washington made Capt. Hugh Goodwin nervous. He was eager—determined—to get a ship and get into action in the Pacific war. After the keel of Hull No. 319 was laid in July 1943, Goodwin watched the reports of ships building and commissioning on the West Coast. By fall, he had settled on CVE-73 as the command he wanted, and every morning after checking in at his desk, he would go upstairs to the detail office and have a cup of coffee with Capt. Bob Hickey, an old friend. There in the office on a board were listed all the CVEs under construction, with their status, and a space labeled PCO—Prospective Commanding Officer. Hicky chalked names into these spaces nearly every day, and the first time Goodwin saw CVE-73 on the board, there was a name chalked against it. He went to the board, picked up an eraser, wiped out the name, and chalked his own name in. Next morning, when he appeared, his name had been erased and the other substituted again. He repeated his performance of the day before, and so did the detail office. It became a sort of game: Every day Captain Goodwin would write Capt. Hugh H. Goodwin in the PCO space of CVE-73. Every afternoon the detail office would substitute another name. This little exercise continued for three months. Finally, one day Goodwin came up to the detail office and found that his name was still on the board opposite CVE-73. He knew then that he had gotten his command.

Goodwin was navy through and through. He had enlisted in the First World War, and served aboard the battleship USS *Delaware* when she was part of the Sixth Battle Squadron, attached to the British Grand Fleet. In 1918, he won appointment to the United States Naval Academy. He graduated with the class of 1922 and was commissioned. His first tour of duty was back in battleships, but in 1923 he transferred to the submarine service, and, in 1924, was assigned to Division 17 in the Philippines. He had two years of Far East service, wintering in the Philippines, then moving to China to escape the typhoon season. The Asiatic Fleet operated then out of Chefoo and Tsingtao. In 1926, he was assigned to a destroyer which was sent up the Yangtze River to "show the flag" at Hankow. Chiang Kai-shek, who was trying to unify China under the Kuomintang banner, had marched up from Canton to Hankow.

At the end of Goodwin's Far Eastern tour, he was assigned to submarine duty in the United States, and then elected to take flight training at Pensacola. From that time, although he wore the gold dolphins of the submarine service, he cast his lot with naval air. He was assigned to VF Squadron 1, Fighter Squadron 1, based on the carrier *Saratoga*. But before he could go to the *Saratoga,* he had to qualify for carrier landings, and for this he was assigned to the old carrier *Langley,* which made 14 knots. He was more than a little nervous, particularly after he saw the executive officer of his squadron make an approach before his own. Goodwin was off the *Langley*'s port beam, at 500 feet, when his "exec" came in and caught a wire with one side of the fixed landing gear. The plane skidded across the flight deck, to the port side, and slid into the water. Goodwin was waved off as a destroyer came by and picked the executive officer out of the water, then he was waved in by the landing signal officer. When he got the "cut"—the signal to turn his engine back to idle—he chopped the throttle. Involuntarily he stretched his right leg, hit the rudder control, and threw the plane into a right skid that carried him over the nettings on the starboard side of the carrier. He righted the plane and caught a wire, but so far up the deck that he hit the barrier, wrapping the wire around the propeller of his plane. He was a "qualified barrier pilot," and forever after he would know what it was like for a pilot to come in "hot."

They flew single-seater F2B fighters in those days, and

they were all "hot" pilots. VF1, the *Saratoga* squadron, was nicknamed the High Hat Squadron, and the pilots painted high silk hats in circles on the sides of the fuselages of their planes. They wore red helmets and the more flamboyant sported red flight jackets. Lt. Cdr. "Pinky" Kneip wore a red Vandyke beard and a pair of Morowitz goggles which gave him a distinctly rakish air. They were "a pretty doggy outfit," they told themselves.

The second commander of VF1 was Lt. Cdr. Arthur Radford. "Raddie" became a good friend to Lieutenant Goodwin, and when the senior officer went up to Washington to join the staff of Commander Air, Battle Force, he persuaded the young "hot pilot" that there was more to naval aviation than waggling his wings, and Goodwin was assigned to the Bureau of Aeronautics. Radford was instrumental in easing Goodwin's way into the Naval War College in 1933 (which readied him for command) and then secured Goodwin's appointment (Radford was detail officer) as aide to Captain A. B. Cook of the carrier *Lexington*. Where Radford left off, Cook took over.

For most of the next ten years Goodwin's star was hitched securely to Cook's career. Aboard the *Lexington*, Goodwin became the first officer to hold the job of air operations officer. Later he was Cook's flag secretary when the admiral took over as commander of the Air Scouting Force. Then came the Argentina assignment, with Radford and Ralph Davison promising to get him out and get him a ship as soon as the task was done.

Captain Goodwin, then, was one of a new bread of naval aviators, experienced in all types of ships, and prepared for command. Whatever the "hot pilot" had been in his youth, by the time he went to the West Coast to pick up his ship and commission her, Captain Goodwin was as knowledgeable about carrier operations as any man in the navy. He had commanded a training squadron at Pensacola, and Observation Squadrons 1 and 2. He knew what was needed to sail and fight an aircraft carrier. The first thing needed was a taut ship, and that is precisely what Goodwin set out to produce when he left Washington with his orders. He was from that moment, what in the old navy they called a "sundowner," a spit-and-polish disciplinarian.

Arriving at Astoria, Captain Goodwin spent two weeks studying various new naval publications, to be sure he was up-to-date on his command and battle procedures. Then he had a chance to see a *Casablanca*-class CVE in action; the *Casablanca* herself was on a training cruise in Puget Sound, to break in the new crews assigned to various CVEs. Goodwin went to Bremerton and rode the ship to get the feel of her. Later, he was to bless the officer who had thought up the idea of the training program, for when his own crew of 1,000 officers and men began to assemble, he was to learn that he had some regular officers, some regular navy enlisted men, and a few merchant navy officers and men. But the vast majority of officers and men were signed up only for the duration of the war. They came from every state; they included city slickers, farm boys, and everything in between. They were, to refine a cliche, of the warp and woof of America, and they knew virtually nothing about either the sea or a ship. If Captain Goodwin was to make a "taut ship" of the USS *Gambier Bay* before she went into battle in a few months, he had his task laid out for him.

Officers and men began appearing at Astoria. It was Captain Goodwin's duty to assemble them, and to integrate the crew into that ship so that she became more than 7,800 tons of steel and copper, zinc, electric wiring, and the thousand inert components that go to make up a 20th-century ship of war. What Goodwin could do in the next few months would mean the difference between a ship and fighting ship, and it might well mean the difference between death and survival for the 1,000 men who would man the *Gambier Bay*.

## CHAPTER FOUR

# The Crew

They came from the four corners of America, these men who were to man the new escort carrier *Gambier Bay,* that far and beyond. Some were veterans of carrier warfare and had been "sunk" in the *Wasp* and *Hornet,* lost early in the South Pacific. Some were veterans of China and the war in the Philippines, some of the Caribbean battle against the U-boats. But most of the young men who came to the base at Bremerton for training, or reported to Astoria, were fresh from the farms and towns of America, and their naval experience had not passed the training stage.

To whip this raw, green crew into shape, Captain Goodwin had a handful of regulars, Annapolis graduates, "mustangs" who had come up to commissions through the ranks, and merchant seamen who had been commissioned in the United States Naval Reserve. The executive officer was Richard R. Ballinger, who graduated from the Naval Academy in 1929. He had come up from Corpus Christi after a year and a half of shore duty. He knew what had happened at Pearl Harbor on December 7, for he had been there, as flag secretary to the admiral commanding Patrol Wing 2.

The air officer was Lt. Cdr. F. E. "Buzz" Borries, of the Naval Academy class of 1935, an All-American football player for Navy. The chief engineer was Lt. Cdr. J. A. Sanders, who had many years behind him in America's merchant marine. He had the thankless task of mastering the tricky boilers.

Captain Goodwin wasted no time in beginning to shape the ship. Lt. G. D. Hazzard had been assigned as navigation officer, but Goodwin took an instant dislike to him for no apparent reason except that Hazzard had been a reserve ensign in World War I. He was also a reserve officer. So Goodwin threw Hazzard back into the officer pool, and brought Lt. George Gellhorn up from first lieutenant, the job he had been assigned, to navigator. He knew Gellhorn; the latter had been Annapolis, class of '25, but had resigned from the navy after a few years and gone into the reserves. Goodwin's attitudes were not unusual; the navy was full of cronyism in the years between the wars, as his own career indicated. A man got ahead by hitching his star to the wagon of a senior officer who was going someplace, and woe betided the man who fell afoul of a senior who could influence his career. One captain, for example, once ran his cruiser aground in heavy fog. The board of inquiry absolved him of blame, but unfortunately Admiral King was aboard the ship that day. Indeed he was the cause of the accident because he had insisted that the captain speed the ship in heavy weather so that King could make an appointment ashore. King never forgot or forgave, and that captain never had another command, although he was one of the most competent men in the navy.

That was the navy way. Many youngsters who came aboard the *Gambier Bay* did not understand or appreciate the navy way, and so from the first, Captain Goodwin was not a popular "skipper" with either the officers or the men. Popularity was not his major concern. He was a disciplinarian, and he forgave no error. "Good intentions excuse only children and fools. When the chips are down and battle is joined, it is the results that count," said Captain Goodwin. He intended to be certain that the results aboard the *Gambier Bay* were positive.

The officers and men came along, and, as necessary, Goodwin judged them and discovered what use he could make of them and what allowances must be made for their deficiencies. When he asked Lieutenant Gellhorn to become navigator, Gellhorn demurred. He had not done any navigating since his student days. Goodwin insisted.

"Well, okay, I will take the job if you will be patient with me."

"Patience isn't one of my long suits, but I'll do the best I can," said the captain. He was as good as his word. Later he recalled that he never could trust Gellhorn's navigation —at least he did not—but he was satisfied that he had the man he wanted in the job he wanted him in.

From the first, Goodwin liked Lieutenant Commander Sanders, the engineering officer. A few swift questions assured him that Sanders knew his engines. That was all that was required. He also liked the appearance of Lt. Richard Elliott, the ship's intelligence officer. Elliott was a reserve officer, older than most of them, and a life insurance agent by profession. Goodwin had known Lt. M. R. Brod, the communications officer, in a previous assignment, and that made Brod go down well with him. A few enlisted men had been in previous Goodwin organizations, but, for the most, they were quantities unknown to the captain and took some sorting out. This, in turn, took time. One young watch officer, for example, never did please Goodwin. From the first day, the captain decided Lt. Ed Coleman would not do, and he proceeded accordingly. Coleman would often feel the rasp of Goodwin's tongue, or be ordered to his quarters for some infraction, real or fancied, of the captain's orders.

As the new men arrived, the future was laid out for them in the captain's first message, written down in the commissioning issue of the ship's newspaper. Goodwin believed in telling it like it is, obviously:

> I firmly believe in the old Navy adage that 'A TAUT SHIP IS A HAPPY SHIP.' I shall require smartness and efficiency of the officers and men of the GAMBIER BAY. I shall demand the accomplishment of difficult tasks as a matter of routine, and the accomplishment of impossible tasks on frequent occasions. . . .
>
> . . . Now the builders are finished, and our job begins. We must complete the work begun by the shipbuilders and make of ourselves the FIGHTING CREW which will complete the GAMBIER BAY . . . always bearing in mind that our ultimate mission is to engage the enemy, we now face the task of preparing ourselves for that hour. . . .

The statement might not have been totally logical, but it was in the naval tradition, intended to inspire the young men coming aboard and at the same time warn them that there would be no mollycoddling.

That commissioning issue of the ship's newspaper had been prepared by a handful of officers and men who comprised the skeleton crew of the *Gambier Bay*, the precommissioning detail. A few days before the ship came down river from the Willamette, the officers and men began straggling in. The navy had secured office space, or what passed for that, in the corner of a wharfside warehouse. Some of the furniture was left over from World War I days when Astoria had been a commissioning port for the old wooden transports that were still lined up in mothballs in a slough a few miles away. Most of the furniture was improvised from two-by-fours and boards, and most of the "chairs" were wooden crates.

Astoria, in winter, is cold and bleak, with winds lashing in across the bar from the Pacific or whistling down the Columbia River, carrying rain or sleet, that could chill a man to the marrow. It was in peacetime primarily a fishing town, populated by Scandinavian Americans originally, a poor town, at best, and in wartime the expanded population had pressed hard on the town's limited housing space and handful of restaurants. The crew began to arrive, and some of them brought their wives for those last few weeks of family life before the men set out to war. The wives settled into drab hotel rooms, and their husbands disappeared early in the morning and did not return until dark.

Christmas was the worst time. Lt. (jg) Rannie Odum had arrived to join the detail on December 22, bringing his wife, Floreid. On Christmas Eve they found the confines of their hotel room stifling and went out for a walk in the evening gloom. They passed neat rows of wooden houses, each with its little garden or yard, and saw the lights of the big Douglas fir Christmas trees inside, and heard the laughter in the bright rooms. For Rannie Odum it was a low point of his life. A few days after the arrival of the commissioning detail, the *Gambier Bay* was sailed down from the shipyard by a civilian crew, accompanied by a handful of officers. Then the work of final outfitting began.

Captain Goodwin gave a dance party for the officers, and one Sunday afternoon he opened the ship to visitors. Thus, the wives had small glimpses of the people and the surroundings in which their husbands would live.

Gingerly, the officers and men got to know one another, as the circle broadened. Lt. Cdr. Neale Curtin, the supply officer, had sailed down the river in the *Gambier Bay* and had already begun to lay in stores. The others began to come aboard and, as their wives left for home, to take stateroom assignments aboard the ship. The *Gambier Bay* began to buzz with activity, as the doctors, dentist, chaplain, and the others came. The chaplain was Lt. (jg) Verner Carlsen, a Lutheran. He had been transferred up from the Naval Air Station at Monterey, California, to join the carrier. He came with some misgivings, for his wife, Mildred, was three months pregnant with their first child. But this was the duty he had requested, and there was no turning back. When he arrived he discovered that in the chaplain's division (and in others) the CVEs had been shortchanged. There was no altar and no organ aboard, and he had to find his own within the narrow resources of western Oregon. It took some doing, but it was done. The chaplain also discovered that many of the men of the *Gambier Bay* could play various instruments, and some of them had brought them along. He sorted out a ship's band (entirely unofficial) and began scouting Astoria's music and secondhand stores for more instruments and sheet music. Before they left Astoria they had what the captain called the only ship's band in the CVE fleet.

Perhaps the busiest man on the ship was Lt. Cdr. Kingston Houlihan, who was responsible for all ship's construction. There were changes to be made, and additions, and Houlihan hurried from the hangar deck to the flight deck and up to the island a dozen times a day.

In January, the men kept coming, many of them from schools and training stations. Tony Potochniak was one of these. He had enlisted in the navy in February 1943, with his father's reluctant consent, and was sent to boot camp at Seneca Lake, New York, for basic training. After leave, he went to the Navy Technical Training Center, Norman, Oklahoma, where he graduated after twenty-six weeks as seaman first class, aviation machinist mate striker. He was sent to Chicago to join the old training carrier SS *Wolverine,* a converted sidewheel steamer that had run on the Great Lakes for years. Then he went to Sand Point Naval Air Station at Seattle, where four more weeks made an oxygen specialist of him. Next point for Potochniak was the

Naval Air Station at Tongue Point, Astoria, and on December 28, 1943, he had joined the *Gambier Bay*.

Seaman Bell's ship, the USS *Trinity*, made a number of trips to the Middle East to load oil and aviation gasoline for the Allied forces, first in the Dutch East Indies, and when they were lost, in Australia. In November 1943, Bell was ordered back to the United States for leave. After his leave he was sent to Bremerton, Washington, to await reassignment, and he went by train, dreaming of Paducah, Kentucky, all the way. At Bremerton, he was assigned to CVE-73, and in a few days sent to Tacoma, and then down with a detail of other new men, to join the ship. As a member of the original crew, Bell was a "plank owner," and the responsibility bore on him so heavily that he decided on January 1, 1944, to dedicate his diary to the story of his ship:

Considering us commissioned and in Astoria, Oregon
this day of January 1, 1944
may we see many battles and kill many enemy and
then return to our mothers and other loved ones
God help us win . . .

If those sentiments seem bloodthirsty, they were the common feelings of the day among these young men who were committed to battle against the Japanese enemy. Captain Goodwin certainly shared those feelings; the scuttlebutt had it that his brother had been a victim of the death march staged by the Japanese to move the captured Americans and Filipinos of Corregidor to Manila prison. It was not true. Captain Goodwin never had a brother; the tale was made up in the mess hall to account for the captain's ferocious attitude toward the enemy.

Some men, of course, had personal scores to settle. Seaman Bell had some strong feelings about the war, after nearly two years in combat, during which the Japanese always seemed to be ahead. The ship's company also numbered several very young warriors. One day Captain Goodwin was on the bridge, when he heard one of his orderlies, Seaman Sankey, over in the corner talking about "the Seventeen Club." He called Sankey over.

"What the hell is this Seventeen Club?"

"Oh, captain, I don't know whether you know it or not,

but we've got a lot of fellows here on this ship who are just seventeen years old. We aren't like those old bastards eighteen years old, who enlisted in the navy just to keep from getting drafted into the army. We didn't have to enlist. We did it because we wanted to do something for our country, and we thought the navy was the place to do it. So we got up this Seventeen Club."

Seventeen . . . they seemed like children. But what the captain didn't know was that about half the members of the Seventeen Club weren't even seventeen, but bloodthirsty fifteen and sixteen year olds, out to win the war.

RM3c Lee McCollum was one of those who came down with the draft from Bremerton to join the ship on the day of commissioning, and his sentiments were shared by most of the young men who were seeing their first warship, the first warship they could call their own:

"Never had a ship looked so beautiful to us! . . . We stood in awe-eyed amazement gazing at her as she lay at anchor in the mouth of the Columbia River. . . . This was *our* ship!!! Blood-tingling excitement, strange adventures, a thousand lives packed into a single lifetime—all this filled our imaginations. This was the goal of grinding work, strenuous training, and endless hours of study . . . Proud? Strutting peacocks . . . were drab by comparison. . . ."

The ship was ready. The captain was ready. The crew was assembling and making ready for the task ahead.

CHAPTER FIVE

# The Pilots

In the spring of 1942, Henry Pyzdrowski, aged 20, was a strange combination of knowledge and ignorance. He was knowledgeable about European politics far beyond his years, but at the same time, his ignorance of the world about him made Pyzdrowski seem naive and younger than those years. Both conditions were a result of family background; his mother and father had emigrated to the United States in 1913 from their native Poland; he had grown up in a religious patriarchy; and he had scarcely spent a night away from home until he joined the navy. Polish was spoken as much as English in the household; his father followed Polish and German politics, and explained Hitler's speeches to the family. By 1939, Henry Pyzdrowski and his two brothers all took it for granted that they would soon go to war to fight Hitler. But that assumption changed for Henry Pyzdrowski when Japan attacked Pearl Harbor. He completed his year at Carnegie Institute of Technology on June 4, 1942, and a few days later left Pittsburgh for Philadelphia and induction into the navy. He was assigned to the Navy V-5 class that would begin June 11 at Chapel Hill, North Carolina.

On the night before Henry Pyzdrowski left home, the famliy had a quiet dinner. Next day Anthony Pyzdrowski took his third son to Pittsburgh's Pennsylvania Station. At the station, father embraced son in the European fashion with a kiss on each cheek and a bear hug, told him an embarrassed little joke to indicate that Henry was now a man of the world ("Candy is dandy, but Liquor is Quicker") quoting Dorothy Parker and then Henry was gone on the great adventure of his life.

At Philadelphia's induction center, Pyzdrowski was pushed, pummeled, examined, and passed as fit for pilot training. He was taken out to a cafeteria with other young men, brought back and told he was an Apprentice Seaman in the United States Navy and would be paid the princely sum of $12.50 per month. Then his group—40 men—was herded aboard another train, this one heading south, to ride all night to Durham, North Carolina, and then put aboard buses that took them to Chapel Hill, and the university campus, where their training would begin.

More tests came next; depth perception particularly troubled Pyzdrowski. The physical program began, to toughen these young men and prepare them for war in the air. They learned to shoot a rifle and read Morse code. They learned aircraft identification, and so much time was spent on Japanese aircraft that they assumed they were headed for the Pacific theater. They did pushups and situps and rolled on their bellies. They marched. They boxed, they swam, they ran obstacle courses. Finally, they graduated to become cadets; they were outfitted in new uniforms, and told they would receive $75 a month. Then they were given leave for two weeks to go home, show off their new navy blues, and impress their families and friends.

Cadet Pyzdrowski came close to washing out in primary training at Lambert Field, St. Louis. His flight instructor did not seem to pay much attention to him and when he was tested in aerobatics, he received two "down-checks" which meant automatic appearance before the "washout-board." He pleaded incomplete instruction and was given another chance. This time he was flying an old Stearman biplane with a check pilot in the second seat when suddenly the propeller flew off and the engine began to race. Uncontrolled, it would tear itself loose from its mountings, and might pull the airplane apart in the process. The correct procedure was to cut the ignition and make a dead stick landing, but young pilots at this stage seldom faced the problem. Pyzdrowski had been posed just that question in the psychological examination given him before his Board appearance. He remembered to cut the power, and landed in a farm field. As the plane stopped, the instructor came forward.

"Young man," he said, "you have just earned your navy wings."

There was no leave before transfer to Pensacola for further training. The pilots learned takoff and landing techniques, aerobatics, formation flying, navigation, and the other tricks of navy pilot's trade. After Pensacola, Pyzdrowski chose "torpedo tactics" as his preference, and was sent to Barin Field, on the Alabama coast of the Gulf of Mexico.

After a few months at Barin, Pyzdrowski was designated as a Naval Aviator, and assigned to torpedo training. He was not quite 21 years old when he was sent to Fort Lauderdale to train in the new Grumman TBF torpedo bombers. His instructors included officers who had flown from the decks of *Wasp* and *Hornet* before they were sunk, sent home to train the boys who would replace them on new carriers. On good days they flew. On bad days they practiced instrument flying in the Link trainer.

At Fort Lauderdale, Pyzdrowski met Jess Holleman, a pilot from Wiggins, Mississippi. Jess was the most popular man in the group; his career and Pyzdrowski's would be intertwined from that point on, although they did not then know it.

Pilot Pyzdrowski was careful. He practiced in his chosen aircraft, the TBF, especially flying to the edge of a stall. He was a disciplined pilot, as befitted a man who would be carrying a one-ton torpedo or its equivalent, and would be responsible for the safety of a gunner and a radio man. He learned to observe and follow the signals of the Landing Signal Officer, *without question.* At the very end of training came an object lesson in flight technique: Ensign Blair, the tail-end-Charlie in formation, overshot, cut the throttle back all the way—forgetting the characteristic heaviness of the aircraft—and mushed into a cypress swamp where the plane burst into a ball of red flame. Blair's crewmen survived but Pilot Blair lived just another 36 hours.

That sobering experience just behind him, Pyzdrowski headed for Glenview, Illinois, where he would make a carrier checkout on the SS *Wolverine* on Lake Michigan. He and Ensign Ely and Ensign Jess Holleman were together, all assigned to go on from there to San Diego, for assignment to a carrier that was going into the Pacific. They had heard that the carrier air group destined for the USS *Enterprise* was training at Sand Point, and the thought came to them that they might be replacement pilots for the *Enterprise.* Excited by the prospect, Pyzdrowski and Holleman took the train to Sand Point Naval Air Station, at Seattle. Their orders said VC-10, but they thought it was a misprint, and meant VT-10, the torpedo squadron of the *Enterprise.* They arrived in Seattle on September 10, 1943.

Quite another sort of pilot was Leo Zeola, a southern California boy who joined the V-5 program in August 1942. Zeola trained at the University of Southern California in Los Angeles, at Delmonte, and then went to Livermore for flight training in Stearman biplanes, which gave him the exciting feeling of "flying by the seat of your pants." Very early in the program, Cadet Zeola, Cadet Bob Zwifel, and another pilot named Hill went out for solos in the Stearmans. Somehow Zwifel and Hill collided in midair and both were killed. When Leo Zeola came down safely, he was met by a group of officials. All they wanted was his name. That was the only way they could determine who had been killed. There was something very impersonal about the experience that shook Zeola severely.

Cadet Zeola was a lively fellow. A few months earlier, after a pilot had buzzed the Livermore rodeo grounds during a show, the commanding officer of the field indicated that buzzing civilians was virtually a capital offense. So Leo Zeola knew, there was no doubt about that. He knew.

One night Zeola met a pretty girl in town. Next day his Stearman came over Livermore, dropped down to treetop level and roared down her street. She came out waving a tablecloth, and he dipped his wings as he went by. Just then, dead ahead, he saw a flagpole. He managed to miss a collision; then he was out of town, and flying ever so carefully back to the Livermore field. He landed sedately and taxied down to the far end of the parking ramp, cut off the power, got out, and began walking toward the control tower. As he walked, he caught the glint of sun on field glasses. As he walked further he saw a knot of people in the tower, and finally he realized the glasses were trained on him. Perhaps, he was beginning to believe, he had a problem. . . .

The nature of the problem became clear when Zeola reached the tower, and a furious flight operations officer came rushing down.

"You are Cadet Zeola?"

"Yes, sir."

"You were flying Stearman No. 3Bx47?"

"Yes, sir."

"Cadet Zeola. You are grounded until further notice."

Cadet Zeola continued to go to his ground school classes, but he found his "pals" avoided him as if he had the measles. Half the people on the field expected Zeola would be washed out at any moment. But he was lucky. A new commander was assigned to the field, and the flight operations officer did not want to present the picture of a station full of troublemakers. He called Zeola in one day.

"Cadet Zeola, if you will forget what happened, so will I."

Zeola was only too glad to cooperate. But he wondered just how he had been caught in the first place. Months later he encountered a senior pilot at another station, the other recognized him and told the tale.

The other officer had been stationed at Livermore as an instructor. On a day off, he was sitting in the living room of his rented house in town, when suddenly just outside the picture window, a Stearman trainer floated by at eye level, so close that he could not fail to make out the identifying numbers on the fuselage. Furious at the idiot pilot who was endangering: (1) the peace; (2) government property; (3) his own life; and (4) the entire community, the officer reported to the control tower at Livermore air field.

Having survived that prank, Zeola went on to Corpus Christi Naval Air Station, where he was nearly washed out by an embittered aviator who had been flying combat with the RAF in Europe, had rejoined the U.S. Navy after the Japanese attack, only to be made an instructor instead of a carrier pilot. But Zeola was lucky again. He survived the embittered officer's bad report, and was sent on to continue training as a fighter pilot.

Zeola was still on the East Coast of the United States when Ensign Pyzdrowski and Ensign Holleman headed for Seattle. At that point, Cadet Zeola didn't know of their existence, or of the building of an escort carrier called the USS *Gambier Bay*.

## CHAPTER SIX

# VC-10

VC-10, the composite squadron of fighter and torpedo pilots who would man the planes of *Gambier Bay*, was born at Sand Point Naval Air Station in Washington on September 23, 1943, with a handful of pilots present. The senior officer was Lt. John Stewart, a "veteran" who was 23 years old, and had been a pilot and instructor at Pensacola for a little more than two years; but by far the most "famous" person in the squadron had achieved his renown in efforts totally unconnected with the navy scene. He was Lt. Vereen Bell, who had left that successful career as a magazine writer and novelist to join the navy. In all, there were 14 officers, three chiefs, and 38 enlisted men in the fledgling squadron; Pyzdrowski, Holleman, Ens. Hovey Seymour, another famous man who had played fullback for Yale in 1939, Ens. Don Kreymer, and Ens. Nick Carter, whose specialties were torpedo launching and cigars. Lt. Cdr. Edward J. Huxtable, the commanding officer, and Lt. Henry Bassett, the executive officer, came a few days later. Since he and Bassett were both torpedo-plane pilots, Stewart became the flight officer and leader of the fighter component.

At Sand Point during those first few days the pilots flew "war wearies"—aircraft returned from combat zones. The fuselages of most of the fighter planes bore flags of the Rising Sun, indicating aerial victories over the Japanese enemy. But the engines of these planes were tired and the wings creaked. And on the ground the aircraft were perhaps more dangerous than they were in the air. The brakes seldom seemed to work properly, a particular problem at Sand Point where the airfield consisted of one runway with water at either end.

Lt. Cdr. Huxtable arrived at Sand Point on September 28, 1943. A week later, the squadron moved to the Clatsop County airport outside Astoria. The change was, if anything, for the worse as far as the pilots were concerned. At Astoria it seemed to rain all the time, and Lt. Stewart recalled the field as "two runways with mud flats between." Those old, tired fighters and torpedo bombers squeaked and slid and scraped along through the mud and rain, day after day.

It was simply coincidence that VC-10 would begin organization and training at Astoria. The squadron arrived two and a half months before *Gambier Bay* came down to the mouth of the Columbia, and by the time the ship came, most of the squadron was gone. But no one would forget Astoria, because of the rain and the cold. Skipper Huxtable had a special reason to remember the place. One day Huxtable decided it was high time to check out in a fighter, since he was commander of all the squadron. He got into the F4F, cleared the ground in fine style, flew easily around the area, and when he came in to land, he followed Standard Operating Procedure, which was to wind the wheels down. But Standard Operating Procedure for the fighter called for 33 turns on the handle to lock the wheels, and he turned only 32. As Huxtable's plane settled onto the runway, the wheels struck, and skidded, and then retracted, and the Wildcat slid along the runway. Gasoline began spilling out of the tanks, ignited, and flames began to chase the plane. The Wildcat came to a screeching halt, with the firemen spraying furiously, and Skipper Huxtable got out and walked away disdainfully.

"It takes a damned athlete to fly one of those," he muttered as he went. That was the last time anyone in the squadron could recall "Hux" flying a fighter.

If the pilots needed "experience," they got it. One day Lt. Stewart took off in his fighter to tow the gunnery sleeve on 1,600 feet of steel cable. He put the Wildcat into a steep climb to go over the mountain that stands behind Astoria. Just as he nosed up, the throttle arm broke off. The RPM gauge dropped 50 percent, and the FM 2 began to nose over. Stewart released the target banner and 1,600 feet of cable over downtown Astoria and then nursed the crippled plane back to the airfield. As he landed he remembered he could not shut off the throttle, and he came in hot. The brakes, as usual, failed, and the Wildcat ended up with its nose in the mud flat.

The chiefs and the mechanics swore none of the fighters was even fit for flying. Ens. Charles Dugan dropped one Wildcat in the bay short of the runway one day. But the most exciting adventure at Astoria was that of Ens. James Lischer.

One Sunday Lischer had three flights. The first two were uneventful, shooting at a sleeve target pulled by another fighter, and Lischer made several runs on the target. On his third hop as he pulled out of a pass, the engine coughed and then began to run rough. Lischer had enough experience in the Wildcat to know its gliding characteristic: similar to that of a stone. He took a quick fix. He was at 4,300 feet, and might make it back to the field. But as he turned toward shore, the engine began to miss and lost power, and then altitude. His hope that he would reach the air field vanished. Still, he might make the beach. But the engine sound was worse, and he began to wonder. He glanced at the altimeter: He still had 3,800 feet of altitude, but smoke was coming from the engine, then flames, and the engine quit entirely. Ensign Lischer pulled the hood release. The canopy popped open. He looked at the altimeter again: 3,500 feet. He undid his safety belt and climbed out of the cockpit; 3,000 feet. He jumped head first, waited a second to be sure he was clear, and pulled the ripcord of his parachute. *Nothing* happened for an agonizing second. Then the parachute popped open, and yanked him into a sitting position. Feeling like a prince of the air, he rode it down, drifting until he was about 10 feet off the surface. Then he slipped out of the harness and dropped into the ocean. The parachute floated away. The Pacific was *cold!* He pulled the CO2 cords on the Mae West life vest, and bobbed like a cork. A TBF flew low over him, and dropped a life raft. He clambered in, and shivered in the bottom in the wind. An hour went by. Then Lischer saw a PBY flying boat. It circled, splashed down, and taxied up to him. He got aboard, and in a few minutes was back at his base, in the dispensary. The squadron flight surgeon Lt. Cdr. Wayne Stewart, gave him a shot of brandy, five cups of coffee, and had him bedded down with hot water bottles for the night. Next day, Ensign Lischer was as good as new and back to duty.

Gradually, the squadron began to take shape. When CPO Morris Montgomery reported at Clatsop Airfield in Astoria shortly after the squadron was organized, Commander Huxtable greeted him like a long-lost brother. Montgomery was one of a tiny handful of "regulars" who had joined the navy before the war. Nearly all the enlisted men were fresh from the civilian streets and farms, and what they knew about naval aircraft could usually be carried in a coin purse. A handful of recruits had been sent from basic training to the service schools and given cram courses in specialties: engines, hydraulics, guns, but most had basic training, a short aircraft indoctrination course, and then assignment to the squadron. There was only one way for them to learn: on the job.

Chief Montgomery was the chief aviation machinist. Chief Walter Flanders, who had made chief petty officer since Pearl Harbor day, was chief metalsmith. Those two and one other, CPO A. A. Andrews, were entrusted with the responsibility of servicing aircraft for training of pilots and air crews, and at the same time training the young boots to do their jobs. No wonder Commander Huxtable was ready to embrace Chief Montgomery that first day. In the next few months, a handful of experienced men would be responsible for training 300 men of the air squadron. Once they boarded their carrier, 260 of those men would be transferred to the ship's complement, and only 40 enlisted men would remain attached to the squadron: the air crewmen and a handful of skilled maintenance people, including Chief Montgomery.

Chief Montgomery took one look around and his spirits fell. Those tired old clunkers from the battle zone would demand constant expert attention if they were to keep flying.

He went to work, then, fighting to catch up and keep all aircraft operational. He never made it, but by the time the new fighters and torpedo bombers were ready, at least all concerned had an idea as to what they were doing. Montgomery, Flanders, and Andrews were thrown together in their efforts to make a fighting team out of a gang of boots.

In December 1943, the new planes were ready for the squadron, and VC-10 was ordered to move south to Holtville, California, where the weather was more conducive to training operations. By train and plane, the men began to move out in the third week of December. Commander Huxtable was one of the last to leave. Before he went south, the *Gambier Bay* appeared at the mouth of the Columbia, and Huxtable went aboard, to call on his new skipper, Captain Goodwin, and to look over the ship. He was only aboard a short while. He had a chat with Goodwin, and renewed acquaintance with Cdr. Buzz Borries, whom he had known at the Naval Academy. Then it was off to Holtville and training in carrier tactics. Neither Commander Huxtable nor the squadron would see the *Gambier Bay* again until April.

CHAPTER SEVEN

# Shakeup

In a way, Slc Tony Potochniak found it a great relief to be ordered aboard the *Gambier Bay*. He knew he was slated for service aboard one of the new escort carriers, but it had seemed a long time in coming. On December 27, 1943, when he came aboard, he had his first look at a CVE, and got into his first "flap." Slc Potochniak was extremely conscious of the importance of his specialty in oxygen. He reported in to V-2 Division, where he was shown the Oxygen Transfer Shop. Within an hour he learned that he was supposed to be responsible to a Second Class Aviation Machinist who knew nothing about oxygen. Indignantly, Slc Potochniak sought out his divisional officer and demanded a transfer.

Obviously, such problems as Slc Potochniak's were going to take some sorting out. The *Gambier Bay* was commissioned next day.

For the three weeks following the commissioning of their ship, the officers and men of the *Gambier Bay* were busy sorting out their affairs, while the ship loaded stores and the first lieutenant built new equipment not planned by Kaiser.

The *Gambier Bay* was organized into departments and divisions, like any ship. The difference between the carrier and a destroyer, for example, was that aboard the *Gambier Bay*, the most important and largest department was the Air Department. Perhaps Captain Goodwin did not see it quite that way; the pilots never believed he was very sympathetic to their cause, and he certainly exerted equal effort and devoted equal attention to every department of his ship. But the pilots, and all those concerned with the Air Department operated on the principle that the *Gambier Bay* was a floating platform, whose reason for being was to launch the aircraft to attack the enemy.

The Air Department was organized in four divisions. V-1 was concerned with the flight deck, but since neither the composite air group nor the landing signal officer were aboard yet, V-1's activity was limited. V-2 was concerned with the activities on the hangar deck, although their area of responsibility included much more. V-3 was the administrative arm of the Air Department; its responsibilities were for radar, aerology, photography, and air intelligence. V-4 was the aircraft ordnance division, concerned with the guns, bombs, and torpedoes of the aircraft. In charge of all these activities was Lt. Cdr. Buzz Borries, the Annapolis football hero, and almost immediately, perhaps, the most popular officer aboard the ship.

The activity aboard the *Gambier Bay* during these three weeks was endless. In the photo laboratory, for example, the men turned the place upside down. Chief Photographer's Mate Weldon Sparrow was in charge of the lab, and with his four photographers he set out to make their installation shipshape. That meant installing two bunks for men on duty, and setting up the permanent positions of the dryers, aerial film equipment, and developing tanks. This had to be done before they went to sea. It was the same in every department, and all this activity came under the eyes of six professionals—Naval Academy graduates. They were the captain, the executive officer, the navigator (Gellhorn), Air Officer Borries, his assistant, Lt. Elmo Waring, and, later, the squadron commander, Lieutenant Commander Huxtable. All the rest were "amateurs" with the exception of a handful of enlisted professionals. In two or three months, the professionals would have to whip the ship into the shape of a fighting machine.

On the day before the *Gambier Bay* was ready to sail from Astoria, Lieutenant Odum, the aerology officer, began saying his good-byes to his wife, Floreid. They had considered the idea of having Floreid come down to San Diego for a few more weeks, for the *Gambier Bay* was destined to be there soon, but she was pregnant, and expecting in March, so they decided it was best that she head homeward to Savannah. Odum boarded the *Gambier Bay*. His new home would be stateroom 206, which he shared with three other junior grade lieutenants, a solid gray environment: gray bulkheads, gray bunks, gray blankets, gray desk, chair, and metal closet on his side of the stateroom. The other side was an exact copy. Odum and Lt. (jg) Sidney Kimball, the assistant communications officer, were the plank-owners, and for a few weeks they would have the compartment to themselves. Each staked out a lower in the two double bunks, and settled in.

Stateroom 206 was the last compartment forward on the second level of the ship, below the flight deck. It was an admirable location in every way save one: Several decks down were the aviation gas stowage compartments. Of course they were surrounded by cofferdams filled with inert gas to minimize the effects of any explosion. Nonetheless, Odum had a vague feeling as he lay in his bunk at night that he was lying atop a giant firecracker.

From his stateroom, Lieutenant Odum wandered back to the wardroom, amidships, just below the hangar deck. The captain, of course, would not appear here often; he had his own private quarters on the starboard side, just below the flight deck and adjacent to the "island," which was the command tower-bridge of the carrier, the eyes, the ears, and the center of operations. At the island's lowest level was the captain's sea cabin, a tiny stateroom. Around the bridge the landing signal officer, the catapult officer, and the arresting gear officer all had their stations. Below the island on the first deck was the operations office (Air Plot) and next to it was the radar control room, or Combat Information Center, commonly called CIC. Across the ship on the port side, connected by a passageway, was the aerology office.

Looking over that office, Lieutenant Odum decided a bunk would have to go here, too, for Aerographer's Mate First Class John Ammon. The inner office of aerology was the map room, where Odum would work at a chest-high plotting table. He would also stand watches as junior officer of the deck, which, with his flat feet, would be torture. He could, of course, plead physical hardship and be taken off the watch list, but after only a few weeks' acquaintance with Captain Goodwin, Lieutenant Odum was sure that if he did so, he would also be relieved as a ship's officer, sent to pool, and probably end up either counting laundry in a shore station or running up balloons on some half-deserted island. He decided to suffer in silence as far as the bridge was concerned.

By January perhaps half the ship's complement was aboard. From the training station at Farragut, Idaho, came Bugler First Class Berman E. Deffenbaugh to join N Division, which was composed of quartermasters and buglers. Hugh Bell, from the oiler *Trinity*, by this time a QMlc, was one of them. Another was a green seaman named Ed Hagerty, and there were half a dozen others under the expert eye of Chief Pomykalski. It was the same in every division: a handful of experienced men to teach hundreds of young Americans the way of the navy.

A week after the ship's commissioning, Commander Ballinger came to the captain's quarters early in the morning, seriously distressed.

"Captain," he said, "I've got four reports of men sleeping on watch last night."

"Who are they?" asked Captain Goodwin.

Commander Ballinger knew what the captain meant. He had checked the service records of the men involved and had the facts in a brief memo. Two of them were under eighteen years of age. The other two were not yet nineteen. All four were brand new sailors who had never been aboard a ship except in training.

"What are we going to do about them, captain?"

The captain paused. "Well, Dick, I have to think this over. Hell, we can't have these guys up the mast for sleeping on watch. If you do, then I have to remember there's a war on and recommend them for general court-martial. There's no way out of it. The example would have to be set. Let me think about it."

All morning the captain worried with the problem. That afternoon he called the executive officer and told him to send the four offenders to the captain's cabin. That was all. He did not give any hint of what he might do.

The four seamen came in, hats in hands. Captain Goodwin saw four young kids, younger than his own boy, who was just then in training at the U.S. Naval Academy, four kids from four different corners of America, standing there, with only one shared attribute: They were all scared.

"Sit down," said Captain Goodwin. Awkwardly the four

sailors sat, not knowing what to do with their hats or hands.

The captain had a book before him on the desk. He picked it up. "You young men were reported for being asleep on watch last night." He looked at each one of them. They looked down at the deck, and the room was as silent as Chaplain Carlsen's chapel. The captain opened his book.

". . . For the crimes of treason . . . sleeping upon his watch in time of war . . . the sentence of death . . . as a general court-martial may adjudge. . . ."

He looked up. The four young men were pale and hanging on every word.

"Well, here we are," said the captain, shutting the book, "you sleeping on your watch, and the United States in a state of war. I think you know that."

The four boys nodded glumly.

"If I have you up to official mast, I have no alternative but to recommend you for trial by general court-martial. I really don't think that would further the war effort a great deal, so I will tell you what I am going to do: I am going to put this conference in a state of suspended animation. Just now I don't recall that you were reported to me for being asleep on watch. But I don't want you to forget it. If you come up before me for mast, for any serious breach of discipline or breach of regulations, then I will be forced to remember this incident. Do you understand?"

"Yes, sir."

"Yes, sir."

"Yes, sir."

"Yes, *sir*."

The four young sailors filed out happily, and Captain Goodwin suppressed a smile as they closed the door to the cabin. There was no more difficulty in the ship with youngsters caught sleeping on watch. Indeed, the whole fabric of discipline seemed to be tightened by this incident. The velvet glove had done its work, and the *Gambier Bay* was becoming more of a seagoing ship every day.

On January 16, *Gambier Bay*'s communications department had a message for the captain: The ship had been discharged from the outfitting dock and was ordered to sea on her first shakedown run. According to the schedule there was plenty of time. It was anticipated that nearly all of

February would be spent in getting the men used to their ship, and accustoming the Air Department to life and operations aboard a carrier.

At midmorning Captain Goodwin was on his bridge and gave the orders to cast off. The *Gambier Bay* left the pier, backed into the down-river channel of the Columbia, and the voyage began. Almost immediately, anyone with a grain of experience at sea could tell that here was a green ship with a green crew. Perhaps all that was needed was a look at the faces, for the forces of nature took over as the *Gambier Bay* crossed the bar.

The Columbia River bar is located just at the point where the continental shelf drops off into deep ocean. Consequently it is always muddy with turbulence, and that same turbulence swirls about the hull of a ship so that she tends to pitch and toss. The *Gambier Bay* with no aircraft aboard, and only about half her crew and stores, was riding high and light in the water as she crossed the bar. Further, a deep low-pressure area had been hanging over the North Pacific for a week, and the winds were very near gale force. So the *Gambier Bay* had hardly gotten under way when the bodies began to fall.

Bugler First Class Deffenbaugh was standing watch on the bridge when the ship began to move. Soon he noticed the swells and began to have a queasy feeling in his stomach. Deffenbaugh's father, who had also served in the navy, had told him that if he stayed amidships he would not get seasick. He was not so sure. At eight bells (1600) he was relieved and told to go down to the mess hall and get something to eat. He was not so sure of that either, but he headed down. Walking along the gangway, he got a whiff of smoke coming from the stack. Then he was sure; his father was dead wrong. Up it all came, everything that had been in his stomach, and over the side it went. Afterwards he felt better, so much better that he thought if he could get to the mess hall and get something to eat, he would be cured. So he resumed his journey, and went to the deck below. When he reached the mess hall, he found it was nearly deserted. Only two men were there, eating. One was the Chief Master at Arms, nicknamed Mr. Five-by-Five for obvious reason. The other was his chief assistant, whom Deffenbaugh knew as Smitty. They were stowing away the food of the day: corned beef and cabbage. One whiff and

Deffenbaugh knew he had made a mistake. He fled for open air, and when he felt he could manage, he went to his bunk and tried to go to sleep. The ship tossed and turned and kept him awake most of the night.

AMM3c Tony Potochniak pulled guard duty that first night out. The swells during the afternoon had been noticeable, but he had managed to avoid getting sick. His guard post was at one of the 20-mm guns, out over the side just aft of the stack. As the wind increased, the ship began swinging. The wind blew across and under the flight deck, and without the usual weight to hold the ship down, the wind had a yawing effect, something like that of a misplaced sail. An hour of this, with gusts of wind blowing smoke into his face from the stack, gave Potochniak all he could bear. He lost his supper, and reached back for his lunch. Finally, his watch ended and he was able to stagger away from the scene of the torture. But for three days he could not eat and even black coffee would not stay down.

Old salt Hugh Bell weathered the blow without a tremor, conditioned by the monsoon and the typhoons of the China Sea on that first tour with the Asiatic Fleet. But even he noted in his diary that "most of the crew were very seasick," and because of it, that first night he had to stand double watch.

The new "90-day wonders" were as badly off as the enlisted men. When the first few hours passed, and Lt. (jg) Rannie Odum was still on his feet, he congratulated himself, and went to dinner in the wardroom. That was his first mistake. His second mistake was to allow the catapult officer, Lt. Henry Pilgrim, to persuade him to go up on the flight deck and take a look at the mountainous waves rising around the ship. They went up. The sight was truly impressive: waves breaking over the flight deck at the bow, although that deck just then was supposed to stand 45 feet above the waterline. About a minute up there, watching the crashing of the waves and feeling the swaying of the ship, and Lt. Odum, too, gave his all to Father Neptune, and then staggered to his bunk and tried to stop the feeling. The bunk kept moving one way while his stomach moved another. He worried for a while lest he die; then he worried lest he keep on living.

To live or to die? The question raged in his body, his brain giving him one message, and his stomach the opposite. At the height of agony, the loudspeaker in the room began to squawk.

"Lieutenant Odum, report to the captain on the bridge."

Bridge? The thought of getting there, being there, made Lieutenant Odum sicker. What if he didn't go? They could only shoot him, couldn't they? And what was wrong with that, asked his stomach? But his brain advised caution, and Lieutenant Odum obeyed his brain. Staggering, clutching, sometimes crawling, he made his way up 40 feet and across 150 feet of gyrating catwalk and passageway to the bridge. He raised his arms to salute, and nearly fell over. The captain caught the arm and steadied him.

"Lieutenant, what's the forecast. Is it going to worsen or slack off?"

Before Lieutenant Odum fell in with the treacherous Lieutenant Pilgrim, he had been well enough to study his maps and reports. They would enter Puget Sound through the straits of San Juan de Fuca in a few hours, and in that protected water, should find haven from the storm, which was moving away from the Seattle area. He was able to give an intelligent, if weak, answer to the captain, and was dismissed. He stumbled down to his office then, to find Petty Officer Ammon there drinking coffee, as saucy as a six-year man could be. Petty Officer Ammon watched the messages and advisories coming in, and called the attention of his officer to the important factors. From time to time, Lieutenant Odum, then, was able to inform the bridge that his original prediction was holding. The weather did soften inside the Sound, and it was not long before they were coming into the protected harbor of Seattle.

This was supposed to have been the beginning of the *Gambier Bay*'s shakedown cruise, but most of the crew could swear that they had never been more badly shaken up in their lives. Later, the captain estimated that eighty-five percent of the crew was ill during the voyage to Seattle. And as for the weather, this particular "Kaiser canoe" would never encounter anything worse, even in far waters of the Pacific.

They could not know that here in Seattle, and the memory of that first brief voyage would be with most of them for quite a while. Days later, RM3c McCollum, sitting in the chow hall, stoking away his dinner, noticed that the sailor directly across from him was looking hungrily at his plate, but not eating a bite.

"What's the matter?" asked McCollum. "What's wrong with the food?"

"There'th nothing wrong with the food," said his companion. "God damith, I lothe my teeth, and I'm hungry ath hell."

CHAPTER EIGHT

# Shakedown

The junior officers and the men of the crew were hoping for shore leave in town, but they had no such luck. Captain Goodwin knew, and they did not, precisely how raw this ship's complement was, and he was determined to rectify that deficiency as quickly as possible. The flight deck view of the Seattle shoreline was the closest they came to mingling with civilian America. Captain Goodwin had a fixed schedule for shakedown, and he was determined to stick to it.

The ship's chronometers and all the clocks aboard were sent ashore for tests and setting on navy time. The ship was demagnetized so that it would not provide homing for magnetic mines. The *Gambier Bay* took on more crewmen from Bremerton. She was fueled and stores were stacked up in the lockers below. She went out into the sound to test her catapult machinery, and it performed satisfactorily. All this done, the *Gambier Bay* sailed south for San Francisco Bay. As she headed out to sea Captain Goodwin had a little surprise for the men. Suddenly he ordered the call: "General Quarters." The alarm bell attached to the public address system began: CLANG-CLANG-CLANG. The bugler on duty sounded the General Quarters call throughout the ship. The squawk box crackled: "MAN YOUR BATTLE STATIONS," and men began running. Shoe leather scraped on steel, shoes clattered up and down ladders, and watertight doors banged with a hollow sound.

An SNJ aircraft laid on for the occasion came out into the sound to make simulated strafing and bombing runs on the carrier, while the gunners tracked the plane with their 20-mm and 40-mm anti-aircraft guns.

When the SNJ disappeared over the horizon, Captain Goodwin ordered the ship secured from General Quarters. Then he spoke into the intercom:

"You men seem to have had some difficulty tracking that plane. That was a single aircraft, and a trainer at that. Where we're going you must be prepared for real enemy air attacks. From now on you are going to have an opportunity to drill and drill and drill. . . ."

The captain was as good as his word. All the way south to San Francisco Bay the gunners drilled and drilled and drilled. They aimed at sea gulls. They tracked blimps. They practiced loading and range finding and readiness to fire, against stop watches. They went to General Quarters every few hours, they practiced abandoning ship, and the captain held several inspections of crew and ship. Needless to say there was fault to find, in every operation from gunnery to streaming the paravanes, the torpedo-shaped instruments designed to sever mines from their moorings.

For most of the crew it was a great thrill to sail into San Francisco Bay under the Golden Gate Bridge, past Alcatraz island, still a federal prison in those days, under the San Francisco Oakland Bay Bridge, and then to tie up at a pier next to Alameda Naval Air Station.

At Alameda there was shore leave, by watches and departments, as the *Gambier Bay* loaded fuel, aviation gas, more provisions, ammunition for the trip south to San Diego. The *Gambier Bay* was moored next to the pier, fore and aft, navy fashion, with the starboard side of the ship inboard. Gangways were fixed fore and aft to connect the ship with the shore, and the enlisted men used the gangways to come and go on liberty, as well as to move supplies into the ship. At Alameda, the ship's security and order were always supervised by the officer of the deck, a senior officer who was directly responsible to the executive officer and the captain for discipline. His station was at the foreward gangway, known as the quarterdeck while in port. The junior officer of the deck stood at the after gangway, and also made periodic inspections of the crew's quarters to see that all was well.

One night in Alameda, Lieutenant Odum had the after

gangway. He was on watch from 2000 to 2400 that night, and it was a quiet night. The port watch was on liberty, and the starboard watch was aboard, all safely bedded down at lights out. That's what the regulations said. But the officer of the deck heard some strange noises from the crew's compartments, and ordered Lieutenant Odum below to investigate. Odum headed toward the bunkroom in question, which he had to reach by going down a ladder. Just after 2300 he started down, and he saw a faint light where there should have been none, and he heard the sound of excited whispers. He put his foot on the first rung of the ladder, which resounded with a clang, and as he did so he could hear the distinctive clicking of dice. He started down, reached the bottom, and probed the compartment with his flashlight. Never in the history of the navy had an officer of the deck come across so still a scene! Not one case of tossing and turning in this bunkroom; no insomniacs here, but a compartment full of happy, angelic sailors, sleeping peacefully, getting the rest they would need to do their proper duty next day. Lieutenant Odum stopped for a moment to appreciate the full beauty of it, then turned and made his way back up the ladder to report that all was secure. He said nothing to the senior officer of the burning flashlight that had rolled beneath one of the bunks, or of the scattered pile of greenbacks on the floor. Nor did he ever ask how they divided up the money.

The officers were able to go ashore, too, for short periods, and Lieutenant Odum and several of his friends made the pilgrimage across the bay to San Francisco where they rode the cable cars up Nob Hill and had steak at the Top of the Mark. But there were no long leaves. Shortly after arrival Captain Goodwin had the word from 13th Naval District that the *Gambier Bay*'s shakedown had been foreshortened. At Pearl Harbor the call had been made for more aircraft to be delivered in a hurry, and several of the jeep carriers had been designated to become aircraft transports. Operation Flintlock, the capture of the Marshall Islands, was just then in progress. The invasion of Truk, the major Japanese base in the South Pacific, was envisioned that year (it never came off), and for that purpose Admiral Nimitz and Admiral Towers, the air commander, and Admiral Hoover, the land-based air commander, wanted more aircraft in the Pacific in a hurry.

The planes were coming off the assembly lines in very satisfactory numbers, the Army Air Force's needs had been adequately met, and the navy had nothing like its old troubles in getting aircraft. The problem was shipping space, with all the demands being made on available transport to support the series of Central Pacific invasions. The *Gambier Bay*'s training program, then, would have to be carried out as she ferried aircraft out to Pearl Harbor and beyond. For she was to deliver planes to the fleet carrier *Enterprise*, thus saving the big ship a long trip to secure replacements.

In haste then, Captain Goodwin sailed for San Diego and arrived on January 30. Lieutenant Odum remembered the day, because he had the duty, and could not go ashore—and it was the first anniversary of his marriage to Floreid. The best he could do was arrange for the wife of a shipmate to send a dozen roses. A day or so later he did get ashore, and, as they loaded planes, he had several brief leaves from duty. He and the padre, Chaplain Carlsen, went ashore together, on a trip to Tijuana, where they went for a long walk through the city. The padre wanted to visit a "typical residential district" to see how the natives lived. Walking down a street of houses with drawn curtains, they saw hands beckoning them from behind the draperies. Just as Lieutenant Odum realized where they were, a Mexican policeman came up to inform them that they were in an "off-limits" area. Only the padre's credentials saved them from an embarrassing set of explanations to the shore patrol, but they got off scot free, and Lieutenant Odum announced that in future he would have to travel in more reputable company. He was not going to get caught in a red light district again.

Early in February the airplanes were brought to the pier, and heavy cranes began loading them aboard the *Gambier Bay*. They were Avenger (TBF) bombers and Hellcat (F6F) fighters. In all, eighty-four planes were stuffed aboard the little carrier, which meant every available space was used, including the flight deck. No flights could be made until the deck was cleared, but that made no difference; the first stop was to be Pearl Harbor, where some of the planes would be off loaded by crane.

On February 7, the planes were loaded, along with a group of passengers—including air crews for the planes and 400 marines destined for Pearl Harbor—and the little carrier moved out into the Pacific. She ran alone, a single ship in a lonely sea, for the navy had no time or available escort ships to form a convoy. Captain Goodwin kept the training program going all the way. Every morning, an hour before dawn, Bugler Deffenbaugh or one of his associates stepped up to the public address system microphone and blared out the reveille call on his horn. "Hit the deck, sailors" were the unwelcome gritty words that followed. Then the day began. When the men were not on duty or at battle stations, they were encouraged to play basketball or volleyball on the forward elevator, which was lowered to hangar deck level. At night the ship was blacked out, but the hangar deck was screened and a movie put on.

Six days after sailing, *Gambier Bay* arrived in Hawaii, and most of these young men had their first look at Pearl Harbor. As they came in, personal visions of the day of the Japanese attack coursed through most of their minds. AMM3c Potochniak thought of home, and how he had enlisted although below draft age, because of the attack on Pearl Harbor; and he thought of his close friend, John Stasko, who had been killed in the sinking of the carrier *Lexington* in the first year of the war. RM3c Lee McCollum stood on the flight deck with hundreds of other sailors as they came in. They passed Battleship Row, where the oil still oozed up from the sunken *Arizona*. They tied up alongside Ford Island, near the *Arizona*, and someone said something about the 1,200 men who still lay down there, trapped inside at the moment of the attack. They were a quiet crowd of sailors that day. "We realized," said RM3c McCollum, "what the enemy could do to us and the danger that lay ahead."

Quartermaster Bell had seen it all before, and he was more or less immune to the spell of Pearl Harbor, but the youngsters were awed by nearly everything they saw. On liberty, Bugler Deffenbaugh and his pals separated as they left the ship. The pals headed for the nearest beer hall. Deffenbaugh was not much of a beer drinker, and what he really wanted was a scoop of "geedunk" (ice cream).

Some of the men on liberty headed for Hotel Street, the red light district in downtown Honolulu, where a girl or a fight could be found almost anytime. Some headed up St. Louis Heights and Wilhelmina Rise, where the more expensive houses were located. Nearly all the new officers managed a stroll through Waikiki, and a look at the Royal Hawaiian Hotel, which was reserved as a rest and recreation center for returning submariners. But an ordinary sailor could still look, poke his toes in the warm Pacific at Waikiki Beach, and drink a glass of pineapple juice (or something stronger) on the terrace of a hotel or restaurant along the strip of Kalakaua Avenue.

After the marines and the airplanes were discharged from the *Gambier Bay,* the officers and men expected to be sailing back to San Diego to pick up their own aircraft, and their air crews. But the moment the cranes stopped lifting aircraft off the flight deck, they turned, and began lifting other aircraft to that same deck. Below deck, the scuttlebutt was overflowing. What was going on? Where were they going now? What kind of sense did it make to take one batch of new planes off and put another batch on board? They counted seventy-nine aircraft before the cranes stopped moving. And what were they going to do with them?

On February 16, the crew had part of the answer. The *Gambier Bay* got under way, and she was headed for somewhere in the Marshall Islands. Quartermaster Bell might not be able to spell the name (Marshel was his phoneticization), but he knew there were still Japanese troops in some of those islands. "The *Gambier Bay* will probably get in her first battle before we return . . . ," he wrote.

No one ever told the crew why they had taken one batch of aircraft to Pearl Harbor and picked up another. The fact was that the planes coming from the mainland were not always in fighting trim, and those going to the war zone had to be. The planes taken to Pearl Harbor had to be checked and sometimes modified for combat. Those going from Pearl Harbor had already been worked over.

But then, nobody ever told the crew very much of anything. Still, with reasonable accuracy, the ship's telegraph functioned on the lower decks, and QMlc Bell's diary entry was more or less correct. The *Gambier Bay* was heading for a point off Majuro Atoll in Bell's "Marshels." Heading into the war zone, the little carrier was accompanied this time by a destroyer to protect her against submarine attack, and they ran a zigzag pattern to avoid becoming "sitting ducks." Every morning began with a call to battle stations, and it was repeated at random throughout the day. As on the voyage from San Diego, Captain Goodwin did not miss an opportunity for training. As they moved out into the open sea, a plane from Barber's Point Naval Air Station approached, towing a sleeve target, and the 20-mm and 40-mm gunners went to work, from their little nests, called sponsons, that lined the edges of the flight deck. The crew now knew why these were called "pom-poms": The noise could be deafening. After the plane had disappeared, the five-inch gun on the fantail was still able to fire against a sled towed aft. Captain Goodwin wanted good marksmen when the time came to fire in earnest.

Captain Goodwin wanted a good deal more than that, too. One of the routine duties of Lieutenant Odum, the aerology officer, was to take two upper air soundings daily, under a directive from the Bureau of Naval Aeronautics in Washington. Coming down the coast from the northwest, Odum made the soundings every day by releasing a 30-inch balloon filled with helium from the flight deck. He and his men tracked the balloon's progress through the telescope of a theodolite, and plotted the results for Washington. This practice, he had been told, would assist the Bureau in its plans. After the ship left San Diego, and headed to Pearl Harbor, aerology continued its daily observations under the benign eye of the captain on his bridge. But on this first day at sea, heading toward the Marshalls, when "weather" released its balloon, Ammon had scarcely begun tracking, when the squawk box began sounding throughout the ship.

"Now hear this. Now hear this. Lieutenant Odum, report to the captain on the bridge."

Lieutenant Odum started. He was in the operations office at the moment. Before he headed for the bridge, he stopped to talk to Ammon. Had someone fouled up?

"Mr. Odum," said Ammon, "I think it was to do with our balloon release. Captain Goodwin has watched us go through this routine many times, and always seemed pleased. But just now, when we did the same thing, he seemed much put out."

Lieutenant Odum made a mental checklist. The others were following his instructions, and he was following the Bureau's directive. He could not understand what the captain might be unhappy about.

When he appeared on the bridge, he gave his smartest salute.

"Lieutenant Odum reporting to the captain as ordered, sir."

"Lieutenant Odum," said Captain Goodwin, "have you ever heard of ship safety at sea?"

"Yes, sir. Of course I have."

"Then why, in the name of almighty God, did you release that balloon just now?"

Lieutenant Odum was about to say that he had not released the balloon, Aerographer Ammon had, but he was smart enough to bite his tongue. The name of the aerology officer was Lt. (j.g.) Rannie L. Odum. "The Bureau of Naval Aeronautics allships directives says. . . ."

The captain turned red. "Lieutenant Odum, I do not give a damn what the Bureau of Naval Aeronautics allships directives say about how a captain shall run his ship in the face of the enemy. Do you realize that the balloon you sent up could help the enemy spot us from God knows what distance."

"Sir, but the allships directive. . . ."

The captain made a rude noise.

"The allships directive, sir, is very specific. Shall I get my copy and show you paragraph . . ."

"No, lieutenant. Do not get your copy. Just listen. I understand that the Bureau wants weather information, and, believe me or not, I also understand why they want it. But if you were captain of this ship, Lieutenant, and you faced the choice of no information about the winds aloft or possible discovery by the enemy by the release of the balloon, what would you do?"

Lieutenant Odum's face cleared. "The former option, sir."

The captain heaved a sigh of relief. "All right, Lieutenant Odum. We are agreed. No more balloons unless you have my express approval. Is that understood?"

"Aye aye, sir."

Lieutenant Odum then left the bridge with a snappy salute. He did not notice the faraway look in the captain's eye.

On February 18, the radio shack picked up news broadcasts that told of an enormous attack by American naval aircraft on the Japanese base at Truk. The scuttlebutt had it that after discharging some of their planes at the Marshalls, they would sail for Truk and join the fight. How they were going to get a squadron of pilots and air crewmen aboard was not considered in the scuttlebutt. Quartermaster Bell, for one, was sure they were heading into their first battle. "If my guess is right, when we leave the Marshel Islands, there will be a few less Japs. . . ."

Next day the *Gambier Bay* fueled its escort destroyer. In the afternoon the planes were gassed up, and some of the engines were started. Late that afternoon they sighted a convoy of eight ships on the horizon. The destroyer went charging off to investigate; then came back. They were American.

On February 20, they reached the rendezvous point. They did not actually have the *Enterprise* in sight, but Captain Goodwin was in contact. Early in the morning, the *Gambier Bay* began launching planes by catapult. That was the only way; the flight deck was so crowded there was no room for takeoff. So the first sixty-five planes were catapulted. The last fourteen took off from the flight deck. Then the *Gambier Bay* turned and headed back to Pearl Harbor, her mission accomplished. Landing signal officer McClendon was aboard. He made the trip with the *Gambier Bay* to Majuro to evaluate the plane-handling crews. Later that day, fortunately for an F6F "Hellcat" fighter pilot in distress, the *Gambier Bay* took him and his plane safely aboard. On February 25, 1944, the ship's log recorded its first carrier landing. Quartermaster Bell did not see much of the action, because he spent the whole day at the ship's wheel. It was double duty, but Captain Goodwin needed an experienced man at the helm. He finally realized there would be no battle for the *Gambier Bay*. The news came that the air battle for Truk had ended in the sinking of many Japanese ships and the destruction of Japanese aircraft on the ground and in the air.

They sailed back to Pearl Harbor then and arrived on February 26. The fleet band came down to the dock to meet them and played as the ship tied up. They were all very proud of their ship and the role they had played in this last action.

Next day, the *Gambier Bay* was loading planes again. But what planes! This time they were taking a load of war wearies back for a set of embryo aviators to crack up in the training fields of America. They sailed on Leap Year Day, February 29, 1944, which meant good luck. It was confirmed soon enough: Captain Goodwin was not satisfied with the *Gambier Bay*'s performance. He wanted her put in drydock for repainting of the bottom, and correction of excessive vibration of the screws at high speed. That meant the ship would be laid up for at least two weeks, and that, in turn, meant liberty and leave for the old salts who now had green verdigris on their brass. USS *Kitkun Bay* joined them on the voyage back to San Diego, and they arrived, pennants flying and hearts as light as they could be.

## CHAPTER NINE

# The First Casualty

Shortly before Christmas the pilots and air crews of VC-10 took off for California to continue their training, and made their various ways down to Holtville, about a hundred miles due east of San Diego, and just above Mexicali on the other side of the border. How they got there depended very much on the temperament of the pilots involved. Ens. James Lischer more or less floated in, having spent two nights and a day in San Francisco en route on the champagne and night club circuit. Almost the moment he arrived he was off on another party. Commander Huxtable let the pilots take their airplanes during Christmas if they had relatives anywhere in the vicinity. Ens. Henry Pyzdrowski's brother was an Army Air Force navigator, stationed at Santa Ana, and he had his TMB for the holiday. He gave Lischer a ride to Santa Ana, and Lischer then went on to see a friend nearby, who took him to his uncle's house. "We spent Christmas eve getting plastered by the fire. Had a swell time but had to leave early the next day so missed out on a big turkey dinner . . ." By the time Ensign Lischer returned to Holtville, the squadron was getting organized. Before the planes had left Astoria, Chief Flanders was assigned to shepherd the squadron ground personnel by train, a job that made him wince. Taking 200 men that far entailed enormous responsibility. The big problem came during a two-hour layover at Los Angeles. A number of the men were from that area, and, of course, they paid no more attention to Chief Flanders' instructions than if he had not issued them. The train left, minus a number of VC-10 personnel, who were eventually sent on by later trains. One of the escapees was captured by the shore patrol and then the SPs came looking for the officer in charge of the detail. When they found Chief Flanders they read him off for inattention to duty and put him on report. When Flanders reached Holtville, he told the whole story to Commander Huxtable, and presented the charges made against him. Huxtable looked at them, grinned, and put them on the table. "Don't worry about it," he said. Flanders never heard of the incident again.

Coming down from Astoria, some of the squadron's planes got separated from the others when they ran into bad weather. Out of Alameda they ran into fog. Some of them, including a TBF in which Chief Montgomery was riding, found conditions so bad the only way they could get their position was to come down onto the deck, follow railroads and highways, and check the names on railroad stations. But they all arrived safely, and soon were at work in the training program.

Holtville, the squadron soon found, was anything but an ideal station. The sun blazed down on them all day, and at night it turned uncomfortably cold. It was so hot in the daytime a man could get a bad burn from just touching the cowling of an engine on the flight line. So they did the maintenance work at night, shivering in the wind. Lt. William Cordner joined the squadron at Holtville to take over instruction in aerial gunnery and bombardment. The torpedo pilots learned glide bombing against a wooden fence in to the Salton Sea. Each day they would demolish the fence; each night the maintenance crew would rebuilt it. They began practicing at night, too, using radar approaches, which meant the maintenance crew stayed up late, because finally the squadron bombers attained an average of eighty percent hits.

At Holtville, the torpedo pilots got their air crews. Each was assigned a turret gunner and a radio-radar operator. These assignments were intended to be permanent, and most of them turned out that way.

Ensign Pyzdrowski was assigned radioman Jerry Fauls and gunner Bob Jensen. Ens. Hovey Seymour, a Yale football hero, was assigned gunner Charles Westbrook and radioman Larry Austin. Westbrook was pleased, for in the training program various crewmen had flown with various pilots and gained different preferences. For a crewman, whose life depended on the skill of the man in the pilot's seat, this was an important selection. In training Westbrook had flown a few times with Lt. Sandy Sanderson, who had been a scout bomber pilot before he transferred to VC-10 and torpedo bombers. Sanderson took delight in barrell-rolling the TBM, which was strictly against orders, since the heavy plane had a tendency to stall in such maneuvers. So while Westbrook liked Sanderson and knew he was a good pilot, he was much more comfortable flying with the more conservative Ensign Seymour.

After hours, when the pilots could leave the base, some headed for the Rice Bowl Cafe in El Centro, and some for the Hacienda DeAnza in Calexico, where most of the married officers lived. The wives played bridge and gossiped, and they all waited. It was apparent the squadron would be moving soon.

On January 20, the squadron was moved to Brown Field, on Otay Mesa, near Chula Vista, again along the Mexican border. During the move, the pilots had leave, and Ensign Lischer took the opportunity to go into Los Angeles with several of his buddies for another binge. They stopped at the Clark Hotel, after visiting a number of bars, and then went out to dinner at Earl Carroll's. Ensign Lischer made a date with a girl he met at Carroll's, and after she got off work at 11:00, they went dancing at the Palladium where Harry James was playing. The other pilots became bored, having no girls, and at two o'clock in the morning stole a taxicab, drove over half of Los Angeles, and then parked the cab in front of the Clark Hotel. They went upstairs and drank the rest of Ensign Lischer's liquor before stumbling into bed.

At Brown Field the men of VC-10 met the officer who in the future could very well mean the difference between surviving and becoming a casualty aboard the carrier. He was their landing signal training officer, assigned to Brown Field to give this new squadron preliminary work in the most difficult task of takeoff and landing from the short deck of an escort carrier. Lieutenant McClendon knew his specialty. After his own training in 1942 as an aviation cadet in the V-5 program, he had been assigned to VF-29,

Fighter Squadron 29, and had served aboard the escort carrier *Santee*. In the fall of 1942, the *Santee*'s planes were involved in the North African invasion. In 1943, the ship was transferred to the South Atlantic on antisubmarine patrol duty between Dakar and Recife. McClendon had been selected for the Landing Signal Officer Training Program and had gone to Lee Field near Jacksonville, Florida, to learn his demanding job. At Brown Field he staked out a piece of runway the size of a jeep carrier flight deck and managed to secure a single arresting wire rig for practice. He began to teach these embryo carrier pilots the techniques of landing on a short runway. When he was finished with them, he expected to take on a new batch, and then another.

For three weeks, VC-10 trained intensively at Brown Field, with the pilots flying long hours every possible day. At Holtville, the senior squadron officers had been able to bring their wives, who lived in a shabby motor court near the field. At Otay Mesa conditions were much better. Lieutenant Stewart, the fighter flight leader, found a "nice" apartment in Chula Vista, close enough to San Diego's North Island Officer's Club and the Coronado Hotel to make it a pleasant short station. Pilot Lischer and the other "hot pilots" did their share of celebrating in San Diego, too, but there was hard work at the field, for Commander Huxtable let them all know the pressure was on. CINCPAC (Commander-in-Chief, Pacific) wanted them out in the Pacific in a hurry. Just before the end of January, VC-10 was given new fighter planes to replace the F4Fs they had been assigned. That meant more familiarization for the pilots. By the end of the month they were flying tactical missions and making mock attacks on U.S. fleet warships at sea out of San Diego. There was still plenty to be learned by all hands. One day, pilot Lischer set out on a mission in his new fighter. Just as he took off, oil began pouring out of his tank, and he had to land. One of the handlers had left the cap off the tank. By the time the oil sump was topped off, and he took off again, he could not find the others and came back. But under the watchful eye of Chief Montgomery and the others, such mistakes became less frequent. By the first of February, the squadron was beginning to shape up. In the second week of February, as the *Gambier Bay* sailed for Pearl Harbor to deliver aircraft to the Pacific Fleet, VC-10 was ready for its first serious carrier trials.

In February, the pilots and aircrews of VC-10 were ordered to the USS *Altamaha* for carrier qualification trials. On March 2, they began, with the experienced Lieutenant McClendon as back-up for the young *Altamaha* landing signal officer. The landing signal officer's station aboard the carrier was the last corner on the port side, aft. Behind the position was a dark canvas windshield that also served to contrast the fluorescent paddles the LSO used to signal approaching pilots. To the left of the LSO station was a padded pit, into which the LSOs could leap if a plane came in too low.

On March 2, the trials began on a good clear flying day. It was the first time that many of the crews had flown together for a carrier landing. The fighter pilots all landed safely, although some of them came in fast and approached the barrier. Then the torpedo planes began to land. Ens. Hovey Seymour was in the pattern, just ahead of Ensign Pyzdrowski. As they turned into the wind, gunner Westbrook looked down at the carrier, which seemed to him roughly the size of a matchbox. Ensign Seymour brought the plane in carefully, and all was going very well until they were just aft of the ship and the *Altamaha* landing signal officer gave Seymour the "come on." But for some reason the TBM dropped too fast.

Suddenly, as Seymour dropped down, Pyzdrowski saw the *Altamaha* LSO signal wildly, with a rowing motion. It meant "you need more power, more power." The TBM was beginning to turn to the left, nose high, which threatened an immediate stall. The *Altamaha* LSO leapt for the pit, and McClendon was right behind him. Seymour's plane managed to clear the end of the flight deck, but there was no way he could recover altitude, and the TBM fell off into the stall. The destroyer escort standing by accelerated, as her captain saw that the bomber would crash. The plane turned over on the port wing and circled back to the port side of the carrier, then hit the water at a thirty-degree angle, nose and port wing first. The tail came back up with the wings above the water line, but the angle was still very steep, and the pilot's compartment was under water.

Gunner Westbrook reached for the turret escape hatch the moment they hit, but it jammed. Then, when the plane came back up, he tried again and got out. Radioman Austin escaped through the tunnel, both ankles sprained from bracing himself against the radio mounts for the crash. Ensign Seymour was not seen again.

The destroyer escort picked up the two men, and they were dried off and sent ashore that night at the destroyer base at San Diego. Next morning they caught a ferry to North Island and then a bus back to Brown Field. On the bus they met a pilot. He too was going to CVE-73 as Hovey Seymour's replacement. The navy lost no time, as Westbrook and Austin learned that day. The new pilot was Ensign Crocker, and the crewmen would fly with him from that time on.

## CHAPTER TEN

# VC-10 Finds a Ship

Although the air crews of VC-10 were sobered by the loss of Ensign Seymour, there was nothing to do but carry on, and the demands of the service soon pushed that unpleasant memory to the backs of their minds. Aboard *Altamaha*, the pilots were awakened at 0515, and called to flight quarters at 0615. Their first hops of the day began at 0700, and they went aloft to practice routine patrol, attack, and navigation. They moved on to predawn takeoffs and late afternoon landings when the light was growing dim. All the while Commander Huxtable was like a cat on a hot tin roof, for only four members of his whole squadron had any previous experience in carrier operations, and the loss of Hovey Seymour so early in the game was a serious blow to squadron morale.

After four days of carrier initiation, VC-10 was moved to Inyokern, California, for final organization. Here the squadron torpedo pilots would calibrate their bombsights and learn to fire wing rockets. There was also some time for leave in Los Angeles and elsewhere. Ensign Lischer, seeking excitement, headed for Hollywood with some of his friends. They spent the weekend night-clubbing, at Mike Lyman's, the Trocadero, and the Mocambo, all famous watering holes of the motion picture crowd in the 1940s. On the following Monday, they went to Metro-Goldwyn-Mayer studio, where Ensign Holleman had a pass. MGM gave them a tour of the sets with the false-front houses and artificial trees, and they recognized some of the scenery from movies they had seen. They visited the sound stage where Lana Turner was making a movie, but she was doing a "bed scene" and did not want any lookers. All the pilots considered that most unfortunate, since la Turner was then in fierce competition with Betty Grable for the title of Pinup Queen of the Navy. Later at the canteen they saw Miss Turner in the flesh, and were most disappointed to discover that beneath that mane of peroxide beat a heart of stone. But they met others, Leon Ames, Mary Astor, little Margaret O'Brien, and Judy Garland, who nearly charmed them out of their hangovers. Then, that afternoon, they went over to the 20th Century-Fox lot, because Jess Holleman knew a producer there, and they saw some shooting on *Wing and a Prayer,* the film glorifying the American victory at the Battle of Midway. Jess Holleman met Miriam Hopkins, and collected a mass invitation for VC-10 to a cocktail party. Ensign Lischer, true to form, picked up the stand-in for Judy Garland and made a date with her. The others were satisfied with less; they were thrilled when on the set they were mistaken for uniformed actors instead of pilots. Reality was just around the corner for them, their performance would be real, not simulated, but at the moment the motion picture set made the war seem glamorous, and the actors were the heroes.

Meanwhile, as VC-10 was preparing to move to its new carrier home, the *Gambier Bay* was made ready to receive its squadron. When the ship docked, Captain Goodwin gave orders to prepare to receive personnel and went ashore. At base headquarters he began to negotiate for drydock availability. Meanwhile, Commander Ballinger supervised the unloading of the war wearies they had brought back from the combat zone. When this task was finished, the *Gambier Bay* was moved to the destroyer base for repairs. The ferrying voyage to the Marshalls had been a most effective shakedown, and Goodwin was lucky to have several weeks to tighten up the ship before going into the combat zone. For the next two weeks duty was easy. Captain Goodwin was forced to wait that long for the drydock. The crew pulled duty for only one four-hour watch every other day, and there was liberty for any man who wanted it. Lieutenant Odum went ashore as soon as they arrived and telephoned his wife Floreid in Savannah.

She reported that their first child might be born any day. Odum applied to the captain for leave but had little hope it would be granted. Captain Goodwin had firmly established his reputation as a martinent, and he had been growling about "readiness." On the afternoon of March 11, however, Odum was called to the captain's cabin. Captain Goodwin sat at his desk, fingering Odum's leave papers.

"I don't know what to do about this," he said, a man aggrieved.

Odum said nothing.

"Do you think you could get to Savannah and back in ten days? That's all I can give you."

"Yes, sir."

"All right. You be back here on the twenty-first."

Lieutenant Odum saluted and turned for the door to make his dash. The captain stopped him.

"Oh, and Odum, I don't know why I'm doing this. You know the old navy saying: It is an absolute must that the sailor be on hand for the laying of the keel, but his presence at the launching is not required." For once, Captain Goodwin grinned.

On that note, Lieutenant Odum retired. Outside he ran into Chaplain Carlsen who had leave under almost the same conditions and was going off to Montana as fast as a No. 4 Air Priority would get him there. The pair were on their way in half an hour, heading by bus for Los Angeles. They parted then and each began his odyssey. Lieutenant Odum managed a flight to Fort Worth, a dash by car thirty miles to Dallas airport, a flight to Atlanta, where he was stopped cold. But he ran into an army sergeant with a liaison plane who was going to Savannah, and he hitched a ride, to reach Floreid's side a full twenty-hour hours before the birth of his daughter, Judy. She was scarcely christened, however, before Lieutenant Odum was on his way again, hitchhiking part of the way back to San Diego.

He just made it, before the drydock became available, and Captain Goodwin moved the *Gambier Bay* around the corner. She was settled in the dock, the cradle hung, water was pumped out, and the ship settled on the cradle. All hands were turned out to scrape bottom paint, and dockyard workers came to change the set of the screws. The ship's band turned out to play for the workers at first, and the strains of "Mairzie Doats," "Sentimental Journey," and "Don't Sit Under the Apple Tree" rang through the yard.

At the end of March, the dockwork done, the *Gambier Bay* was put to work qualifying pilots for carrier operations, just as the USS *Altamaha* had been used by the pilots of VC-10. This exercise, too, served a double purpose, for it would give the *Gambier Bay* crew experience in plane-handling. At this time, Lieutenant McClendon came aboard after becoming acquainted with the VC-10 pilots ashore. *Gambier Bay* then put to sea with a squadron of F4U Corsair fighters, the first ever to land aboard a "baby-flattop" carrier, flown by Marine Corps pilots, who were as green as grass about carrier operations. The scuttlebutt had it that Captain Goodwin asked for assignments like this one because he was an eager beaver, bucking for his flag and two stars. Whatever the reason, the whole ship was tense as the marine pilots took off and particularly as they landed. But McClendon did his work efficiently, and not a single Corsair went into the drink. When Lieutenant McClendon was assigned to the ship, he moved in with Odum and Lieutenant Kimball in stateroom 206.

On April 3, the *Gambier Bay* was back at San Diego, and that day she began loading her own carrier squadron, VC-10. Various members of the crew had been assigned to temporary duty elsewhere to perfect specialties and make themselves more useful later. AMM3c Potochniak, for example, had talked over his oxygen specialty with Lt. J. C. Edmondson, his divisional officer, and Edmondson had asked the captain to send Potochniak ashore for further training in the oxygen shop on North Island. The captain had agreed, and Potochniak had spent a fruitful month working under an old navy chief who knew more about oxygen than many university chemists.

Soon the *Gambier Bay* was heading out to sea on the last phase of her shakedown: the marriage of the squadron and its pilots to the carrier. They would practice carrier air operations for ten days.

Most of the officers and men aboard the *Gambier Bay* were a little surprised to learn that the captain's son was aboard for this exercise. There was nothing irregular about his presence, even if it was a bit unusual. Hugh H. Goodwin, Jr., was a midshipman on leave from the United States Naval Academy to check out naval aviation, which he had declared as his future specialty. Of course, not all midshipmen had the run of a carrier at sea, but that simply offered proof that the navy could be a human institution. As long as he did not get in the way, he could observe to his heart's content. What young Goodwin observed was one of the toughest trials ever to befall a green carrier squadron. His father was determined that the *Gambier Bay* would be the best ship of her class in the fleet, and that meant in the air as well as on the sea.

Flight operations began on April 5. Commander Huxtable had butterflies in his stomach that first day. He looked down the length of that 480-foot flight deck, and the memory of Ens. Hovey Seymour's last attempted landing flashed into his mind. To be sure, he had put his boys "through the paces" in the past two months. They had practiced field carrier landings over and over. On the day the air crews and pilots came aboard, Commander Huxtable let his pilots know that their ship captain was a "spit-and-polish officer," that he was both a submariner and a pilot, and that he expected a very high degree of performance. Then Commander Borries came in, and most of the pilots recognized this legendary figure from Naval Academy football days, the man they used to say "singlehandedly" defeated Knute Rockne's Notre Dame teams two years in a row for Navy.

Commander Borries began to talk. Every sentence was prefixed with "The captain wanted me to convey" or "it is the Captain's wish that. . . ." At the end of it, the pilots of VC-10 were asking each other why the captain didn't come and tell them these things himself. Already they sensed that life here was going to be different.

How different was indicated almost immediately. First flight operations consisted of learning to ride the catapult, under the direction of Lieutenant Pilgrim. One afternoon, having catapulted off the deck, Ensign Pyzdrowski was flying formation, when Bob Jensen, his turret gunner, accidentally tripped the latch to the turret hatch, and the hatch cover flew out and embedded itself in the vertical fin of the empennage. Commander Huxtable saw what had happened and flew over to inspect the damage. He instructed Pyzdrowski to land, and the young pilot dropped down toward the carrier. Lieutenant McClendon told him to go once around the carrier so he could look over the damage. When he did, he decided it was safe for Pyzdrowski to land, and brought him in, so carefully that the TBM hooked the No. 1 restraining wire, and got a "well done" from the bridge. When pilot Pyzdrowski got out of the cockpit and inspected the hatch cover, he saw that another six inches in and the fin and rudder controls would have been destroyed.

The pilots soon learned that there was a great advantage to having Bill McClendon as their landing signal officer. They trusted McClendon because they knew he knew his job. So in spite of Commander Huxtable's misgivings, his young men proceeded to perform admirably. On April 6, Captain Goodwin headed the *Gambier Bay* into the wind and the ship began operations. Not a plane was lost or hurt that day. Nor was the second day blighted, but on April 8, as Ens. Nick Carter brought his TBM in for landing, the engine failed, and he had to ditch alongside. Pilot, gunner, and radioman all got out safely and were soon picked up by a destroyer and taken back to North Island. Next day, they had a brand new Avenger and flew out to join the carrier. Again, on the landing approach, the engine failed, and Ensign Carter had to ditch. Again, all three men escaped the sinking bomber, and were picked up by a destroyer that delivered them by breeches buoy to the *Gambier Bay*. Commander Huxtable did not blame pilot Carter; his two forced landings had been due entirely to mechanical failures. But Carter was badly shaken up, and decided his luck had run out. He asked for transfer out of the air service, and a sympathetic Skipper Huxtable agreed that under Carter's circumstances it might be best for him.

After four days, then, the squadron seemed to be in fine shape, and Commander Huxtable's butterflies began to disappear. Then Air Plot notified Captain Goodwin that a transport plane in distress had radioed from 500 miles west of San Diego. He broke off the normal exercises to conduct a search for the transport, and this took them into a storm. The search area itself was clear, but the *Gambier Bay* moved into high winds and heavy swells. Commander Huxtable flew in the first search group. When he returned to the carrier, he found her bouncing like a cork in the heavy sea, the stern with a forty-foot pitch. He came in on the approach, and Signal Officer McClendon gave him a high cut. That meant land. Automatically, Commander Huxtable lined up with the bridge, and then looked at the carrier's deck. It was going down! But he had been trained to accept the orders of the landing signal officer. This time, said Huxtable, he hoped to God McClendon knew more than he did. He slammed the stick forward, gave the plane full left aileron, and dived for the deck. When he saw it coming at him, he pulled the stick full back, and "let her slam in." On the flight deck, his plane captain, AMM2c Gutzweiler, said he saw the left tire go so flat as it smacked the deck that the rim of the wheel hit the deck and chipped. But the tire held, and Huxtable was down, safe.

The squadron skipper was worried that he might lose some of the young pilots to the wicked weather, and he went up to the island to talk to Commander Borries, the air officer. He said he was afraid they would have a bad accident if they continued to operate in these conditions. Borries agreed and passed the complaint on to Captain Goodwin. The captain was obdurate: They must continue the search, he said. Lieutenant Stewart, the fighter flight leader, came in shortly afterwards. On his downwind landing leg, he noticed that the bow of the carrier dropped so far into the trough of the last wave that the next wave broke over the flight deck, which was supposed to be sixty feet above water. He came in to land, he said, only because there was no place else to go. He, too, wanted operations suspended, but Borries and Huxtable gave him the bad news: The captain insisted that they keep on.

The flights continued all day. They never found the passenger plane, and the next day they were in no condition to operate, because only three of the torpedo bombers and four fighters were undamaged. The impact of landing on a rising deck had flattened tires and bent the landing gear of the bombers, and snapped the tail wheels off the fighters. Three fighters ended up in the barrier. By the time the fighters were landed, it had taken an hour. The TBMs had it even rougher. Ensign Pyzdrowski popped both tires, and one came off the wheel rolled down the deck, and washed overboard as the bow dipped into a wave. The pilots and air crews gained the impression that Captain Goodwin was more concerned with having a showdown with VC-10 than in the welfare of his men.

As they came back to San Diego, someone told them the transport plane did not ditch, hence no survivors in the sea. The pilots began to believe the whole exercise was an opportunity for Captain Goodwin. That view was given substance when Captain Goodwin wrote a fitness report on the squadron that listed many deficiencies. The report soon reached Cdr. James Flatley, chief training officer for ComFleetAir. If the squadron was that bad, either the commanding officer was incompetent or the training was insufficient. If Lieutenant Commander Huxtable was incompetent, he should be relieved, or if the training was improper, perhaps Flatley ought to be relieved. He was concerned enough to pursue the matter and call Huxtable for an investigative conference. Flatley raised serious questions about the endangering of the young pilots, and the danger to military equipment caused by the captain's reluctance to land the planes ashore where the weather was clear.

In the end the fitness report was amended. One point was certainly proved: Composite Squadron VC-10 was prepared to operate anywhere, under any conditions. Even years later, Lieutenant Stewart claimed that in all his flying days he had never operated under worse conditions than those the *Gambier Bay* faced in that April storm west of the Catalina Islands off the coast of California.

## CHAPTER ELEVEN

# War Zone

The month of April was spent tidying up at San Diego, installing the last of the equipment, integrating the air squadron with the ship, and taking on more carrier personnel. Ensign Carter transferred out on April 16. The squadron's aircraft and air crews went off for amphibious support training at the naval air station in San Diego. Here they learned that the mission of the *Gambier Bay* was not going to be what many had thought. Unlike the Atlantic, where the German U-boats were a major menace, in the Pacific the Japanese used their submarines as arms of the fleet, not as commerce raiders. So while the jeep carriers that went east became parts of antisubmarine warfare teams, that tactic was not needed in the Pacific. What was needed was every bit of air support for the invading forces that moved against the Japanese-held islands of the Central Pacific. A major lesson of the ferocious struggle on the beach at Tarawa was the need for softening up, and the *Gambier Bay* was to become a part of the amphibious landing teams. At the Gilberts and the Marshalls, Adm. Richmond Kelly Turner had been developing the tactics of amphibious landings. He required constant air cover. At the same time, Admiral Towers and the "Young Turks," which included "Jocko" Clark and Arthur Radford, Captain Goodwin's friend, were agitating for the independent use of the fleet carrier force that grew so rapidly. They were supported by Adm. William F. Halsey and Adm.

Marc Mitscher in their exuberant campaign to turn the fast carrier task force loose against the enemy, rather than pin it down at a landing operation in support of troops. They wanted Turner and his subordinates to use the escort carriers for this purpose, and to a certain extent they managed to win their point. Turner, of course, would have liked to have every airplane in the Pacific supporting his landing operations, but, by the spring of 1944, it had become apparent that Japanese air power in the outlying reaches of the empire was badly depleted. The attack on Truk had wiped out a large segment of that power. The strikes on the Marshalls before the Gilberts landing had done much to wreck Japanese air power in that area, and when the Americans attacked the Marshalls, the defenses were not as strong as they had expected them to be. But the closer the Pacific Fleet came to the Inner Empire, the harder the going was to be, and everyone knew that. Admiral Towers and the other aviators advocated a course of hitting hard with air strikes, knocking the power out before the troops approached the beaches. Admiral Spruance, Admiral Turner, and, to a certain extent, Admiral Nimitz, wanted to be conservative, and keep the big carriers within calling distance of the landing forces. But the small carriers would play an integral role just off the beaches.

While the operating arm of squadron VC-10 was training, the squadron structure was being changed aboard the *Gambier Bay*. Some 300 men had been training at Astoria. Now the squadron was trimmed down to 80 officers and men.

Other personnel came aboard the carrier. A draft of men just out of boot camp was taken aboard from Balboa Park. Most of them were seventeen and eighteen years old. One of these was Charles Heinl, son of a mortician from Minster, Ohio. They came aboard very green and had to be taught that ropes were not ropes, but lines, and the floor was not a floor, but a deck, and all the other intricacies of life at sea.

At the end of April, VC-10 returned. This time, the officers, too, had to come aboard to stay. The time had come for the married men to part from their wives. Lieutenant Bassett, Lt. Vereen Bell, and Lt. (Dr.) Wayne Stewart pulled their duffel together, kissed their wives good-bye, and came aboard the carrier.

Louise Bassett, Flonnie Bell, and Virginia Stewart set

out together in the Bassett car for the south. Louise Bassett was going home to Madison, Florida, to reclaim her little boy. Virginia Stewart would stop with her for a while before going on back to Pennsylvania to her home. Flonnie Bell was going back to Thomasville, Georgia, to await the return of her husband Vereen. As they left, Vereen Bell went up the gangplank of the *Gambier Bay*, the last officer to come aboard, and took his duffel to Stateroom 206, where there was just one bunk remaining, the upper above Lt. Rannie Odum.

There was one last bit of liberty. AMM3c Potochniak and George Zubbrick decided to go down to Tijuana. They stopped at the Brown Bear tavern in National City, and the Tropicana Club. The Shore Patrol came in at the Tropicana, but fortunately Potochniak had his second I.D. card that showed his age as 21, so he managed to escape a pair of very suspicious sailors. Then, it was time to sail, and the ship loaded a contingent of Marines from the Second Marine Air Wing, who bedded down wherever they could find a spot on the crowded ship. The sailors, playing old salts, took the "gyrenes" under their wings. AMM3c Potochniak befriended an upstate New York marine named Andy Horvot, who gave him a 10-inch bayonet as a souvenir.

At the naval air station on North Island, the *Gambier Bay* loaded stores and supplies. Her own contingent of aircraft stowed, the flight deck was filled with more new planes for Pearl Harbor. So they were to do another ferry job. But this time, the men of the *Gambier Bay* sensed that they would not be coming back, but going on the other way, toward Tokyo.

On that last day, Captain Goodwin brought a party aboard the ship for a tour. He was proud of his ship and what he had done with the crew to make a fighting unit of the *Gambier Bay*, and he wanted to show off a little. With him on the tour of the ship this day were Mrs. Eleanor Goodwin, her friend Mrs. Beattie (wife of a classmate of Goodwin's at the U.S. Naval Academy), and Miss Anne Beattie, a California high school senior whose features, form, and red hair had the Seventeen Club falling all over themselves to make sure she got whatever she desired. Captain Goodwin sent for the ship's photographer, Chief Weldon Sparrow, and had him take pictures of Miss Beattie sitting on a 2,000-pound bomb. She autographed the bomb with chalk: "Best wishes to Tojo," and a dozen pilots swore that they would deliver the present personally.

On May 1, the *Gambier Bay* sailed from San Diego in company with the *Kitkun Bay* and the *Hoggatt Bay*, all bound for Hawaii. It was a foggy day, so shortly after they left North Island, the land was obscured from view. Still, many men clustered around the fantail and on the flight deck, looking back. "It was sort of hard to realize we weren't coming back for months instead of days or weeks," Ensign Lischer wrote home the next day.

The journey to Hawaii would take eight days. To pass the time profitably, Lt. Vereen Bell, the intelligence officer, gave daily briefings on the Japanese, their war tactics, their traditions, and their code of honor—*Bushido*. He reviewed plane and ship identification. He talked about survival at sea.

Some of the pilots played cribbage in the ready room. Ens. Bucky Dahlen did needlepoint. Lieutenant Bell, when not lecturing, went off to stateroom 206 and pecked at the typewriter. He was just starting a new novel, *The Renegade Queen*.

Down on the hangar deck, the marines were packed in like sardines; it had been turned into an 80 by 400-foot bunkroom. Suspended from the flight deck joists above was a Stinson OY-1 observation plane that belonged to the marines. The pilot, a marine major, spent his days in the wardroom, where he organized a poker game, which lasted five days. At first the major lost, but in the middle of the game his "luck" changed, and at the end there was no beating him. The navy pilots borrowed and borrowed from nonplaying pals to keep in the game, and in the end the major won thousands of dollars. The game ended when some onlookers tipped the players that the major had marked at least one deck. But there was no going to the captain, for naval regulations outlawed gambling aboard ship, and the innocent would have been tried right along with the guilty man. But as the game broke up, there were a dozen navy pilots who asked nothing more than to have that Stinson observation plane in their gunsights over some invasion beach.

As the *Gambier Bay* drew closer to Pearl Harbor, an air of solemnity permeated the ship. Lieutenant Odum looked around the wardroom at dinner one night, and seeing nothing but sober faces, he wondered how many of these pilots would be delivered to a watery grave in the coming months. Padre Carlsen had not been pleased with church attendance on Sundays during the early days of the ship's life. But suddenly, after they left San Diego, the hangar deck filled up on that first Sunday at sea, and the men sang the hymns with feeling:

> Eternal Father! Strong to save
> Whose arm hath bound the restless wave;
> Who bid'st the mighty ocean deep,
> Its own appointed limits keep:
> O, hear us when we call to Thee
> For those in peril on the sea!

On May 8, the little squadron approached Pearl Harbor. Commander Borries was launched in a Wildcat to take messages to Pearl Harbor, and he arranged for their reception. They tied up at Ford Island, and the marines and the cargo of airplanes were moved ashore. Next morning the ship got under way again, this time in conjunction with the *Kitkun Bay* and a number of other vessels of various sorts. Although none of lesser rank than the captain could have known, they were training for the forthcoming invasion of the Marianas Islands, to be the first breach in the Japanese Empire's secondary perimeter of defense. Admirals King and Nimitz were already talking about the next move, which they planned to make against Formosa, in the heart of that empire.

This particular exercise involved a simulated landing on the beach of a small Hawaiian island. The old battleships *California, Tennessee, Colorado,* and *Maryland* were all to give fire support with their guns, as they would in the Marianas. They were escorted by destroyers, which also would be called upon to lay fire on special points on request. The escort carriers would supply combat air patrol to protect the force from air attack, and air strikes, where called for.

Lieutenant Bassett led one section of TBMs out on a mission. Coming back, he flicked the switch on his radio transmitter to tell Air Plot he was on his way. But mistakenly, he hit the long-wave transmission switch instead of the short wave. Captain Goodwin heard the transmission. When it had ended, he turned to Lieutenant Odum, who was on the bridge.

"Who is leading that flight?"

"Bassett, sir."

"You go down to the flight deck. When Lieutenant Bassett lands bring him up here immediately."

Lieutenant Odum did not know what was on the captain's mind except that he was annoyed. But the junior officers of the *Gambier Bay* had grown used to the captain's harsh application of discipline. At least Odum knew that Bassett had trouble waiting for him on the bridge.

Bassett landed. When he had cut his engine and stepped down from the cockpit. Odum escorted him straight to the bridge. The captain speared Bassett with a withering look.

"Lieutenant Bassett. Do you know what you just did?"

"Landed, sir."

"I perceived that. No. I am speaking of what you did on the radio. Do you know?"

"I told Air Plot we were coming in."

"Yes, Lieutenant Bassett, and you also informed every enemy vessel within 5,000 miles of Pearl. Do you know, Lieutenant Bassett, the difference between short-wave and long-wave radio?"

"Yes, sir."

"Do you know that there are different switches to be pulled for different purposes?"

"Yes, sir."

"Do you also know that your instructions were to use the short-wave frequency assigned to this ship for communications?"

"Yes, sir."

"I am not sure Lieutenant Bassett. I am not sure at all. You will return to your quarters and consider yourself under close-quarters arrest until further notice. Perhaps you will take the opportunity to study the radio manual."

"Yes, sir."

Captain Goodwin got a faraway look in his eye. Would they ever learn?"

The captain's concern was amplified next day. One of the FMs came in for a hard landing and flipped on its back. The airedales brought up a small truck-mounted crane, called a cherry picker, to lift the wreck. They should have secured the crane for stability; that was what they had been taught. But they were in a hurry because there were more FMs circling above them. So they hooked the crane to the airplane and began to lift without stopping to tie the crane down. The same swell that had caused the flight deck to lift up on the wrecked FM caught the carrier again, and the crane toppled over on its side. Every man on the flight deck jumped, but one. Larry Ransome did not make it and was crushed between the overturning crane and the deck. The captain suffered as another victim was chalked-up to inexperience.

Captain Goodwin became so concerned with the performance of the ship's crew and the squadron that he called Padre Carlsen to the bridge, and asked him to make a copy of a certain quotation from the Bible. A day or so later a notice came up on the bridge weather shield:

"Even as Jesus Christ admonished his disciples (Mark 8:18) so do I admonish you—Having eyes, do you not see? And having ears, do you not hear, and can you not remember?"

That night, they practiced night carrier landings. Captain Goodwin insisted on that extra margin, for how was he to know what conditions they would encounter in combat? The pilots, and particularly Lieutenant Stewart, the fighter leader, looked upon the whole maneuver with extreme distaste. A night carrier landing, said Lieutenant Stewart, was like a parachute jump: There was no use practicing because if you didn't do it right the first time, you didn't have a problem. But the captain issued the orders, so up they went. Coming down was something else again. Stewart took his FM-2 up, and when he came in on the carrier for landing all he could see was a red suit, luminous in the night, red gloves, paddles, and hat, but no landing signal officer. Lieutenant McClendon was there, underneath all that finery, but Stewart walked away to the ready room muttering that he felt like he had been brought in by the Devil himself. That was also the night that one fighter pilot, misjudging his approach, bounced, gunned his engine, flew directly across the deck full of parked planes, and came in for another shot. Lt. Elmo Waring, the assistant air officer, swore that was the night his gray hairs started sprouting.

When it was over, however, even the captain brightened a bit. Steaming back to Pearl Harbor he gave the crew a "well done" and told them they were now ready to go out and meet the Japanese. It would not be long, the scuttlebutt said. They were going to be part of a striking force to go after the enemy.

## CHAPTER TWELVE

# The Hot-shot Pilots

The *Gambier Bay* had a hot reception when she arrived back at Pearl Harbor on May 20. That same afternoon, a fire started aboard one of a group of LSTs loading ammunition at the Pearl City ordnance dock. The LST blazed, blew up, and spread the fire throughout the little fleet. Several more ships blew up. Fire fighters and fire trucks scurried across the base, but the fire continued to rage, punctuated all afternoon and night by explosions of high-velocity ammunition. Tugs stood off and sprayed the stricken ships, with no apparent effect. Before the night was over, six LSTs had been destroyed, as well as a number of smaller vessels. The scuttlebutt had it that the new operation had to be delayed. That was not true, although a little more time was needed to put everything right on board.

To Captain Goodwin, putting everything right meant having aboard the *Gambier Bay* men he felt confidence in. One of these was Lieutenant Coleman, who as predicted, had never pleased the captain at all as a watch officer. The captain would not let Coleman stand watch unsupervised. He did not want an officer aboard who could not stand watch alone if necessary.

Fortunately, as he was turning the matter over in his mind, Captain Goodwin discovered that Lieutenant Coleman had the same idea. The lieutenant came to his cabin and saluted.

"Captain, may I speak very frankly with you?"

"Of course, Coleman."

"You know, I'm sure, that I am never going to be able to stand officer of the deck watch which will satisfy you."

"Well, I have about reached that same conclusion."

"I have a friend here in the assignment desk in the CINCPAC officer's pool. Would it be all right with you if I arranged to be detached and ordered to that pool for further assignment?"

Would it? Would it ever! The captain was all smiles. "I think you have hit on a perfect solution." he said.

So they shook hands on it, and next day Lieutenant Coleman was gone. Two or three days later Lieutenant Brod, the communications officer, came back from base, chuckling as he stepped onto the bridge.

"Captain, I've got some news that's going to knock you over backward."

"What's that?"

"You know Coleman? You sent him to the pool."

"Yes, of course. He and I agreed that was the best thing to do."

"Well, Coleman now has orders as the commanding officer of an LST!"

"Good God!" said Captain Goodwin. "What is the navy coming to?"

Down below the bridge, in his cubbyhole of an office, Commander Huxtable was putting things right in another fashion. Three new fighter pilots had reported aboard, just before they headed out for maneuvers. Huxtable had heard about two of them, Ens. Leo Zeola and Ens. John Tetz. Their records contained some interesting reading.

After Zeola had narrowly escaped washout during training he had been assigned at Christmastime to the naval air station at Sanford, Florida. There he became friends with another pilot in his flight, Johnny Tetz. They flew together day after day, learning operations in F4F Wildcat fighters. They advanced to the air station at Glenview, Illinois, and qualified with their six landings aboard S.S. *Wolverine*, "the old ferry boat," a converted carrier, and then they were assigned to Trenton, New Jersey.

At Trenton, the two hot pilots were introduced to the FM-2, which was the newest model Wildcat, originally called the F4F, when made by Grumman, or the FM-1, when made by General Motors. The new FM-2 weighed

700 pounds less than the planes Zeola and Tetz were used to flying, but it had an additional 200 horsepower in the engine, "a hot aircraft," as Ensign Zeola put it. But it had some troubles. The valve seats tended to come loose in flight. When the navy learned this, a new program was started. Every General Motors FM-2 delivered by the plant at Linden, New Jersey, had to be taken to the naval aircraft factory at Philadelphia to correct the deficiency. Then the planes were flown to the West Coast. Soon pilots Zeola and Tetz were being flown in a transport to Linden each day, where they picked up FM-2s to fly to the factory. Sometimes, when Zeola and Tetz picked up a plane, they found it had less than an hour's flying time on its record. That meant they must fly around for more than two hours to give the aircraft its proper test before landing.

One day a dozen Trenton pilots boarded the transport and were duly delivered to the field. On the way there, they began talking about New York.

"Gee," said Ensign Zeola, "wouldn't it be nice to see the Statue of Liberty."

"And the Empire State Building . . . ," Tetz piped up.

The talk became general and enthusiastic. The transport plane landed and the pilots picked up their planes. Soon, in twos and threes, they were taking off. About half an hour later, the newspapers, radio stations, and New York City Hall began getting telephone calls.

"Hey, I just saw an airplane fly underneath the Brooklyn Bridge . . . There goes another . . . and another . . . !"

"Hey, I'm looking out at Central Park. There's half a dozen airplanes out there, buzzing the trees. What is it, are the Japanese attacking . . . ?"

"Hey, I'm up here on the thirty-third floor of the Empire State Building. I'm not crazy or anything. You know what I just saw? An airplane circling around the building. What did it have on the wings? You know the white star and the red and blue. What kind? I don't know what kind. . . ."

The calls kept coming. Soon the switchboards of the newspapers and radio stations and City Hall were ringing. So were those of the FBI, where the appearance of airplanes was not regarded as a joke, and the Eastern Sea Frontier, with its offices down by City Hall, where it was not funny either. Rear Adm. Adolphus Andrews, in particular, found it was no joke when he received a telephone call from Admiral King, who had apparently just been talking to Mayor Fiorello La Guardia. Everyone concerned was extremely hot under the collar. Admiral King had assured the civilian authorities that New York was not under attack, but when the civilians wanted to know just what was happening, the commander-in-chief could not tell them.

During the next few hours, all the army air bases were checked out, and all the Coast Guard and navy air stations were asked to account for their aircraft. Inexorably, the finger moved toward Trenton. Only here were there planes unaccounted for.

Ens. Leo Zeola and Ens. John Tetz had filed Trenton local flight plans before taking off that day. Did they go up over Trenton and stay up there? That was the question. It was asked next morning when all the pilots reported to the flight line after breakfast. They were sent to the operations office, and lined up. An officer came forward and asked each pilot: "Were you there?" Every man vigorously denied any knowledge of New York City on the day before. "All right," said the operations officer, "you will each write out a statement and you will sign it." All did so, but before the morning was over, several of the culprits realized that they had perjured themselves in a legal, written document and came forward to admit their part in the prank. The whole dozen were grounded immediately, and the confessors were shipped out—where Zeola and Tetz did not know. Those who did not confess were not shipped away, just then. But in a matter of days a military detail showed up, and the four remaining pilots, including Ensign Tetz and Ensign Zeola, were hustled into a DC-3, the armed guard stood in the aisles of the plane, and they were flown, under arrest, to the naval air station at Brooklyn. Zeola and Tetz did not confess as they, alone among all those pilots, had their local Trenton flight plans to back them up. So they were put back aboard the transport plane and returned to Trenton, free of charges. The commanding officer at Trenton, however, wanted no more part of these particular birds, so they were assigned to a detail picking up aircraft and ferrying, with the West Coast as their ultimate objective. They flew down to Philadelphia and picked up modified FM-2s. There Ensign Zeola got to talking with Ensign Tetz. "Gee," he said, "wouldn't it be nice to see Washington, D.C.?" He had never been there. Neither had Ensign Tetz. Their flight plan had marked out a large restricted area over Washington, and the lieutenant leading the flight of planes observed the orders perfectly. But somehow, near Washington, Ensign Zeola and Ensign Tetz, in the back of the formation, dropped out, and flew directly over the White House, nice and low, so they could have a good look. Then they poured on the speed and caught up, and next time the flight leader looked around, it was as though they had never been out of formation. The telephones at the newspapers, radio stations, the FBI, the White House, the Pentagon, Navy Annex, and the police department began to ring. High officialdom got on other telephones, and wanted to know "where the hell those airplanes had come from" and "what in the hell was going on" when the president of the United States was not safe from air attack even by his own troops.

Soon after, Zeola was assigned sea duty and sent to Barber's Point Naval Air Station in Hawaii, to the pilot pool there. Johnny Tetz soon joined him. They began making the transition into the F6F Hellcat fighter, which was the standard airplane for the fleet carriers by the spring of 1944. But for these hot pilots, the F6F seemed a tame bird indeed compared to the FM-2. After a few weeks, he and Tetz asked if they could not stay in FM-2s. So their orders were changed; they no longer headed for fleet carriers, but would become pilots in the composite squadrons that manned the *Gambier Bay*-class escort carriers, for that was where the FM-2s were going.

Ensigns Zeola and Tetz were assigned to VC-10.

As Commander Huxtable read all this information about the travels of his new pilots, he also had access to the newest information, which dealt with the Empire State Building incident, the Brooklyn Bridge, and the White House flight. Nothing had actually been pinned on these officers, but the information was right there with their official jackets.

Huxtable looked at Zeola and Tetz narrowly. "You are a pair of hot pilots, I understand."

On his first refresher flight out to the escort carrier conducting the operations, Zeola turned down wind, made a cross-leg in approved fashion, and then an approach. The landing signal officer gave the signal to cut, and he did just as he had in the Great Lakes; he dumped the stick and dove for the deck. The FM-2 struck with a clang, and jumped back into the air. The hook was three feet above any arresting wire, and suddenly he found himself floating at eye level with the bridge above the barrier and at low speed. He poured on the gas and got out of there. Miraculously he stayed in the air and came around for a second pass. Once again, he got the cut and dove for the deck. This time, he managed to catch a wire and careen to a halt. The airedales rolled him around and back, and off he went again. The third time he repeated the performance of diving for the deck, bounced off again, and came eyeball to eyeball with the captain, who was glowering at this incompetent flyer.

Into his earphones came the message: "Get that crazy son-of-a-bitch back to the beach." And shortly after came a more restrained message from the Combat Information Center, ordering him back to Barber's Point. After that, for the next three days he lived in a flight suit and flew practice missions landing on the runway, and learning to take a landing signal officer's cut for what it meant: Not to dive for the deck, but to release the back pressure and let the aircraft float in and land. Finally, he got the message, went back out to a carrier, and had fewer problems.

So when Commander Huxtable asked Zeola if he was not the hottest pilot in the navy, Ensign Zeola was a bit more modest than he would have been earlier. This probably saved his neck with Huxtable, for there before the squadron commander was a full report on all the incidents and a request from higher authority for an equally detailed report of disciplinary action meted out to the miscreants. Huxtable read bits from the papers, and chewed Zeola and Tetz out unmercifully. "We do not," he said icily, "need any hot-shot pilots in this squadron." Finally he had exhausted the issue. It was either keep them or send them back to the beach. And both young pilots looked satisfactorily cowed.

"Okay," said the squadron commander. "You've had your last chance, from now on it's shape up or ship out."

Pilots Zeola and Tetz went quietly out of the cabin and onto the flight deck to get some air.

## CHAPTER THIRTEEN

# Pearl

The men of the *Gambier Bay* waited. They knew now what they were waiting for: the day when the invasion force of which they were a part would move out to strike the Japanese. The men of the ship had liberty every other day, according to watch. The officers, too, drew duty only every other day. So for the ship's complement, luxury was the watchword. For the pilots and air crewmen of VC-10 the last two weeks of May 1944, were occupied by tactical training.

Shortly after the ship tied up, Commander Huxtable was called to a meeting in the movie theater at Pearl Harbor. When Huxtable got there, he found the theater filling up with officers from dozens of ships. A marine colonel stepped forward, and the briefing began. It was going to be a tough operation, said the colonel. The Japanese had proved at Tarawa and in the Marshalls how valiantly they could fight, even when outnumbered and outgunned. The difference was going to lie in the quality of effort the Americans could bring to this battle. The navy, Nimitz, Spruance, General Smith, expected the best that every man could offer, and he was sure they were going to get it. Let them make no mistake: Men were going to get hurt, and men were going to die. But the United States forces were going to take the Marianas, and move on from there until they entered Tokyo.

The colonel's briefing was inspired, and Commander

Huxtable came away from it exalted. Then came another briefing for the airmen by Capt. John Crommelin of CINCPAC staff. That officer got down to cases. The aviators were supplied with maps of Saipan and with detailed information about their mission, with battle maps to show where the American ground forces would land and their objectives. After the Crommelin briefing, Commander Huxtable began training VC-10 for the task at hand, specifically, the torpedo pilots.

Commander Huxtable took his torpedo planes to Kauai to practice supply drops, in case the marines encountered difficulties at Saipan like those that had plagued them at Tarawa. Ensign Pyzdrowski was sent to aerial photo school at Barber's point. From 1000 to 1500 every day he flew along the coast of Oahu Island practicing high-speed photography. Other pilots from the squadron went to school to learn aerial minelaying on the island of Kahoolawe. They practiced firing rockets on the north side of Molokai. This invasion of the Marianas would mark the first use of a new variety of rocket, and each torpedo plane would carry six of them. They also learned the use of napalm, the fire bomb introduced by Adm. Harry Hill in the Marshalls invasion.

The officers of the squadron spent much of their spare time at the Barber's Point Naval Air Station officers' club, where they gathered at the bar to drink "Barber's coolers" made of rum and pineapple. Two or three Barber's Coolers tended to encourage somnolence or hi-jinks. Quiet understatement—Hemingway style—was in fashion. The young men would raise their glasses high.

"Hell is war" was the toast they chanted, and then, with all the insouciance they could muster, they would chug-a-lug the drinks, quite unmindful that thousands of miles away young Japanese airmen were quaffing their *sake* in much the same fashion. Some of the American flyers would gather around the piano then, to sing "Deep in the Heart of Texas," "Waltzing Matilda," and "Bless Them All." These were the only war songs most of the young heroes knew. One day when one flyboy broke into "Anchors Aweigh" the room joined him in a line:

"Anchors aweigh, my boys. Anchors aweigh. . . ."

And then the room lapsed into embarassed silence. Nobody knew the next line. General laughter covered the gaffe; these innocents forgave one another, for none of them had been at the war business all that long.

Off-duty officers and men played softball (separately) in an old cow pasture at Pearl City. They went to the movies. Some chased girls in Honolulu. As May drew near its end, the tension grew. Seaman Heinl and Seaman Elbert Covington were on liberty in Waikiki one day when a siren sounded for an air raid drill. They were sitting in a bar, drinking beer, when the noise began, and the S.P.'s came in to order them to an air raid shelter in Kapiolani Park. The bar was full of sailors and marines, most of them fully aware that in a few days an air raid siren would mean the real thing to them. They shouted at the S.P.'s to go away, and leave them alone. The Shore Patrol, outnumbered, called on the army for assistance. Soon trucks came lumbering up, carrying armed soldiers, and again the recalcitrant were ordered to participate in the drill. Again they refused, so the M.P.s and S.P.s began throwing tear gas grenades. One grenade struck a marine in the head and knocked him cold. Some of the sailors began throwing the grenades back at the army men. A full-scale riot was only narrowly averted when the servicemen finally went out into the park, but they never did enter the shelter.

During the last two or three days of May everyone knew the *Gambier Bay* was about to sail. Trucks brought fresh provisions—a sure sign of departure within seventy-two hours. The word got out that grape juice was a good vitamin supplement. The officers went out by the dozen to buy grape juice at the navy exchange. The enlisted men also had juice on their minds, but of another sort. Some men came aboard carrying bottles. Three Feathers whiskey, gin, and rum, which were promptly confiscated by the officers of the deck. Naval regulations prohibited consumption of alcohol except for medical purposes. Some men came aboard with mysterious bulges at waist, armpit, or trouser leg, all of which had to be investigated, usually to the discomfiture of the smugglers. A store of beer was brought aboard legally, and promptly locked up in the ship's brig, which, in fact, was never used for any other purpose. The beer would be drunk on liberty parties off-ship, later on.

The junior officers and enlisted men still did not know where they were going but had a pretty good idea from the scuttlebutt. On May 30, two marine passengers boarded the *Gambier Bay*, and a crated Stinson OY-1 "Grasshopper" observation plane was hoisted aboard. So it was to be an invasion, that much was clear to everyone by the end of the day.

With the invasion forces massed, Admirals Nimitz and Spruance were confident enough that they risked a breach in security by calling the senior fleet officers and pilots to a meeting and briefing them on the objective of Operation Forager. Admiral Spruance was in command. The Joint Expeditionary Force would be commanded by Adm. Kelly Turner, who by this time, after experience at Guadalcanal, the Gilberts, and the Marshalls, was the world's foremost expert on amphibious operations. The small carriers would support the landings, while the fast carrier force, under Adm. Marc Mitscher, and the landbased air force, under Adm. John Hoover, moved far afield to destroy any enemy aircraft or warships that threatened the invasion forces. In all, the force consisted of 535 ships, more than a thousand carrier aircraft, and 127,500 troops. Once the troops were ashore, they would come under the command of Gen. Holland M. Smith, the marine chief of Nimitz's ground forces in the Central Pacific. The *Gambier Bay* was going to cover the Saipan and Tinian invasions of the Fifth Amphibious Corps, which consisted of the Second and Fourth Marine Divisions. Another force would attack Guam.

At that briefing the major target—Saipan—was revealed, insofar as the Americans knew it. They estimated that 15,000 Japanese defenders would face them on Saipan. The actual figure was 32,000 troops. They also underestimated the nature and extent of the enemy's defensive establishment, and, above all, they underestimated the Japanese naval high command's reaction, which would be to send its Combined Fleet against the Americans.

But that was the big picture. As far as the *Gambier Bay* and VC-10 were concerned, they would be part of a fleet of four escort carriers, two destroyers, and four destroyer-escorts that would cover the beaches of the Saipan-Tinian attack force. First, the fast carriers would move in and plaster Saipan, Tinian, Rota, Guam, and Pagan. Then Hoover's land-based airplanes would strike Truk, Woleai, Palau, and Yap to prevent the Japanese there from sending reinforcements to the Marianas. The fast carriers by this time would be hitting Iwo Jima and Chi Chi Jima to prevent air assistance from moving down south. Admiral Mitscher's fifteen carriers would mount more than 800 planes for this purpose.

The strikes would actually begin on June 11. On June 13, the *Gambier Bay* and the other ships of the Saipan invasion force would be in position, the old battleships and cruisers would begin the firing, and the air squadrons would begin bombing Saipan to soften up the enemy. On June 14, the troops would land, and then VC-10's job would be to cover them and provide air support for the invaders and the invasion fleet. All this would begin for the men of the *Gambier Bay* on May 31. Early that morning she would weigh anchor and move out. All liberty would end at 9 P.M. (2100) on May 30.

May 30 dawned, Memorial Day, the holiday to honor Americans dead in a war nearly a hundred years before. Commander Ballinger managed to secure leave for any and all men who wanted to go ashore, as long as the watches were covered. When that word came, the ship began to empty. An enormous beer party was held by enlisted men ashore. The officers trooped over to the Barber's Point club for a last fling—but not all of them. A few, like Ensign Pyzdrowski, were affected by the solemnity of the holiday and by the enormity of what lay before them. Pyzdrowski headed across Ford Island to Battleship Row, and looked down into the water at the hulk of the USS *Arizona*. There she was, the broad deck outline visible, but only her superstructure rising to the surface. She had gone down, he remembered, on the very day that he had soloed for the first time in an airplane at Butler Municipal Field outside Pittsburgh. It was a very solemn young ensign who turned away and began to walk back to the *Gambier Bay*.

That evening Pyzdrowski remained ashore until after dark. He lay down on the grass near the ship and listened to the sounds of loading. He looked up at the stars and prayed that God keep him in the palm of his hand the rest of the way on the long journey. Suddenly he was pulled from his somnolence by the sound of the squawk box aboard the *Gambier Bay*.

"Ensign Pyzdrowski. Ensign Pyzdrowski. Report to the quarterdeck."

It was time to go. The war beckoned.

# CHAPTER FOURTEEN

# Saipan

Captain Goodwin told Navigator Gellhorn to fix the course for Roi in Kwajalein Atoll of the Marshall Islands. These islands had been captured five months earlier and quickly turned into a staging base for the fleet. Gellhorn was not familiar with them since before the war they had been part of Japan's "forbidden empire" and the Americans had very little knowledge of the sea around them. So Gellhorn depended, as he would for most of the voyage, on Ens. Al Beisang, a reserve officer, but one who knew his navigation. Just before Lieutenant Commander Gellhorn left the captain's cabin, Captain Goodwin had another idea.

"By the way," the captain said, "while you're at it, you'd better prepare a Napier Diagram."

Lieutenant Commander Gellhorn merely nodded and left the cabin. When he got back to the chart room, he passed the assignment on to Beisang, as if it were nothing at all. In fact, the preparation of a Napier Diagram was extremely complicated, and if Gellhorn might have done it in his academy days, he probably had forgotten how. It required the precise plotting of data that involved the compass deviation, magnetic reading, and variation, to obtain a true heading in case of failure of the ship's gyroscope. No one expected the gyroscope to fail; in the navigation department they regarded the captain's assignment as just another bit of harrying designed to keep them on their toes. Gellhorn said no more about the Napier Diagram, but Beisang spent many hours with his slide rule and logarithm charts and finally produced the diagram.

On the morning of departure, as usual, Captain Goodwin took his coffee on the bridge. As the land faded away that morning, Junior, his steward came up with the captain's silver service and two cups, in case Commander Borries or another officer had been called to the bridge, and the captain felt like entertaining. Junior came up the ladder into the pilothouse below the open bridge, a feat of balancing worth watching, and then on up through to the captain's station. The helmsman, boatswain's mate, quartermaster, and bugler looked greedily after him, but anyone noticing would see that their greed was tempered with anticipation. As usual, no one else was on the bridge, the captain drank a single cup from the full pot and sent Junior back below.

This was the moment the pilothouse watch had been waiting for. Junior, a dark-skinned native of Guam, was relegated under the naval code to stewardship, but he really wanted to be a sailor.

"Hi, Junior," said Bugler Deffenbaugh warmly. "Hullo, Junior," said all the others. Junior flashed them a big smile and began to step around, toward the ladder.

"Wouldn't you like to run the ship?"

"Whadda you mean?"

"I mean steer?"

"You mean I really could?"

"I don't see why not. He could do it, bo'sun, couldn't he?"

"Sure, as long as Bell watches him."

So Junior, in great glee, took the helm of the mighty ship. To do so he had to put down his tray, whereupon three sets of willing hands reached for it, because it was well known aboard the *Gambier Bay* that the captain's coffee was the finest in the ship. Junior steered, the captain above unmindful, and Bell supervised, casting anguished glances over his shoulder at the other three men who drank coffee from the captain's silver service. Finally, the boatswain's mate took pity and made Quartermaster Hagerty supervise Junior so Bell could share the proceeds of their chicanery.

Captain Goodwin took no notice of such shenanigans, even if he was aware of them. His mind was focused on more important matters, particularly the coming action in which he, his men, and his ship would be tested. There was still a little time for more training, and he was not going to miss a moment of it. They were traveling with a large element of Task Force 52, the Saipan invasion team. The *Gambier Bay* and *Kitkun Bay* began to launch planes in a battle exercise. Down on the flight deck, the activity began, as planes were brought up from the hangar by the elevators. Air Officer Borries passed the word to Lieutenant Waring, his assistant, and Waring alerted Lieutenants Pilgrim, McClendon, and Krida, the junior officers who worked the flight deck. They would practice some fighter catapults in the course of the program. The fighter pilots, when they heard that news, began to groan. The catapult was an understandable necessity for the lumbering torpedo bombers, but Wildcats did not need catapults. Or so they said. The captain said otherwise, and otherwise it was.

So on the flight deck, the sailors in the green T-shirts got busy. The boys in the red T-shirts gassed up the planes, and the boys in the blue shirts began spotting them under the direction of the men in yellow T-shirts. "Charlie Butterworth" (Lieutenant Pilgrim) hummed to himself in the manner of the actor for whom he had been nicknamed, and gloated in his power. He would give the zoomies a little extra kick; those extra "gs" would teach them to laugh and call his catapult a "turkey." When the *Gambier Bay* turned into the wind, the launching began. Lieutenant Krida ran up and down the deck, checking on everything; he was the jack of all trades on the flight deck. He lumbered along, singing "blood on the saddle, blood on the ground, great big puddles of blood on the ground. . . ." Lieutenant McClendon, slim, intense, and worried over his charges, took his irridescent paddles and waited for the boys to come home so he could bring them down.

On the bridge, the captain ordered General Quarters. Down in the mess hall, in the spud locker, Seaman Chenry Quinn was organizing a little game. Quinn was a plank owner, who had joined the ship at Astoria in the First Division. But after a few months he had been put on mess cooking, and he liked that duty, so he stayed after BMlc A. J. Smith, who had also joined the ship after service with Quartermaster Bell in USS *Trinity*, offered Quinn command of the spud locker. For a man of gambling bent, this was a choice assignment, with plenty of privacy and virtually no chance that an officer would disturb it. For weeks, Quinn had operated a game of Seven-Over-Under, with the suckers betting and Quinn paying off. When seven came up he won all. If the bettor believed in fives, and an eleven came up, Quinn also won. It was a nice little hobby, and lucrative. But this day as the alarm rang through the ship, Seaman Quinn tucked away his dice, waved the gamblers away, grabbed his steel helmet, and headed up toward his battle station. He was a gunner on a 20-mm gun on the port side. As he came up, on the flight deck the first planes were preparing to launch.

All day long the *Gambier Bay* and *Kitkun Bay* circled in operations. At dusk, the planes were called in, and shortly afterward, the *Gambier Bay* found herself in company with the large force, the old battleships *California, Tennessee, Maryland,* and *Colorado,* and four transports loaded with troops. Next morning, June 1, at General Quarters, Captain Goodwin gave the men of the *Gambier Bay* the word: As they all knew in their hearts, they were going into battle.

First, he said, they would stop in the Marshalls where the invasion force was making ready. Then their destination was the Marianas islands. They could be proud, the captain said, because this invasion force was the largest yet mounted in the war. The *Gambier Bay*'s task was to cover the marines while they landed on Saipan. They must expect attack by Japanese planes and perhaps by ships, for the enemy could not be expected to take this invasion without a fight. There was no question of the outcome, the captain said, for American might would win. The Japanese were going to remember Pearl Harbor when the Americans reached Saipan.

That afternoon of June 1, the men of the *Gambier Bay* heard the general message sent to the invasion force by Admiral Nimitz. Their commander wished them "good hunting and good luck." The hunting would not begin for ten days; they could use the luck, but they did not have it. On June 2, as the planes of VC-10 lined up on the flight deck for takeoff to begin the day's exercises, the guns of one of the fighters went off suddenly and struck an airedale, wounding him in three places.

The *Kitkun Bay*'s planes and those of the *Gambier Bay* shared the tasks of mounting daily antisubmarine patrols and combat air patrols, to protect their convoy from Japanese attack. The other planes of the two carriers flew off to join several other squadrons in war games each day. They practiced aerial rendezvous and simulated attacks on their own ships. On June 2 and June 3, these exercises were carried out satisfactorily, but, on June 4, Lt. Owen Wheeler landed his torpedo plane in the water. A destroyer was nearby and Wheeler and his two crewmen were rescued. On June 6, the weather roughed up. Ensign Zeola, who feared virtually nothing, described his flight that day as "one of the hairiest I ever made." He also lost two friends who were pilots aboard the *Kitkun Bay;* one spun in on takeoff and the other was killed on landing. *Gambier Bay*'s Landing Signal Officer McClendon had a rough afternoon, with the carrier pitching and tossing in a rising sea. Lt. Bob Weatherholt brought his torpedo plane in but did not make the carrier and had to put down in the sea. His radioman, P. E. Collins, became the squadron's first air crew casualty when he failed to emerge from the tunnel before the Avenger sank.

On June 7, the pilots were edgy. Wheeler's engine failure of June 4, and Weatherholt's almost duplicate trouble two days later had made the torpedo pilots suspicious of the planes they would have to fly in combat. That day Lieutenant Bassett's TBM also began acting up immediately after the catapult launching. The symptoms were the same: black smoke which meant an oil problem. Bassett immediately turned and headed back to the carrier for a landing. Captain Goodwin looked on in shocked surprise; what was this pilot doing coming back immediately after launch? But Lieutenant McClendon saw the smoke and understood the problem, so he ignored grumblings from the bridge and brought the ailing plane aboard, safe and sound. Chief Montgomery took a look at Bassett's plane and found that the oil return line was rubbing against the firewall. A few miles more and the line might have parted, and then Bassett would have faced the same problem that had sent those other two TBMs into the sea, a frozen engine. The TBMs were all checked out, and the pilots began to regain confidence as no more incidents developed. But they had left Pearl Harbor with sixteen fighter planes and twelve torpedo bombers. Now they had only ten bombers.

The nineteen fighter pilots and fourteen bomber pilots moved into a lifestyle that was to become habitual at sea.

In the morning, at reveille, those who would fly combat air patrol and antimsubmarine patrol were alert before dawn. Those who were not scheduled to fly went from their quarters to the head to shave, then to the wardroom for breakfast, then to the ready room, where they spent most of the day, listening to the squawk box, reading, playing cards, or napping.

The food aboard the *Gambier Bay* varied, depending on who and where you were. The officers ate well, plenty of steak and ice cream. They were nearly as well off as the chiefs, whose messes, throughout the navy, were always the best because the chiefs managed to scrounge delicacies no matter where they went. The enlisted men's mess was something else again, and from the outset the men had complained. Finally, out of Pearl, the grease and grit became so deadly that the word "mutiny" was mentioned, and the officers complained enough to Commander Ballinger that the cooks were racked up and the food improved. The *Gambier Bay* was shaking down fast.

On June 7, Lieutenant Bell briefed the ship's company on the nature of the mission ahead of them. Some of the material repeated the all-fleet briefing at Pearl Harbor before their departure. He repeated the warning that the pilots of this carrier were responsible for antisubmarine patrol and combat air patrol to provide safety for the whole Saipan landing force. He did not need to repeat the warning given at Pearl, that *Liscome Bay*, a sister ship, had been sunk in the Gilberts operation by a Japanese submarine, and that they must be constantly on the lookout.

That day came another incident. One of the plane captains sitting in a TBM with folded wings decided he would make like a combat pilot. He pulled the trigger switch of the 50-cal. gun. Several 50-cal. shells pierced the flight deck, and one went down into the air crewmen's ready room and sliced through a book in the hands of one man, then smashed through the deck and injured several men in a compartment below.

On June 8, the *Gambier Bay* reached Roi. She anchored in the midst of what Lieutenant Odum called "a limitless armada of American ships." Quartermaster Bell, perhaps a little less romantic, counted seven battleships, eight cruisers, four carriers, and about thirty destroyers, plus many smaller craft and transports. "It is sure going to take a lot of Jap ships to put this task force to the bottom," Bell wrote in his diary, "& I don't think they can bring that many around. . . ."

At Roi the ships all loaded supplies and ammunition for the fight ahead. The mail came aboard, and with it an Alnav (directive from Washington) which brought word of a number of promotions aboard. That summer most of the junior officers got promoted; ensigns became lieutenants (jg) and jg's became full lieutenants or two stripers. Borries and Huxtable became full commanders. The officers and men who stayed with the ship were moving along. So, for that matter, were some of the others, who had "peeled off" at various points. One of them, Lieutenant Coleman, was in command of one of the LSTs assigned to this operation, and his ship may have been an element of Lieutenant Odum's "armada."

On June 9, the *Gambier Bay* continued to load. The men had to stop work three times during the day, for Japanese planes were reported to be snooping around. Snoop they did, but that was all; the land-based aircraft were alerted and took off, but the Japanese never appeared to challenge them.

The Marianas invasion, Operation Forager, was already in motion. Admiral Spruance had come from Pearl Harbor in his flagship, the cruiser *Indianapolis,* to Eniwetok. The fifteen carriers of the fast carrier force were poised, and ready to strike various islands around the Marianas to prevent a Japanese air attack from starting.

At Roi Captain Goodwin and Commander Borries went ashore with Commander Huxtable to try to bargain with authority for two TBMs to replace the planes lost on the voyage from Pearl Harbor. They would find a snowball in hell first, said the supply officer cheerfully. The answer was a quick no; if there had been any spare torpedo bombers they were long ago spoken for by the "big boys," the fast carriers.

There was no other shore leave, except on official business. Lt. J. W. Patterson, the ship's athletic officer, organized his first boxing show to amuse the men. In San Diego he had bought a ring and all the equipment. He had help from the "old hands" who had seen dozens of navy boxing smokers. When he called for volunteers, it was not a question of finding warriors but ot separating the sheep from the goats. Finally they arranged a seven-bout card that supposedly pitted matched competitors. The ring was set up on the forward elevator and the crew sat on the hangar deck and on the edge of the flight deck above. The ship's band was assembled and played between matches. AMM3c John Smorda, the ship's "jazz singer" was the announcer. Chief Joe Russell served as referee, and Commander Ballinger kept time. It was a highly successful promotion, and for an hour or so most of the men forgot what lay ahead of them. That day the crew also got mail from home, and in the afternoon the last mail was delivered into the hands of the censoring officers for shipment back to the United States. It was apparent on the evening of June 9 that the time had run out.

On June 10, the Saipan invasion fleet sailed from Roi. Next morning the call to General Quarters rang out at 4:30, and the men of the *Gambier Bay* ran to their action stations, while the pilots and air crews of VC-10 prepared to man their planes. They would conduct antisubmarine patrols and combat air patrols to protect the invasion force.

That morning Captain Goodwin gave the crew a pep talk over the loudspeaker. Quartermaster Bell found it inspirational. There was a difference this first day of the *Gambier Bay*'s war: The men had breakfast at their action stations. The ship was secured at nine o'clock in the morning, and the invasion force steamed on. *Gambier Bay*'s planes returned to the carrier after several hours, and flights from other escort carriers took over the protective action. They were all part of Rear Adm. H. B. Sallada's Carrier Division 26, which also included the *Kitkun Bay, Hoggatt Bay,* and *Nehenta Bay,* and they would split the defense on the way to their objective. In the afternoon, Lt. Vereen Bell gave another talk over the squawk-boxes, telling the men the nature of Saipan and Tinian islands, and what was known about the Japanese defenses. Bell was scarcely finished when the captain informed them that two Japanese planes had been sighted by the combat air patrol. One was shot down, but the other escaped in the clouds. That meant the invasion force must be even more alert against possible attack. At 3 o'clock that afternoon, once more it was *Gambier Bay*'s turn to take the patrols; four fighters were launched as combat air patrol and torpedo bombers went off low to look for submarines. They did not find any submarines on that day, or the next, but, on June 13, a TBM pilot from VC-10 believed he saw a periscope. He dropped several depth charges. Immediately a pair of destroyers moved in, and gave the area a heavy attack. They reported an oil slick on the surface, which, if not illusory, meant that the charges had sunk or damaged an enemy submarine. The bridge kept up a commentary during such actions as information was received over the talk-between-ships (TBS) radio frequency. Thus, the men of the *Gambier Bay* felt very much a part of the action.

Just before noon on June 13, *Gambier Bay*'s combat air patrol was relieved by that of the *Kitkun Bay*, and the fighters landed. The wheels of the last plane had scarcely ceased turning when over the TBS came the word that the combat air patrol from the *Kitkun Bay* had "spooked" a Japanese Betty, a twin-engined bomber. They were going after it, the *Kitkun Bay* reported. Almost immediately a report followed: They had lost the plane in the clouds. The men of the *Gambier Bay* groaned, but then came another report. The Betty had just been shot down. The captain had no sooner said the words than an enormous cheer went through the ship. That afternoon, Captain Goodwin hooked the TBS system into the ship's squawk-boxes, so the crew could follow all the action of their force. He also told them that the next day, June 14, at daybreak they would be thirty miles off Saipan, and VC-10 would begin its attacks.

After dark the ship was secured and those men not on watch turned in to sleep. They were awakened at 11 o'clock that night by the alarm and the bugler: General Quarters. Quartermaster Bell was lying in his bunk, wondering what tomorrow would bring. He jumped up and into his shoes and hurried to his action station, the helm. He was the man who would steer the *Gambier Bay* in battle. On the bridge he learned that the ship's radar had picked up a blip at 4,000 yards. A destroyer was dispatched to investigate, and the whole force was standing by for action. The destroyer opened fire on the target, which returned the fire, and then disappeared. Was it a submarine? The destroyer circled, dropping depth charges and after a few minutes reported an oil slick.

The task force now took credit for sinking two Japanese submarines. Had they actually done so? The best Japanese account of submarine activity, by I-boat Captain Zenji Orita and the American account by writer Joseph Harrington, indicate that RO-114 may have been the submarine sunk on the night of June 13, and RO-111 may have been the submarine sunk the following night.

During the night, the *Kitkun Bay* and *Gambier Bay,* left the task group and joined the *Coral Sea* and *Corregidor,* two more escort carriers, and the bombardment force off Saipan. At 8 o'clock in the morning the air strikes began. No *Gambier Bay* planes were lost to enemy action that day, although three cracked up on landing on the carrier deck, and one fighter was so badly damaged that the airedales pushed it overboard.

The troops were to land on Saipan on June 15, and the bombardment by battleships, cruisers, and destroyers began two days earlier. The fast carriers were supposed to work over the Marianas beginning on June 12, but on the morning of June 11, Japanese planes were seen by the task force, which meant that the enemy knew the Americans were coming. There was nothing further to be gained by delay, so Spruance told Admiral Mitscher to go ahead. For four days the planes from the big carriers bombed and strafed the islands of the Marianas. They had no opposition until June 12, when a group of ten Japanese bombers appeared but were driven off. On June 15, two more groups of Bettys appeared, but they did no damage and several were destroyed. From Admiral Spruance's flagship, it seemed unlikely that, after all these days of bombing, strafing, and naval gunnery, there could be anything left to worry the marines when they landed on June 15. But they were in for a surprise. As the Americans had learned new techniques of attacking, the Japanese had learned new ways of defending themselves. They were dug in so deep and their blockhouses were so heavily reinforced that the bombardment had relatively little effect. The marines landed and encountered such heavy opposition that they fell behind schedule the first day.

The first air strike from the *Gambier Bay* was in the air at 8 o'clock that morning. The first target was a sugar mill at Charon Kanoa. Commander Huxtable led the TBMs and Lieutenant Stewart led the fighters. Huxtable had to give up the lead to Lieutenant Bassett midway in the approach when his radio went out. For several days, they had been hearing stories of the heavy anti-aircraft fire put up by the Japanese against the fleet carrier raids, and the bomber pilots were worried. But on this first attack, they found the anti-aircraft fire very light and came back to the carrier quite elated. All came back, that is, but Lieutenant Stewart. During a strafing run, Stewart's Wildcat was hit in the engine by groundfire, and began to cough. He managed to nurse the plane out over the sea and land in the water beside a destroyer, which promptly picked him up. But he would not be seen by the men of the *Gambier Bay* for two weeks. There was no time during the battle to stop and decant stranded airmen.

Lt. James F. Oliver took over as acting squadron fighter commander after Stewart's crash. All day long the pilots of VC-10 flew support missions. The other escort carriers had responsibility for the combat air patrol. Lieutenant (jg) Pyzdrowski flew one antisubmarine patrol early in the morning, northwest and ahead of the carrier force. On his return he and his crewmen had a first-rate view of the landing craft moving in from the invasion fleet. On their second scouting rotation that day, they passed over Marpi Point at the extreme north end of the island. Lieutenant Bell had briefed them about the enemy several times, and on the last occasion he had told them the defenders of Saipan were Japanese marines, most of them six feet tall and committed to death rather than surrender. Nor could they expect to encounter any friendly natives on Saipan or Tinian, the second point of invasion. The Marianas were a part of the Inner Empire; the housing, customs, and language were all Japanese. They had taken in this information but it had not prepared them for the sight they saw that day at Marpi Point. As they passed over the cliff top, they saw men, women, and children holding hands, leaping from the cliff 900 feet to certain death. These were civilians, who also were determined never to surrender. Their deaths, before the invasion was well launched, were an indication of the amount of faith they put in the claims on the radio of Toyko Rose that Saipan would never fall. On the third rotation of their scouting mission that day, they flew along the bottom of Marpi Point cliff and saw the bodies pounded in the heavy surf. There were hundreds of them.

Aboard the ship, the men of the *Gambier Bay* had ringside seats to watch the battle, plus the commentary of the radio. Captain Goodwin had the pilots' communication band piped into the public address system, and they listened to the aviators talking. Admiral Turner had given the signal to land the troops at 5:42 that morning. The Second and Fourth Marine Divisions were making the assault, and they would hit the beaches of the Charan Kanoa and drive for the air fields at both ends of the landing area.

At 8:44 the first wave hit the beach, and by nine o'clock troops had landed on all designated beaches. They came under intense fire from the Japanese, who had constructed their defenses with concrete and logs so that the firing range of one machine gun overlapped the next. On the mountains behind the beaches, the Japanese had placed 77-mm and 105-mm guns, and surprisingly few of these were affected by the three-day bombardment and the heavy air attacks of the fleet carriers. By the time the fourth American wave of troops landed the Japanese had begun to lay down a barrage on the beaches. In several places, the Americans were stopped, and at 10 o'clock, Col. James P. Risely of the Sixth Regiment called for his reserve battalion. That was an indication of the difficulties the landing force faced. They called for gun support from the battleships and cruisers, and Torchy called for air strikes as he toured above the battlefield and observed the movement of Japanese troops. VC-10 sent its fighters out first to strafe, and then the bombers, each loaded with ten 100-pound fragmentation bombs. That evening, Tokyo Rose broadcast to the Americans and warned them that they would all end up in watery graves when the Imperial Nipponese forces descended upon them and destroyed them. Already, she said, the Americans had tried twice to land on Saipan and had twice been repelled. Knowing how untrue that remark was, the men of the *Gambier Bay* laughed at Tokyo Rose's warning that the Japanese Combined Fleet was coming out to get them.

Just after Tokyo Rose's show, the general alarm sounded aboard the *Gambier Bay,* and it was back to battle stations for every man. The captain reported that a flight of enemy bombers had been spotted, apparently heading their way. But a few minutes later came the order to secure; of the five Bettys in the Japanese flight, four had been shot down by the combat air patrol from another carrier.

That night of June 15, the men of the *Gambier Bay* expected some sort of attack. They were worried and frightened, and many of them wrote letters to loved ones at home to express their feelings.

"It is night time and very hot in two ways," wrote Ensign Lischer to his father and sister. "I must admit I'm scared as I think everyone probably is . . . With some of my experiences I have believed in God more and felt him closer than ever before. I haven't turned strictly religious, but to feel Him in there helping is a helpful feeling. . . ."

Padre Carlsen noted the same phenomenon that night. The ship was unusually quiet, and the men were unusually respectful and comradely toward him, even men he had never seen in chapel. Very few atheists went to bed aboard the *Gambier Bay* that night of June 15, 1944.

## CHAPTER FIFTEEN

# Beachhead Secured

On June 16, 1944, the men of the *Gambier Bay* were awakened at three o'clock in the morning. The alarm bell rang over loudspeakers throughout the ship: Clang-Clang-Clang. The bugler blew the call to General Quarters, and the bosun called: "Man your battle stations." Lieutenant Greenfield, the assistant supply officer, was sleeping in his underwear because of the heat. He groped for the light above his bunk, found his shoes and slipped into them, grabbed his trousers and shirt from the end of the bunk, struggled into them, leaving shirttails flying, and grabbed up his life preserver in one hand and his awkward gunbelt with the .45 Colt automatic in the other, and then fumbled for his steel helmet as well. He dashed for his battle station, a race against the men dogging down the watertight doors. Panting, he reached his station, one of the port batteries of anti-aircraft guns and began counting the noses of his men.

A little later the captain explained that enemy planes had been picked up on the radar screen, about sixty miles out. Radar, the great boon from the British, made all the difference; the ship was alert long before any enemy could approach. But this group of enemy planes apparently had business elsewhere, for after moving in to a point ten miles off the carrier, to seaward, the enemy changed course, and moved away. Still, the captain kept the ship at General Quarters until seven o'clock.

By that time "the strike" had left the *Gambier Bay*, to assist the marines on the beaches. Later in the day, some of the TBMs carried supplies and ammunition for the troops. Twenty thousand men had been landed, but they were moving slowly against strong opposition. Early in the morning the Japanese launched a *banzai* attack. Officers screaming that they would drive the marines into the sea, brandished their samurai swords and came down the hills. But marine tanks and troops stopped the attack, and by the time the Japanese had reformed their forces, the air strikes were beginning. On the radio circuit, Quartermaster Bell heard two of the *Gambier Bay*'s TBM pilots arguing about which one would have the privilege of going down and destroying an enemy truck and a squad of men. One of them yielded, the other was off the air for a few moments, then came back to report: no more truck, no more Japanese.

Aboard the *Gambier Bay* a good deal of romantic talk developed during the day. The fact was that the going was extremely difficult for the marines, but Admiral Turner was not advertising that fact, so the impression in the fleet was that this invasion was a walkaway. The planes struck Garapan, the principal town on the island, and set fire to the cane fields. The explosions and the fires gave a satisfactory feeling of success but actually did relatively little damage to the defense effort.

That day the torpedo bombers were loaded with 500-pound bombs and assigned to find and destroy enemy artillery which was pounding the marines who were moving toward Aslito airfield. East of the air field, Lieutenant (jg) Pyzdrowski's radioman, Jerry Fauls, spotted four small guns placed at the points of a square. He thought perhaps a big gun might be in the middle, camouflaged, and told Pyzdrowski it might be worth an attack. Pyzdrowski nosed the bomber over. The four anti-aircraft guns (for that is what they were) began firing, but he dove through the flak and bombed. Behind him came two other bombers. All three 500-pound bombs struck the target and wiped out a piece of heavy artillery.

It would take more than air power to win control of these islands, however; the fast carriers learned this much on June 16, when they sent planes against Guam and Tinian to neutralize the airfields there. The Japanese anti-aircraft fire was strong and accurate, and a number of carrier planes were shot down. On Saipan, the pilots of the *Gambier Bay* did not seem to have the same difficulty, perhaps because the big guns of the battleships and cruisers were available to keep the anti-aircraft gunners down.

For the men of the *Gambier Bay* June 16 was a relatively quiet day. June 17 would be a little different. It began with a routine call to General Quarters an hour before sunrise. The captain then got on the public address system with some exciting news: The Japanese fleet was out.

One of the reasons for attacking the Marianas, he told the men, was to draw the Japanese Combined Fleet into open battle. A dozen Japanese carriers were coming at them from the Philippines, and so Admiral Spruance had ordered the fast carriers and fast battleships to "go get 'em." They had gone off, leaving to the escort carriers the entire job of supporting the landings. So far, at least to Quartermaster Bell, "this has been too easy." He estimated that the whole of Admiral Sallada's escort carrier command had lost only half a dozen planes (which was about right), and with the word that Lieutenant Stewart had been picked up, the *Gambier Bay* had not yet lost an airman.

The Japanese had indeed launched their strike, which they hoped would be decisive in their favor. They called it the A-GO Plan, and its purpose was to tempt the American fleet in the area south of the Marianas. But when the Americans attacked Saipan, Vice Adm. Jisaburo Ozawa, the fleet commander, was forced to act.

The Marianas were only 1,500 miles from Japan, and public opinion would be shocked if the enemy invaded this ring of the empire. Admiral Ozawa's force was smaller than Admiral Mitscher's, and the American carrier planes outnumbered the Japanese by two to one. But the Japanese fully expected to have the support of more than 500 aircraft sent previously to the Marianas, the Palaus, and other islands in the area. Their planes, which were not armored, were lighter than the American and had greater range. Finally, Ozawa had the "weather gauge" as long as the easterly trade wind held. He could launch and recover planes while approaching the enemy, while the Americans had to turn into the wind to launch and recover, which meant turn the wrong way.

On June 17, Admiral Spruance was getting ready for the battle, and he issued his battle orders. But the men of the *Gambier Bay* knew virtually nothing about this major action. Their job was to stick with the invasion and protect the ships and the troops. On June 17, operations continued as they had for two days. The *Gambier Bay* now carried a marine observer, who flew in the Grasshopper with Captain Goulet, the pilot, and kept in communication with the ground. But on the night of June 16, his contact with his counterpart on the island had been broken off, and he worried that this man might be dead. He wanted to get down to Aslito that day, although only part of the field was held by the marines.

He asked Captain Goodwin for the use of a TBM and pilot for the mission. Captain Goodwin assigned Pyzdrowski the task. The TBM took off from the *Gambier Bay*, and on the way to Aslito, the marine officer briefed Pyzdrowski on the approach he must take to avoid friendly fire: a very low pass over the channel between Saipan and Tinian. The field was rough and full of potholes caused by artillery, but the marines had filled a path fifty feet wide and it was possible to land. They landed safely, and the observer warned Pyzdrowski to move fast and keep his head down since pilots were a favorite Japanese target. Since no planes had landed on Aslito yet, Pyzdrowski wondered how he knew. He listened, not quite believing.

"As you leave the plane, run ahead of me and keep your head down."

"Sure," said Pyzdrowski, and he proceeded to stop halfway along their transit to stare at the first Japanese prisoners of war he had ever seen. Immediately came a "zing" past his right ear, and he was tackled from behind. It was the observer.

"For Christ's sake, lie low and keep your head down."

Marine machine-gunners began peppering the trees across the runway. They must have shot the sniper, for a few moments later someone signaled them to go on in. The observer went to find the commander, and Pyzdrowski was directed to the mess hall to wait. The marines had not been in occupancy of the territory for twenty-four hours, but they had already adapted the Japanese facilities and were socked in. He was befriended in the mess hall by a marine cook who was making doughnuts. The cook glanced at Pyzdrowski's name on the brown patch of his breast and smiled.

"I'm a Polack, too," he said, "from Milwaukee." So

the navy Polack and the marine Polack exchanged anecdotes about their service careers. "Your first combat?" said the marine.

Pyzdrowski nodded. "Where was yours?"

"Tarawa."

The marine gave Pyzdrowski a bottle of sake and a bag of fresh doughnuts which would certainly prove to the ready room that Pyzdrowski was the first navy pilot to land on Saipan. Then the observer returned, and Pyzdrowski took him back to the *Gambier Bay*. They landed on the carrier, and when the engine stopped they got out. From time to time, over the radio, they had heard reports of action by the combat air patrol, but the ships of the carrier force had not been bothered. Still, the observer and Captain Goulet decided that the time had come for them to leave. The marine commander at Aslito had said the field would be totally secure in another few hours, and that the observer might as well begin operating from Aslito on the morning of the 18th. So the Grasshopper found a new home. The observer went below to pick up his kit, and Captain Goulet got the little plane ready for take off. When the observer came up on the flight deck again, Lieutenant (jg) Pyzrowski stopped to say good-bye.

"How many spotting missions have you flown?" asked the junior lieutenant.

The other man looked at him, with a calm and businesslike eye. "Oh, about two hundred and eighty hours, I'd say."

"That goes back quite a way," said Pyzdrowski.

"Yes," said the observer. "Back to Guadalcanal. . . ."

So that was how the observer knew about the sniper.

Other than that, the *Gambier Bay* and VC-10 had a relatively uneventful day. At least that was true until six o'clock in the evening as dusk was settling in. The call to General Quarters sounded again. The men had settled into a sort of routine by this time, and most of them believed the signal was no more than standard dusk routine. But this time there was more.

Chaplain Carlsen's General Quarters station was on the bridge with the captain, and his assignment was to be the "talker," to give the ship's crew a blow-by-blow account of activity during battle. It soon became apparent that Chaplain Carlsen was going to get his feet wet as interlocutor this day. The Combat Information Center reported that Japanese planes—"bogies"—were heading toward them, but were still sixty miles away. The *Gambier Bay* had just recovered her combat air patrol after four hours of flight, and the decks were cluttered. One of the Wildcats had crashed into the barrier on landing when he bounced and his tail hook failed to engage the arresting gear. AMM3c Potochniak was working with the airedales, preparing to slide the fighter over the side so they could clear the decks in a hurry. A carrier with a fouled deck was always the enemy's choice for attack, and Captain Goodwin gave them a sense of urgency.

The combat air patrol was launched by another of the escort carriers. Then came a second report: more bogies at 126 miles. And a third, more Japanese planes at forty miles. That third group kept closing—forty, thirty-five, thirty, twenty-five miles, twenty-four miles. . . . At that point, the combat air patrol intercepted the Japanese bombers, and shot down several of them. But the others came on in, and at 6:50 they launched an attack on the *Gambier Bay*. As they came, Lieutenant Bell, at least, recognized them as Judys—Japanese dive bombers.

A ramp was set up and the fighter was slid over the catwalk on the port side. As they pushed the plane, the specialists were cannibalizing it: The radiomen stripped out their gear, and Potochniak climbed into the cockpit to salvage as much of the oxygen equipment as he could. In a few moments the fighter slid over the side, and the deck was cleared—not a moment too soon, for just then the 20-mm and 40-mm guns forward on the starboard catwalk began firing.

Potochniak saw a black shape hurtling down and tracers churning the water alongside the ship. One moment he was standing on the deck, and the next he was lying full length in a light lock for the protection it would give him. He did not see a bomb, but he felt it go off and the ship shudder from the impact. He popped his head out of the light lock to see what was going on.

Quartermaster Bell was at the helm. When the talker reported the Japanese aircraft at ten miles, he began straining his eyes. It was hard to see in the growing darkness. But then his eye caught a flash of motion and there it was, a bomber coming down on them. The gunners saw the airplane and began firing. The plane came in on the bow. On the bridge, Captain Goodwin looked up, watched the

Japanese bomber and raised his right arm to measure the angle of deflection of the bomb. He saw it start down, and he waited as it came. Then at the last moment he gave the order: hard to starboard. On the deck below Quartermaster Bell swung the wheel as fast as he could move his hands, and the carrier turned. The bomb kept coming, and Quartermaster Bell could see it miss narrowly just off the port bow. Then came another, and another, the captain ordering the helm moved so that all three bombs missed the ship.

All this time Chaplain Carlsen was on the bridge, carrying on a play-by-play report for the men below who could not see the action. The men below could certainly hear. Quartermaster Bell said he was virtually deafened by the sound of the ship's guns all firing at the bombers overhead.

"We got him," shouted Chaplain Carlsen, and Bell looked up to see a Japanese plane hit the water and explode in flame. And then came another shout from the chaplain, and another.

All those weeks of training, all the dry runs and hours spent in learning nomenclature and the method of taking apart the guns and putting them together, all these apparently useless exercises now paid off. The young men at the 20-mm and 40-mm guns suddenly discovered that they knew how to use their weapons, and they fired them with remarkable accuracy for "first timers" in combat. As the captain's skillful maneuvering of the ship showed his experience, so did the shooting down of two torpedo bombers show how training had paid off for the men of the *Gambier Bay*. Yes, men. Some of them had still not turned eighteen, but they were men that day.

Lt. Rick Roby was strapped in his Wildcat on the catapult when the bombs fell so close by. The fin of one landed against the right wheel of the plane. Ensign Zeola was sitting on one wing of the plane at that moment, and Lieutenant Pilgrim, the catapult officer, was sitting on the other. Both were splashed by the spray from the bomb blast, and they jumped down from their perches soaking wet.

Excitedly, Chaplain Carlsen continued his account, as the Japanese planes fell. One last plane came under fire by a destroyer and was shot down, and then the guns ceased firing. The *Gambier Bay* had emerged virtually unscathed. Four men were hit by flying shrapnel from the near misses, and one man sprained his ankle in the excitement. But the Japanese attack had failed, and the *Gambier*

*Bay* had credit for two planes shot down by her gunners.
The *Gambier Bay* had launched her fighters to help drive off the Japanese attackers, and by the time the combat ended it was quite dark. So the fighter pilots and Lieutenant McClendon had a new exercise: night landings under combat conditions. Captain Goodwin turned the ship into the wind, steaming as close to the nineteen-knot limit as he could because of the lack of breeze, and McClendon brought out his irridescent suit to match his paddles. He brought all the men in safely but one. That pilot landed in the water and was saved, although the fighter was lost. All in all, as the ship was secured for the night, the men of the *Gambier Bay* could look back on a very successful day, except for one new loss suffered that evening. Ens. Lee Giger did not return with the others and was at first reported missing. It was learned later, however, that his Wildcat had been shot down while chasing those bombers, not by an enemy airman, but by the now celebrated anti-aircraft gunners of Tinian. He managed a water landing near a destroyer and was picked up, and the word was passed that he would be coming back to the squadron. Relief at this news made the day seem even better. Then came more good news from Admiral Sallada's flagship: The beachhead was safe. Saipan was far from taken. In the air attacks that evening a landing craft had been hit by a torpedo. An LST was set afire in that same attack, but she was saved. *Fanshaw Bay* had received a bomb hit that exploded on the hangar deck, killing eleven men and forcing that carrier back to Eniwetok for repairs. But the marines were ashore, and with the help of the *Gambier Bay,* they would remain there. The men of the *Gambier Bay,* from the lowest swabbie to the captain, were dedicated to delivering that help, and were also certain that God was on their side. Chaplain Carlsen, however, wanted to give God all the help he could, and his commentaries from the bridge were no less than inspirational. That night he signed off after the Japanese air attack: "All enemy aircraft are burning satisfactorily."

CHAPTER SIXTEEN

# The Enemy Bites

The Japanese had discovered that ships at sea were most vulnerable in the hour just before dawn and just after sunset, and these were the times when they pressed home their most vigorous attacks. On June 18, the men of the *Gambier Bay* were aroused by alarm and bugler at 4:10 in the morning. Japanese aircraft were on the radar screen, coming in. One group came within seven miles of the *Gambier Bay,* but none closed on the fleet of carriers operating off the eastern shore of Saipan. The ship was secured from General Quarters at seven o'clock, and the "normal" battle day began. From before dawn the hangar deck and flight deck were busy, with men in different colored T-shirts gassing the planes, loading bombs and machine-gun belts, and spotting them on the decks for takeoff. Out of the ready room streamed the pilots and their air crews, to man the planes and fly their missions.

On June 18, Admirals Ozawa and Mitscher were searching for each other. The Americans had a string of reports from U.S. submarines, but search planes had not located the Japanese carrier force. The Japanese had reports from land-based search planes, but they were unable to locate the American carriers. Next day, the Japanese found the Americans but did not launch a strike against them. Meanwhile, planes from Tinian and Guam were attacking the Saipan landing force. The nature and effectiveness of the attacks showed what was happening to Japanese land-based air power, which was supposed to make the difference in the Ozawa attempt to wipe out the American fleet. At ten o'clock on the morning of June 18, a single Betty approached the *Gambier Bay*, obviously a suicidal gesture, which was confirmed five minutes later when one of the carrier's combat air patrol planes shot the two-engine bomber down. From time to time during the day, the talker on the bridge reported air activity, but always it was the same, a single or a pair of enemy planes, which were quickly destroyed. At each such report the flight deck erupted in cheers. The men of the *Gambier Bay* were bloodthirsty fellows these days, stimulated by patriotism and navy indoctrination. "Our boys sure don't waste time on these yellow rats," wrote an excited Quartermaster Bell in his diary. This spirit, of course, was necessary for the successful conduct of the war, and it was shared in every measure by the Japanese enemy.

That day, June 18, when VC-10 torpedo planes attacked the town of Garapan with 500-pound general-purpose bombs, Jess Holleman's TBM was set afire by anti-aircraft guns. He might have jumped, but he did not know what his crewmen would do, and besides, he was over enemy territory. So Holleman kept the plane flying although the flames were all around, burning him. When he reached Tanapag harbor, he ditched, successfully enough that the plane floated long enough to let him search for his air crew. Neither man was aboard the plane, so he assumed that they must have parachuted and climbed into the rubber raft. From the shore the Japanese began firing on him and continued until he drifted out beyond their range. He was picked up by a landing craft and rushed to a hospital ship. The crewmen, AOM3c J. Bacon and ARM3c H. Rivers, were never seen again. Probably they did jump and landed behind the Japanese lines. If they were not shot while hanging in their parachutes, they could hardly have survived much longer after landing in the midst of an enemy determined to kill every American they saw.

The experience of June 17 had warned Captain Goodwin to expect an attack at dusk, so he ordered a change in the mess schedule. The evening meal would be moved up half an hour; they would eat at 4:30 in the afternoon, and then if the Japanese came in a 5 or 5:30 they would be ready. The idea was sound, but the timing was a little off. The Japanese came early. At 4:20 the alarm rang for General Quarters. Enemy aircraft were approaching; distance seventy miles. Then came other reports, and the fighters scrambled to go up and find the enemy. In the radar room, Lt. (jg) William Cuming discovered that all these flights were coming onto the screen at the same point, and with a little calculation he saw that they were coming from Guam. So in spite of the fast carrier strikes by Adm. Jocko Clark's four-carrier task group on June 12, the enemy had plenty of striking power left. Only after the war did the Americans learn how crafty the Japanese airmen had been. They camouflaged and hid their aircraft quite successfully and left out in plain sight mockups of Zeroes and Bettys made of bamboo and straw. When the pilots came into bomb and strafe these "planes," they burned most satisfactorily. As a result, the Americans went back to their carriers to report on scores of aircraft destroyed, when the real figures were only fractions of the number.

At least three groups of bombers were approaching the *Gambier Bay* that afternoon. The combat air patrol was up and knocked down several torpedo bombers comfortably away from the carriers, but they could not get them all. Too many of them were coming from too many directions. The combat air patrol radioed that the carriers had best make ready for air attack. They had counted a hundred planes in the wave.

The *Gambier Bay*'s fighters were in a tough spot. They could not engage the Japanese because they had flown for nearly four hours and were nearly out of gas. There was only one answer: Land the fighters and refuel them. This was dangerous; it meant running the risk of being caught with a deckload of planes and the gas hoses exposed. But it was a risk that had to be taken.

The captain gave the orders and Lieutenant McClendon began landing the fighters in a hurry. Everything went perfectly; there were no wave-offs and no accidents on the flight deck. The chiefs began spotting the planes and refueling. The task was just completed and the first fighters were in position for takeoff, when the men on the flight deck of the *Gambier Bay* saw the Japanese coming.

Lieutenant Patterson ducked behind a deck tractor and watched the six torpedo bombers come in at about 100 feet altitude, out of the sun. They were about four miles away, and had obviously set a course directly into the broadsides of the carriers on the starboard side.

*Gambier Bay*'s guns began to fire before the planes came into range, and from the flight deck Patterson could see the tracers falling short and dropping off like spent roman candles. As the bombers closed, the gunners began to find the mark, and the tracers (every third shell) showed that they were hitting the lead plane. But, incredibly, it kept on coming. Then, when he was about a quarter of a mile out, both engines burst into flame, and the plane sailed across the flight deck of the ship, a ball of fire. He was too high to do any damage to the *Gambier Bay*, but apparently he was heading directly for the side of the ship on the carrier's port. He misjudged, skimmed across the deck, and plunged into the sea.

Commander Huxtable was in the radar shack when the first reports came in, and he counted a hundred blips on the screen. As the American fighters went to work the number of blips decreased, but they they scattered, and the fighters had to disperse, too. When the bogies were reported just fifteen miles off the carrier, Huxtable went out onto the catwalk. As he stepped outside, the first Japanese torpedo plane came in over the destroyer screen, heading for the carriers.

Some of the fighters were still forward, and the plane handlers were respotting the bay, where the planes were assembled for takeoff. There was a mad scramble then to get the fighters into the air. One of them, in the way, had been shot up in the tail section. Chief Flanders was looking over this plane when the Japanese began to come in. He ran for the island and the safety of its interior passageway.

Meanwhile a second bomber headed directly across the deck of the *Gambier Bay*, coming in from the starboard bow. He, too, was hit and lost control. The plane zoomed up in a steep climb, burst into flames, and went into a spin, then broke off into a gliding dive and plunged straight into the sea and sank. He must have missed by only a few yards.

Lieutenant Roby was sitting in his FM-2 fighter on the after end of the flight deck when the Japanese planes zoomed in. Next to him was a TBM, and when the Japanese plane came in strafing, one shell passed through the folded wings of the TBM and the fuselage, and went right on over the deck and out to sea, without exploding. AMM3c Potochniak was underneath that plane. He was feeling gun-shy after that attack and dropped into the catwalk and hurried into the head, with the thought that the steel bulkheads offered more protection than the open deck. There he found Alvin Maki, the ship's painter, who had the same idea.

"Jesus Christ," said Maki. "Somebody could get killed around here." Then he laughed. "If it was us, what would they write home to tell our families? That we got killed in the shithouse?"

The pilots were warming their engines as that torpedo bomber came to attack. The other carriers nearby, *Kitkun Bay, Coral Sea,* and *Corregidor,* were all firing as the torpedo planes skated in among them. As the first Wildcat took off from the *Gambier Bay,* enemy bombers were off the ship's bow, and several other ships were firing on them. Ens. Charles Dugan and Ens. Joe McGraw both flew directly into American anti-aircraft fire. Part of the wing of Dugan's Wildcat was shot away, but he managed to climb above the battle and stay in the air. A 20-mm shell struck McGraw's plane just behind his head, tearing away the glass canopy and damaging his flap-control mechanism. He, too, remained in the air. Lt. Gene Seitz, pilot of the fourth plane to take off, charged his guns as the plane left the deck, with his wheels and flaps still down, for he saw an enemy bomber converging on his course. He left the end of the flight deck, banked left, and fired at a plane a hundred yards ahead. It winged over and crashed. Lt. Herman Harders climbed out of the "friendly" barrage safely, and saw down below him a plane with the Rising Sun insignia, trying to escape. He went after it and damaged it, but the plane did not crash, and he suddenly found himself engaged with others. But as he broke off the attack, Lieutenant Bassett's TBM appeared, coming back from antisubmarine patrol. Bassett attacked the Japanese bomber, and his turret gunner, AMM3c Don Blanford, shot the enemy down.

Operations continued. The *Gambier Bay* kept her combat air patrol in the air, for Lieutenant (jg) Cuming was reporting bogies all afternoon. Lieutenant Odum and Yeoman Lyerly had spent most of the time the past two days in Air Plot where they had heard all that was going on and seen the action on the radar. But they had not seen any actual Japanese planes, and they wanted to have the thrill. Odum asked Lt. Cdr. Elmo Waring, the assistant air officer, if they could go up on the flight deck during an attack. Waring was not enthusiastic. They would be a lot safer with the flight deck over their heads, he observed soberly. But they were insistent, and he was too tired to argue. He was on twenty-four-hour duty and had been for three days. Between operations he napped a little on a camp cot set up in Air Plot. On June 18, he was not getting much rest, although Lieutenants Buderus and Cuming kept spotting for him.

Shortly after the torpedo bomber attack, another group of blips appeared on the screen and on the big plotting board in Air Plot. Odum watched, fascinated, as the plane came in. It looked, on the board, like a big bug crawling across a table, then suddenly picking up speed. Waring said it must be a horizontal bomber, from the tactic used. Just then, the bomber altered course and speeded up more, and Waring said he was sure the *Gambier Bay* was the plane's target. Yeoman Lyerly and Odum went out onto the catwalk to watch.

Commander Huxtable was on the flight deck, looking for enemy planes. He spotted two, very high, and thought at first they belonged to the *Gambier Bay*'s combat air patrol. But suddenly one peeled off, and began to dive. He was standing near the 40-mm guns forward of the bridge.

"Here they come," he yelled.

The 40-mm guns began firing. The distance was still too great for the 20-mm guns.

Commander Huxtable saw that the lead plane was coming at the *Gambier Bay*, and he ducked for cover. He ran for the door leading into the bridge, but men were stacked in there six feet deep, so he ran to the after corner of the island and hung out over the flag bag. From that point he was "safe," comparatively speaking, but he could still watch the Japanese plane dive. The ship's guns fired steadily; smoke and the smell of cordite filled the air. The Japanese plane came on, apparently unhurt, and dropped its bomb. Lieutenant Odum saw the yawning doors of the open bomb bay and watched the plane as the wings waggled; apparently the pilot could not get the bomb release to operate properly, for although the Betty crossed from starboard to port just forward of the island and barely cleared the radar mast, the bomb dropped a hundred feet ahead of the ship. The plane flew on for a second, but the pilot must have been hit, because he never pulled out of the dive and went into the water fifty yards off the *Gambier Bay*'s starboard quarter, just as the spray from the bomb splattered the flight deck all the way back to the island. Lyerly saw the bomb and the spray and ran into Air Plot, hurled himself onto Commander Waring's cot, and pulled the mattress up over himself until only the soles of his shoes were visible. That was Lieutenant Odum's primary recollection of the event. He was right behind Lyerly, and all he could see were those shoes. Commander Huxtable came back up toward the island, shaken, thinking for a moment of that Japanese pilot with the respect of one airman for another. He had to give credit to someone who pressed home an attack that way.

As the Japanese attacked, the guns of the *Gambier Bay* were firing. Quartermaster Bell was at the helm, and Chaplain Carlsen was at the loudspeaker, recounting the action to those who could hear him. Certainly Seaman Chenry Quinn on his 20-mm gun could not hear in all the noise on the flight deck and in the gunpockets, but down below the engineers and the men on the hangar deck and the men in damage control could hear. Then suddenly, the guns were quiet, and the chaplain's voice rang out. "We got six of them."

It was growing dark and Captain Goodwin had many planes in the air. Ensign McGraw's plane was in bad shape. It had more than thirty holes in it from friendly fire, no radio, no flaps, and no lights. So as the other planes landed, McGraw was told to stay up top and wait. His plane was the most likely to crash on landing, and that was the procedure, bring home the healthy chickens first, and the sick ones could wait—if they were not too sick. It was questionable at best whether or not McClendon and McGraw, combining their skills, could bring the plane down.

Lieutenant Roby also had some trouble. His Wildcat had lost its hatch. So he, too, was left circling above the carriers, while the others landed.

As the darkness increased, and several planes suffered damage on landing and fouled up the deck of the *Gambier Bay*, the captain instructed Roby and McGraw to land on the *Kitkun Bay*. Roby turned, made the approach and landed on the other carrier on his first pass. McGraw was having more trouble. He made two passes at the *Kitkun*

*Bay* and was waved off both times. Then, the landing officer obviously decided that McGraw's Wildcat was a hopeless case and waved him away entirely. It was too late at night, said the *Kitkun Bay,* to try to take the damaged plane aboard.

McGraw then flew back to the *Gambier Bay*. Ensign Dugan's shot-up fighter had caused part of the trouble, but it had been cleared away and the deck was free. But now it was almost totally dark, and McGraw faced a virtually impossible landing. Captain Goodwin decided to risk calling enemy attention to the *Gambier Bay* and ordered the carrier's lights turned on. Ensign McGraw was told to bring his damaged Wildcat in. On the flight deck, Lieutenant "Mac," as he was called, had donned his shining coveralls and picked up his irridescent wands. Ensign McGraw began edging the plane down. He had never made a night carrier landing before, and tonight he was coming in at ninety knots, twenty knots faster than normal speed, because he could not operate his flaps. He was further hampered by the wind whistling all around his head in the open cockpit of an airplane not designed to fly that way. But he brought the Wildcat down, it hit the deck with a bang, and bounced up to crash into the barrier. All considered it was the best landing of the day, because with the luck of the Irish, Ens. Joe McGraw walked away from the wreck.

Ensign Shroyer came in that evening in his TBM, and the engine failed as he was "in the groove" on the last leg of his approach. He landed just astern of the carrier and all three, pilot, gunner, and radioman, were picked up by an escort.

Within two hours, all the planes of VC-10 were down, more or less safely, and operations were suspended for the night. The men had been expecting chow at 4:30, but it took them until 8:30 to get squared away. The *Gambier Bay* carried thirty fighters and bombers, and all but the ones on the hangar deck under repair had flown several missions during the daylight hours.

Ensign Dugan, who was called "Mr. Daring" in the squadron, told intelligence officer Vereen Bell in his debriefing the story of his first kill. He and Seitz, Courtney, Lischer, Harders, Gilliatt, and McGraw had spotted a Betty at 24,000 feet. They had chased the Japanese plane which had tried to escape by hitting the deck. Dugan had

NAVY PHOTO

When the smoke lifted over Oahu, more than 2,400 Americans, most of them naval personnel, were dead or dying, and 1,300 more were wounded. Some 230 aircraft had been destroyed or heavily damaged, and in Pearl Harbor 18 ships had been sunk. The USS *Arizona* was a total loss.

"TORA... TORA... TORA!"

Admiral Yamamoto's surprise tactical objective achieved, he realized the Imperial Japanese Navy had "merely awakened a sleeping giant, and filled it with a terrible resolve."

"A DAY OF INFAMY," PEARL HARBOR, DECEMBER 7, 1941.

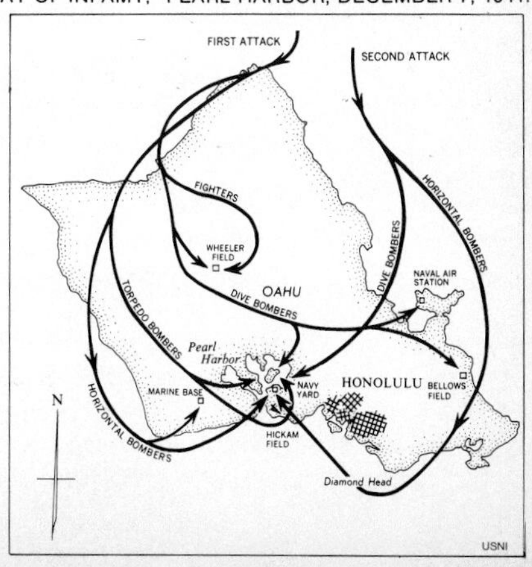

CVE-73, the *Kaiser* "bonus-baby" built in a record 171 days, the 19th of its class commissioned in 1943. The "baby-flattop" became a home for 990 shipmates and an air base for 18 "Wildcat" fighters and 12 "Avenger" torpedo bombers. Top speed 17 knots (19 mph). Four Battle Stars and the Presidential Unit Citation later, the USS *Gambier Bay* was sunk in action, October 25, 1944.

"Three Rounds, Two Minutes Each."

"Pay Day, Pay Day."

"Movies at 1900 (7 PM)."

"Lord, give us safe passage, Amen."

Not so safe landing! The tailhook failed to snag an arresting cable, but the alert flight deck crew raised the "wire-barrier" in time to stop the runaway Grumman TBM "Avenger."

Good safe landing! The Grumman FM-2 "Wildcat" snagged the #3 arresting cable for a positive stop; the "wingman" got the "wave-off" to go around while the flight deck was cleared for landing.

The safety destroyer retrieved dunked pilot and, sailing alongside, conveyed him to his carrier via the breeches buoy.

Opposite page:
The hangar deck became a gym, a credit union, a movie house and a chapel where young sailors came to keep physically fit, to send money home, to relax and to pray with Chaplain Carlsen.

June 19, 1944 off Saipan a Japanese bomber shot aflame by carrier anti-aircraft fire was foiled in suicidal crash of the USS *Gambier Bay* on the eve of the "Marianas Turkey Shoot."

A quick-thinking USS *Gambier Bay* fighter pilot, wheels and flaps still down (circle), charged his "Wildcat's" guns as he left the deck, bagged his first "meatball" as he "fired" the enemy bomber (bogey) a hundred yards ahead.

Captain Hugh Goodwin (fifth from left) and the men of the USS *Gambier Bay* in a relaxed moment during the invasion of Saipan. The "jeep-carrier's" anti-aircraft guns shot down the first four Japanese bombers which attacked her.

Liberation of Saipan, Tinian and Guam secured, called to higher duty, the "spit-and-polish" Captain reviewed his now veteran "men-of-wars-men" as he disembarked the USS *Gambier Bay*.

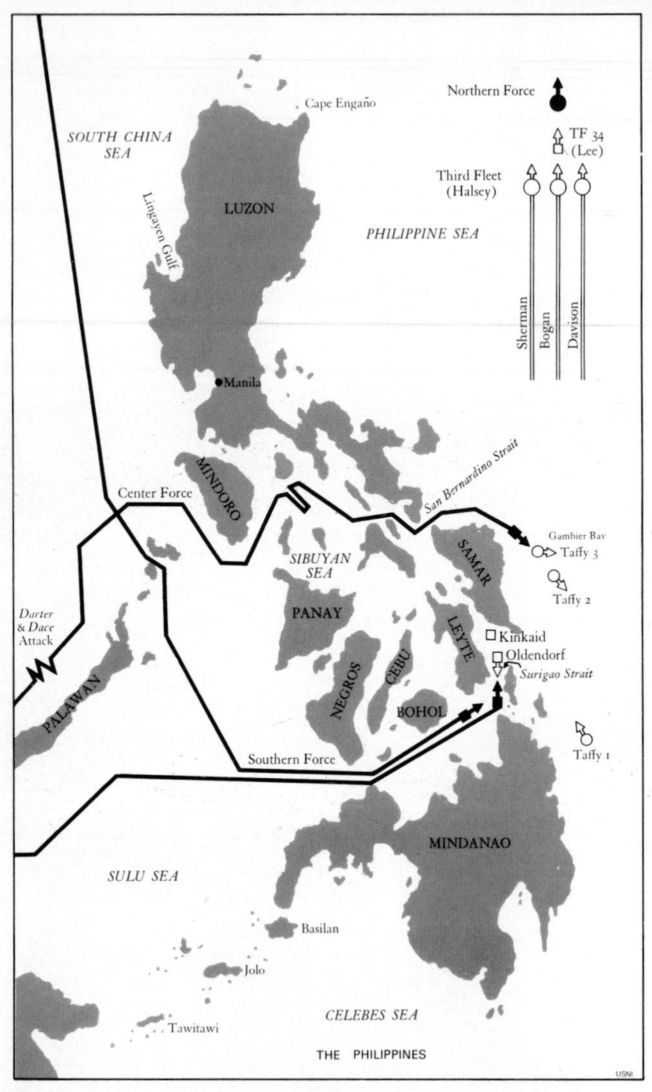


October 20, 1944, 2 PM, General Douglas MacArthur declared: "People of the Philippines, I have returned!" Her escort mission completed, the USS *Gambier Bay* joined carrier Task Unit "Taffy 3" stationed off Samar to provide air cover for the landing forces in Leyte Gulf.

NAVY PHOTO

Captain Viewig surveyed his ship hopelessly. The steering was gone, the power was gone, a shell pierced the engine room, the boiler and the generating tubes. That single shell sealed the fate of the USS *Gambier Bay*. The ship was "dead-in-the-water." The Captain called: "Abandon ship!" It was 0850.

USS *Gambier Bay* mortally wounded and adrift, ships of Task Unit "Taffy 3" sailed away.

Sister ships desperately launched all aircraft as the USS *Gambier Bay* became focal point of Japanese fleet shellfire.

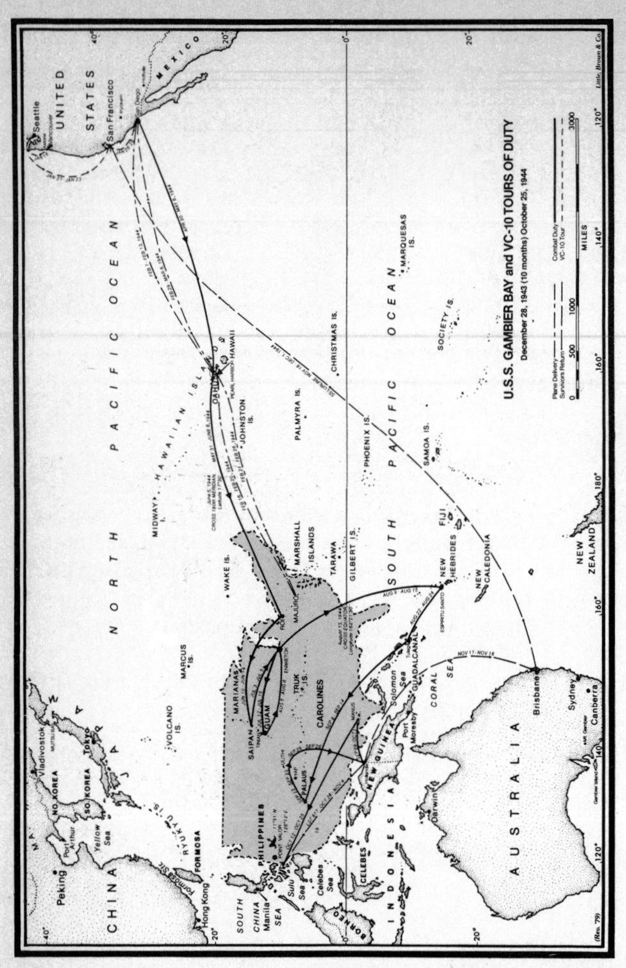


October 25, 1944. War Cruise ended; for the IJN forever infamous, for the USN forever glorious. Admiral Takeo Kurita's annihilated fleet "high-tailed" it for Japan. In its wake, however, were the sinking destroyers DD *Hoel, Johnston,* and DE *Samuel B. Roberts* who sacrificed themselves to protect the USS *Gambier Bay*—the only USN carrier ever sunk by enemy gunfire. The crew of the IJN cruiser *Tone* came to attention as she slid past the men of the sunken American ships struggling in the water—for the Japanese knew that they had indeed faced stalwart "men-of-wars-men."

gotten ahead of the others, and just as he thought he had missed the plane in the gathering darkness, he came on it head on. He had fired most of his ammunition in the chase and had just one more burst of 50 mm. He fired that, and watched the Japanese bomber nose over and make a beautiful chandelle turn, right into the drink. When Lieutenant Bell heard the story, told in Dugan's rich Irish accents with gestures and much laughter, he took Dugan to the captain, and the captain was so impressed that he asked Dugan to repeat his star performance over the intercom. So for fifteen minutes, Dugan relived the story of his day's combat, and the men of the *Gambier Bay* relived it with him. It had been quite a day.

CHAPTER SEVENTEEN

# War Wearies

During the daylight hours the pilots flew their planes into enemy territory and got shot up. During the nighttime hours, the maintenance men put the planes back together again, or if they were too far gone pushed them over the side. Theoretically, Commander Borries made the decisions to jettison aircraft. Actually, Chief Walter Flanders, the leading metalsmith, was the man whose opinion counted, and he was very stingy about losing planes. He knew replacements would be hard to come by, and every wreck that he could cannibalize meant that much more security for the ship. But if a plane came in smashed up during flight operations and could not be moved, there was no choice. Over it must go. Chief Flanders's nightmares centered around Air Officer Borries standing on the bridge with his bullhorn shouting at the mechanics: "Well, make up your minds." And then came the pain of pushing the injured airplane over the side and watching it splash into the blue sea.

Chief Flanders was in charge of metal work for VC-10, but since the *Gambier Bay* did not have a chief metalsmith, he also watched over the work of the ship's company. Because of this command situation, the *Gambier Bay*'s metal department functioned as well as any in the navy. This week, in battle, some of his men worked forty-eight hours at a stretch to get a plane back into action. The procedure was to bring a wrecked aircraft down the elevator from the flight deck as soon as possible and put it in a bay where several men would be assigned to treat its ills: electric, hydraulic, and perhaps a shattered tail section. Chief Flanders would assign metalsmith Hess or Hewitt, Jones or Britt to oversee the work on a particular plane, and others would work with them. Sometimes the repairs were nothing short of ingenious. Early in the Saipan action one of the fighters came in badly shot up. The ribs in the tail section had been broken. The *Gambier Bay* did not carry the equipment to make aluminum extrusions for those ribs, but Chief Flanders took a piece of one-inch angle iron, a razor blade and a roll of scotch tape, and repaired the tail. Next day the fighter was back in action, and flew from the deck of the *Gambier Bay* until the very last day of her life.

On June 19, action began early for the men of the *Gambier Bay*. They went to General Quarters routinely, an hour before dawn but just before six o'clock several groups of Japanese planes were spotted by radar, and one of them closed on the carrier formation. At twenty-four miles out, the ship's fighters were directed to the Japanese and mixed with them, shooting down a number, but a few got through. These were Bettys, and they did not come down, but flew high above the carriers and bombed. One of the destroyers shot down a Betty with its five-inch gun, but the smaller weapons of the carriers could not reach so far.

June 19 was the day on which the Japanese carriers found the American fleet, sandwiched between the Japanese force and Guam and Rota. So far the A-GO plan was working perfectly. Admiral Ozawa would dispatch his aircraft from the carriers, they would attack the Americans, land on Guam or Rota, rearm and refuel, and come back to attack again. The shuttle system should be deadly. But the A-GO plan had not taken into account the heavy destruction of Japanese aircraft throughout all the Pacific islands in recent weeks. Guam was supposed to have 500 planes available for A-GO. Actually, Guam had fifty operational planes, and this morning of June 19, as they took off, they were met by fighters from the *Belleau Wood, Cabot, Yorktown,* and *Hornet*. Some were shot down, some landed and were immediately rushed into concealment. Not only afterward the Americans discovered a large force of enemy planes coming up, apparently from Yap, to reinforce Guam. They shot down most of these planes. By midmorning Admiral Ozawa had four separate attacks in the air, heading for the American ships from the Japanese carriers. In all, more than 250 Japanese planes attacked, and the vast majority of them were destroyed. This was the beginning of the "Marianas Turkey Shoot," as the fliers called it, or the Battle of the Philippine Sea, as the historians would term it. It was fierce and deadly fighting, but aboard the *Gambier Bay* nothing would be known of the struggle for five days. The escort carriers kept on with their important job, which was to protect the transports and warships from aerial attack, and to destroy enemy air facilities in the Marianas.

The American strikes this day were aimed at Tinian, to neutralize the airfields there. Ensign Lischer and Lt. Richard Roby discovered a Kate bomber just entering the traffic circle over Ushi airfield on Tinian, and together they shot it down. When they came back to tell their tale, Ensign Lischer came in hot, hit the barrier, and his Wildcat flipped over. He reached up, or down in this case, and unlatched the harness and climbed out without a scratch. With his chart in his hand, he walked across the flight deck, forgetting that after a landing the barrier posts were dropped hydraulically to be flush with the flight deck, until the next plane came in. He stepped squarely on one of the posts just as it was being raised. It came up fast and catapulted him into a swandive. Unfortunately, the flight deck was not a comfortable landing place, and Lischer ended up in sick bay having his head stitched.

That was an "operational" accident, as opposed to a combat injury, and entitled him to no separate distinction except for the hoots of his fellow pilots. Another operational accident that day was far more tragic to the men of the *Gambier Bay*. The carrier that day was responsible for two combat air patrol groups. Each patrol was carried out by four airplanes, who searched predetermined patterns above the carrier force, ready to be "vectored," or dispatched to any point on the orders of the Combat Information Center. Lt. (jg) Dean Gilliatt was flying one of the planes of the second patrol. From the bullhorn on the bridge came the order, "Pilots man your planes," and the four fighter pilots scrambled from the ready room to the flight deck and got into the cockpits. "Stand clear of propellers," came the next order, and then, "Start engines." The pilots engaged the starter mechanisms, the engines whined, coughed, and started, and they were ready to launch.

Since the fighters were expected to be in the air for an extra-long time, they were hung with wing tanks. Normally, the wing tank was attached to the starboard wing of the Wildcat, and the pilot adjusted the controls before takeoff to compensate for the additional weight to the starboard side. But this day, the plane captain of Gilliatt's fighter was unable to fix the tank to the starboard wing, so he moved it over to port. He forgot, and so did Lieutenant Gilliatt, that the plane was trimmed for extra weight to starboard, when actually the weight was on the other side.

Lieutenant Gilliatt began a "free-run" takeoff. The moment the plane began to move he knew he was in trouble, but the short and narrow deck of the Kaiser carrier gave him no margin. As the wheels left the deck the port wing was dropping, and the plane nosed over to the left side of the centerline in spite of the pilot's obvious frantic efforts to maintain the proper attitude for takeoff. For a moment it seemed that he might make it—the Wildcat needed only a foot more altitude to clear. But the landing gear caught in the top of a port side 40-mm gun mount just forward of the island, and sent the plane over the side, into the sea at a forty-degree angle. The plane went down, but came up and floated horizontally, as if flying on the surface of the sea.

The crash alarm sounded at the moment it became apparent that Gilliatt was going to hit the gun. Commander Huxtable was in the ready room, and he rushed to the catwalk, and came outside just as the ship passed by the floating plane. He could see Gilliatt in the cockpit, his head slumped forward on his chest, unmoving. Either he had broken his neck on impact or he had been knocked out. The ship moved inexorably past the wreck, and men on the flight deck prayed that the pilot would come to and unsnap the safety belts. But they went past, and the plane sank, and when the escort came up, the sea was empty.

Lieutenant Harders, Gilliatt's best friend aboard the *Gambier Bay*, stood on the catwalk outside the Aerology office, watching with Lieutenant Odum. Tears began streaming down Harder's cheeks. "Oh, why couldn't it have been me instead of Gil? He had so much to live for," sobbed the flyer. Gilliatt had married in these frantic war years, and he had learned just before they left for the war that his wife was about to have a baby. So much said, there was no more to say. The call came from the bullhorn for another pilot; the combat air patrol required four planes and only three were in the air. In a moment another fighter pilot was manning his plane, and in a minute he was off the deck, taking the place of Lieutenant Gilliatt. The demands of the war left no place for personal sorrow.

The combat air patrols ran into a few Japanese planes and shot them down. Each time a plane fell the word was passed around the ship and the men of the *Gambier Bay* cheered.

"Those yellow bastards are taking a licking but they don't seem to know when they are licked," wrote the bloodthirsty Quartermaster Bell in his diary, unmindful of the tribute he was paying to Japanese bravery. As the battle so obviously turned against the defenders of Saipan, their courage became no less than suicidal. Each plane shot down was a potential missile, and as the days went by, the men of the *Gambier Bay* noticed a changed approach by the enemy. On this June 19, the Japanese pilots began trying to crash their falling aircraft into American ships. These were not kamikazes; that development was yet to come. These were brave warriors of the emperor giving their lives for their country, and trying to make those lives count to the last.

By the night of June 19, the men of the *Gambier Bay* were worn out after five consecutive days and nights of battle. They did not know then, but the Marianas Turkey Shoot of Admiral Mitscher's force was just then decimating the enemy. Admiral Ozawa would lose ninety-two percent of his carrier planes and most of those Guam planes on which he had counted. The *Gambier Bay*'s troubles with Japanese air attack at Saipan were over.

CHAPTER EIGHTEEN

# The Five-fingered Salute

On June 19, many of the Japanese aircraft from Guam and Rota had attacked the invasion fleet off Saipan, but as the "Marianas Turkey Shoot" continued, all available planes were sent to help Admiral Ozawa and his carriers. Thus, on June 20, when the Battle of the Philippine Sea was at its height, the escort carriers and other ships of the invasion fleet were virtually left alone. A few Japanese snoopers came around during the day, but these were almost certainly observation craft, which made no attempt to attack. The beachhead had been secured by the marines, and the Army 27th Division began landing elements of its infantry combat teams. On June 19, Gen. Holland Smith took command of the ground forces from Admiral Turner. The Japanese faced certain defeat as the Battle of the Philippine Sea ended in an American victory. But the Japanese commander, General Saito, was determined to fight to the end.

Even after the enormous destruction of Japanese planes in the Turkey Shoot, the Japanese were able to mount a few attacks from the air, from as far away as Truk. The battleship *Maryland* was torpedoed, and a raid on the American-held anchorage at Charan Kanoa caused damage to several ships. After June 19, no enemy aircraft managed to enter the defensive area of the carrier fleet offshore, but that did not mean the *Gambier Bay*'s task was completed. The marines and army troops ashore still faced tough going against determined defenders, and they needed air support, in case of enemy air attack.

On June 20 and 21, the *Gambier Bay* launched its fighters, but no bombers. On June 22, the ship did not conduct any aerial operations. The hunting was definitely slowing down. On June 28, Sallada's task group moved around the island to the west side, for the marines needed some help. The army forces had bogged down in a drive on Mt. Tapotchau, the highest point on Saipan, and the situation was serious enough that Gen. Holland Smith relieved Army Gen. Ralph Smith of command of the 27th Division. But the change of command did not speed the drive. The Japanese resistance became more fierce as it became more suicidal. Mt. Tapotchau was not captured until June 27. The next day, General Smith called for help from the carriers, and the TBMs were brought out to carry out selective bombing.

On June 29, Commander Huxtable and Lieutenant (jg) Pyzdrowski shared one exciting mission. The marines were driving on the town of Garapan. They were crossing a series of ridges, but each one was contested by the Japanese, whose fire by mortar and machine gun was most effective. Huxtable and Pyzdrowski went up, each TBM carrying ten 100-pound antipersonnel bombs. They were called by the ground controller, who directed them to the area he wanted bombed. Each plane made two dummy passes down the ravine where the Japanese were holed up, shooting at the marines coming up the other side. Then they made final passes, and dropped the bombs. They never knew, of course, how effective their bombardment had been, but it was most satisfying to be a part of the action, so close in that they could feel the concussion of their own bomb bursts.

Despite the bombing of the Charan Kanoa sugar mill on Saipan, the tall smokestack of the factory still stood because higher authority had cautioned the pilots against bombing it. They wanted to save the stack as the base for a radio aerial. The plan was already in motion to make Saipan a major base for B-29 bombing of Japan proper, and the Seabees were ashore, building the extra-long airstrips before the last snipers were wiped out around the runways. But as the battle continued and General Saito's forces resisted strongly, it became apparent that Japanese aerial observation of marine and army ground movement was extremely accurate. Since the Japanese had no spotter planes in the area, they must have an observer located in some high point. Commander Huxtable said it was that smokestack and asked for permission to knock it down. Permission was refused. The *Gambier Bay* had her duties to perform; let the men of VC-10 stick to those.

On June 20, Admiral Sallada took the *Kitkun Bay* and *Gambier Bay* east of Saipan to pick up two convoys of supply ships and escort them to anchorage off Saipan. No air attacks were made in support of troops for the next three days. VC-10 fighters flew air patrol and found no enemy aircraft. The torpedo bombers flew antisubmarine patrol missions and found no submarines. On June 22, the destroyer *Berham* reported a torpedo wake passed under her stern, but she was not hit. That same night after dark a lone Japanese bomber came in on Charan Kanoa Roads, where the battleships were anchored abreast, firing in support of the ground troops. The Betty dropped a torpedo that hit the *Maryland* and scooted off before a gun could be fired. The battleships had gotten careless, and Admiral Oldendorf, commander of the fire support unit, was nearly blasted the next night when another Betty dropped a stick of bombs that landed just behind his flagship, the cruiser *Louisville*. But June 23 marked the virtual end of effective Japanese air harassment. That day, Army Air Force P-47s arrived in Aslito airfield, which was rechristened Isely Airfield after a navy pilot who was killed there early in the operation. The next day, a group of P-61 night fighters, equipped with radar, came in, too, which put an end to effective Japanese effort after dark.

The *Gambier Bay* was not called upon for air strikes against land targets again until June 28. By this time, all the fighting force had the good word about the success of the fast carriers in the Battle of the Philippine Sea, and morale had never been higher. "It sure does feel nice to be on the giving end of the war instead of the receiving end as I always was before I came aboard this ship," wrote Quartermaster Bell in his diary. It had been dull duty, flying combat air patrol where there was no combat and antisubmarine missions where there were no submarines. The only excitement was "operational." Ensign McGraw's fighter got into trouble when, on combat air patrol, he jettisoned his detachable wing tank, and the release failed. The tank came back and sliced off a piece of the fighter's horizontal stabilizer. Thereafter McGraw could control the plane only by turning in shallow banks and turns. Leo Zeola was flying on McGraw's wing, and he stayed with him all the time, but as they approached the carrier, Zeola became very noisy.

"I wanted wings, until I got the things, but now I don't want them anymore," he sang over the radio.

Ensign McGraw was just then trying to get into the traffic circle. The maneuver demanded a sharp rudder and elevator adjustment, and the crippled Wildcat would not take it. Twice McGraw had tried, and twice he had been waved off by Landing Signal Officer McClendon.

"Shut up, Leo," McGraw shouted into the radio. "This is not funny."

Down on the deck, where the maneuvering was being piped into the address system from the Combat Information Center, nearly everybody agreed with McGraw. Zeola and Ensign Lischer were the two bad boys of the squadron, forever cutting up and making jokes, and Buzz Borries, in particular, was often short with them.

This time Ensign Zeola did shut up, for he knew very well that his pal McGraw was in trouble. On deck and on the bridge, Commander Huxtable, Commander Borries, and Captain Goodwin advised McGraw of all the tricks in their bags, but none of them worked. Finally Captain Goodwin told the pilot he would either have to ditch or parachute. McGraw had never jumped before, and that was what he decided to do, although ship captains did not much like that solution to the problem. There was always the chance that an unattended aircraft could circle around and become an unguided missile to strike an American ship. But in this case, Ensign McGraw parachuted, the Wildcat disappeared over the horizon, and a destroyer picked up the pilot almost before he had his feet wet.

By June 27, the American control of Saipan was exemplified when Gen. Holland Smith hiked up Mt. Tapotchau, where the Japanese had built a little shrine. From here, the highest point on the island, General Smith could see all around him. He knew very well, however, that, although eighty percent of the Japanese defending force had been destroyed, the Japanese were going to fight on to the last. They still had a few tanks and a number of artillery pieces. General Saito established a new "final line of resistance" that ran from Tanapag to the eastern shore of the island.

With the enemy herded into the narrow north end of the island, General Smith decided to make more use of naval gun and air support. At the same time, VC-10 was assigned to the task of beginning the softening up process against Tinian, which would soon be invaded. So June 28 marked the end of the lassitude for the pilots and the men of the ship. The fighters strafed, and the bombers hit Garapan and Tanapag and targets called out by the spotters. All this while, the Japanese troops were staging suicide attacks, and the Japanese civilians continued to leap from the height of Marpi Point, which the navy had now nicknamed Banzai Cliff. Admiral Sallada heard about the mass suicides there, and decided he wanted photos for the record. VC-5, the flagship's air squadron, had lost its photo plane, so he called on VC-10 to take the pictures.

Ens. R. L. Crocker had just brought the photo plane back from antisubmarine patrol. The engine was running rough on the way back to the carrier, and in the last few minutes Crocker had so much trouble getting home that he turned thumbs down, when he landed and gestured to the crew chief. That meant the plane was inoperable and should not be flown again without a major inspection. Captain Goodwin did not know of this development, however, and he had already told Admiral Sallada by TBS "willco" with a speed that to the airmen demonstrated their captain's urgent desire to get ahead in the navy world. He was taken aback for a moment, but then he ordered the plane onto the flight deck, ready to launch, and Lieutenant (jg) Pyzdrowski to pilot her. Chief Sparrow was to go along and take the pictures the admiral wanted.

Pyzdrowski was not only the pilot, he was also engineering officer of VC-10. He heard that Crocker had "downed" the plane, and conferred with Chief Montgomery and Chief Flanders. They all agreed that the photo plane should have a check before it flew again, and Pyzdrowski took that decision to Commander Huxtable. Hux discussed the matter with Buzz Borries, the air officer, and Borries, caught between squadron and the captain, decided that they would let a plane captain make the judgment. By this time everyone on the flight deck knew what was happening: The captain wanted that plane flown, and the squadron did not.

The plane captain did not want to be caught in the middle. He ran up the RPM as high as he could and came back with a "thumbs up" signal. The captain was happy. The photo mission would go.

Pyzdrowski was furious. Not only was his judgment overruled for what he considered to be a matter of the admiral's personal vanity and the captain's toadyism, but he was the one who was supposed to fly an airplane he had said was not operational. He carried his argument to Commander Huxtable, the skipper. Huxtable agreed with everything he said. But there was one more point. The captain had issued a direct order. It was either fly or face a general court-martial. Pyzdrowski accepted that, and said he would fly the "suicide" mission. But the plane still was carrying several depth charges. Could these not be unloaded to lighten the TBM?

There was no time, said the captain. The mission had to get off.

"Why doesn't the plane captain fly the mission?" Pyzdrowski muttered.

Chief Sparrow showed up with his extra equipment and Pyzdrowski winced. It was bad enough to have to take up a crippled plane, but to have 300 pounds added, and a man who could be nothing but a liability in a crash, was worse. Pyzdrowski ordered his gunner, Robert Jensen, out of the gun turret. Only radioman Fauls would come along if Chief Sparrow needed all that equipment to take the pictures. Pyzdrowski put on his helmet and goggles and prepared to take off. He revved up the engine as Lieutenant Pilgrim operated his catapult, and the plane went off the end of the flight deck, low over the water, as these heavy planes almost always did.

After the plane was launched, flight operations were suspended, and the *Gambier Bay* was secured for lunch. No one noticed, then, that the TBM never rose more than twenty-five feet above the sea, and when they had gone out about two miles it finally gave up altogether. Pyzdrowski made a neat water landing, radioman Fauls pulled a sputtering Chief Sparrow from the tunnel, and in a moment they were in the rubber raft, and a destroyer was hurrying toward them. As the destroyer approached, Pyzdrowski realized that the crash might have snapped the wires that armed the depth charges, and the plane was going down. He signaled the destroyer off, and it stood to one side, waiting. The raft was directly in the path of the *Gambier Bay*, where nearly everyone was out to lunch, including the lookouts. The carrier was coming up on the raft, and moved so close that when one of the depth charges went off, it shook the whole ship.

The destroyer picked up the plane's crew and sent them back aboard the *Gambier Bay* by breeches buoy. Buzz Borries and the plane captain were the first to congratulate him on the narrow escape, which Pyzdrowski considered to be 100 percent their fault. His disposition was not made better when Borries told him the captain wanted to see him.

What for?

Well, for one thing, the captain seemed to feel that Pyzdrowski might have been responsible for the depth charge explosion.

On the bridge, an angry Captain Goodwin threatened to have Pyzdrowski court-martialed for insubordination. He virtually accused Pyzdrowski of sabotaging the mission. The argument was deteriorating so rapidly there might have been two court-martials, not just one, when Commander Borries stepped between them. He ordered Pyzdrowski to his quarters "for rest." The captain had the last word: He grounded Pyzdrowski for two weeks. But even that did not take. In less than an hour, a call came for a special antisubmarine search. Lieutenant (jg) Cuming had seen some strange blips on the radar screen and someone had to investigate. Commander Borries decided that it was best to get Pyzdrowski off the ship for a time, and this was a long mission. Pyzdrowski took off again for the second time in two hours.

The flight crew got into the TBM for catapult launching. As the plane was made ready on the catapult, Commander Borries gave a thumbs-up sign. Lieutenant (jg) Pyzdrowki responded by grabbing his nose between thumb and forefinger. He looked at the bridge and delivered a salute. Anyone watching would see that it was a five-fingered salute, and that his thumb touched the end of his nose.

## CHAPTER NINETEEN

# The End of the Action

Either Captain Goodwin did not see the five-fingered salute, or, when Lieutenant (jg) Pyzdrowski returned from the four-and-a-half-hour mission, the captain had calmed down, for the only immediate result of the affair was that Chief Sparrow was so immensely impressed with himself that he founded The Dunkers' Club, whose members all had survived a water landing.

Pyzdrowski and other pilots continued to fly, mostly missions against Tinian in late June and early July. Some Saipan points still needed attention, so the fighters and bombers also worked over gun positions and troop concentrations. Meanwhile, the planes were growing tired and needed some shore maintenance and engine changes.

On June 30, Lieutenant Stewart returned to the squadron. He had been brought back to Saipan by the destroyer, and sent ashore to Isely (Aslito) Airfield. He spent one night there, acquired a Samurai sword, and next day was picked up by a torpedo plane and flown back to the *Gambier Bay*. What a fascinating tale he had to tell.

On D-Day his plane had been shot down by a freak incident. As he nursed it out to sea, he saw only one small hole in the cowling eighteen inches ahead of the cockpit. It had severed an oil line, for the pressure dropped, and the temperature rose. It was obvious that he would not make it sixty miles back to the carrier, so he found a destroyer out beyond the transports. He came down to make a water landing, the black smoke pouring from the engine, as if he were trying to lay down a smoke screen. The prop froze, the Wildcat splashed and went under. He jumped out, climbed along the wing as it bobbed up for a moment, and then the wing fell out from under him, leaving him bobbing alone. He managed to get into the little rubber boat after several flip-overs, and he lay down in it exhausted. When the destroyer came up, it sent a swimmer out to get him and they pulled him aboard with a line. That was the beginning of his adventure, for shortly after he was picked up the big Japanese air attack of that day occurred, and the destroyer on which he was now a passenger was ordered to make smoke.

Stewart had expected to be sent back aboard the carrier that day, but in the evening the destroyer was pulled from the invasion force and sent to join Admiral Mitscher's attack on the Japanese fleet.

Lieutenant Stewart now became the destroyer's air intelligence officer. He stayed on the bridge when aircraft were around, identifying them as friend or foe for the gunners. In slack periods for the next few days, he relieved the junior officers at the decoding machines. And he had a ringside seat at the "Marianas Turkey Shoot." On the second day the Americans hit the Japanese carriers and sank the carrier *Hiyo* and several smaller ships and damaged the carrier *Zuikaku* so severely that at one point she was nearly abandoned. They wrecked the flight deck of the carrier *Ciyoda*. On the night of that attack the carrier planes, coming home, began to run out of fuel. Admiral Mitscher ordered the lights of the ships turned on, but some planes did not make it. Stewart's destroyer then spent two days looking for downed seamen, before it came back to the fleet, and on June 30, Lieutenant Stewart rejoined the *Gambier Bay*. Captain Goodwin welcomed him aboard, asked a few questions, and then turned the ship's intercom over to Stewart, so he could tell the tale of the Turkey Shoot. And he did, for forty-five minutes.

Next day, July 1, the fighters and bombers of VC-10 were sent to strafe the remains of the Japanese force east of Garapan and the gun positions that still stood at Marpi Point. They also attacked caves around the point, where some Japanese soldiers had holed up for this last stand at the very end of the island. On July 2, Captain Goodwin finally found a use for the 1,000-pound bomb autographed by Miss Beattie: a fortified Japanese command post. The torpedo pilots held a lottery to see who would have the honor of delivering Miss Beattie's personal message to Premier Tojo, written on that bomb so long ago.

Ensign Crocker won the lottery. He and gunner Charles Westbrook and Larry Austin would have the honor. Miss Beattie, said Ensign Crocker, would owe him a date when they returned home. They took off, delivered the bomb on target and came back, and Ensign Crocker wrote Miss Beattie about the date she owed him. It was actions of this sort that never failed to remind Captain Goodwin, the professional, that he was fighting a war in command of almost a thousand American boys, most of whom really ought to be still in school. Overall, he was so pleased with the performance of his men that he sent a message to Admiral King in Washington:

> The relatively inexperienced crew of this vessel, the *Gambier Bay,* proved itself far beyond the most optimistic expectations of the Ship's Captain. Six months ago, this vessel had just been commissioned, 97% of the crew had never been in action, 85% of them were seasick the first time the ship had blue water under her keel; now they have the appearance and confidence of veteran men-of-wars-men! Their conduct under attack left nothing to be desired and is another shining example of the adaptability and courage of the young men of our country.

This message was duly posted for the men of the *Gambier Bay,* and even Lieutenant (jg) Pyzdrowski was pleased by the captain's praise. Their battle at Saipan and Tinian was over, for Admiral Sallada had decided that the attrition to aircraft had made the *Kitkun Bay* and *Gambier Bay* of limited usefulness in the remainder of this operation. They needed a rest, but even more they needed new aircraft and some new pilots and air crew to fill up the gaps that war had made in the ranks. So the very afternoon of Ensign Crocker's strike with the 1,000-pound bomb, the *Gambier Bay* was ordered to set an easterly course for Eniwetok in the Marshall Islands. The first battle had ended for the men of the *Gambier Bay.*

## CHAPTER TWENTY

# On to Tinian

When the order came to withdraw to Eniwetok, the atmosphere aboard the *Gambier Bay* became more relaxed than it had been for the past three weeks. The men dreamed ahead of shore leave and at least a beer bust, maybe more. Eniwetok ought to have some shore facilities by this time; it had been an American base for over four months. Captain Goodwin left off chewing on Commander Huxtable, which he had been doing for weeks. Commander Borries left off chewing on Ensign Zeola and Lieutenant (jg) Lischer, who were not flying any more missions or combat air patrol at the moment, and spent much of his time playing basketball on the hangar deck, where he was the most skilful ballhandler on the ship.

Borries also made many mysterious trips to one crew shelter beneath the flight deck. This was the hangout of Chief Montgomery and his airedales. They had an ancient hot plate there, whose original heating element had long since burned out. They made a new one almost every day from stainless steel aircraft safety wire. Each element lasted about twenty-four hours, but they had plenty of safety wire aboard. They also had plenty of coffee, courtesy of the cooks in the galley. The real shortage was of fresh water, for the *Gambier Bay* was a small ship with a large crew and faulty condensers, so water was rationed at all times. The fresh water taps in the crew spaces were turned off most of the day, but in some sections of officers' country it remained on. Chief Montgomery's problem was to beguile an officer into fetching water for them in a No. 10 bean can.

At first everyone in Montgomery's crew tried his hand at making coffee. Some of the java was wonderful, some was not so good, and some was just plain lousy. Finally, the coffee making was turned over to AE3c Eugene Martin, a small man from Oklahoma, where he had learned the proper technique of boiling coffee in a bean can. When the wind was right, Martin's coffee could be smelled all the way up to the Fly One Space in the island, where Buzz Borries kept his office. This coffee, everyone swore, was as good as the captain's and a lot more easy to obtain. So Borries would head for the airedale shelter, and when he got there he would dutifully fetch a can of water and then get a cup of coffee and a roll or two scrounged from the CPO mess. One day Montgomery was relaxing with a cup of coffee in the shelter, when he was paged on the flight deck bullhorn. He dashed out onto the flight deck to report to Air Officer Borries.

"Chief," said the air officer solemnly, "do you have any of that good coffee?"

Yes, the trip back to Eniwetok was relaxed; that was the precise word for it. Since VC-10's fighters were in rough shape, the *Gambier Bay* was not asked to supply any combat air patrol on the way back, only antisubmarine patrols with the TBMs. A day or so before they reached Eniwetok, all the fighters were assessed and tested. For a week the metalsmiths and mechanics had been working them over. Commander Borries had eleven of them flown off; six passed the test and five were sent on to Eniwetok, either to be dispatched back to the United States as war wearies or to be overhauled by the shore facilities that could manage the job.

On July 10, the *Gambier Bay* anchored at Eniwetok. Again, there was no shore leave, which came as an unpleasant surprise to the men. But there was little time for grousing among the crew of the ship; they had to take on supplies and ammunition and new aircraft to replace the worn-out planes. The crew was busy loading for the next twenty-four hours. Most of the pilots sat around the ready room, reading, playing acey-deucy, or writing letters. Lt. John Sanderson wrote a poem celebrating the various characters of the flight deck:

"Carrier life is something," we've all heard people say.
"If you've missed this *grand* experience,
get your transfer in today."
But when it comes to flying, you can put me on the shore.
For life on a CVE is something worse than war.
They get you up at three o'clock with a whistle and a bell,
And you stand by in the ready-room just sleepier'n hell.
Word is passed to man the planes, and you race out
on the double.
Then word is passed to go below, there is no end of
trouble.
You'll be sitting in the cockpit when Borries says
"fly off!"
You jam the throttle forward, and the engine starts to
cough.
You go rolling down the deck, but you always feel
the need
Of just one extra knot to keep above your stalling speed.
Or you're up on ASP or combat air patrol,
Your gas is almost gone, and your belly's just a hole.
You'd like to eat, your plane and you have both been
cruising lean,
But Air Plot says to orbit, there's a bogey on the screen.
Sometimes we're told to scramble, and you go charging
to your plane,
But you sit there twenty minutes, while the shrapnel
falls like rain.
Then the enemy is gone, the Admiral says "Let's go!"
So you retire with your gear to the ready room below.
They put you in the catapault, and secure you in the gear,
Pilgrim sticks his finger up, and looks up with a leer.
You're drawing forty miles when Charlie points "away!"
And you hope to hell you've power to get in the air
and stay.
It's when you're landing back aboard that you find it
really rough,
You're high, you're fast, you're low,—Christ Mac!!
that's slow enough!
You're cut, you're on the gear, and now Krida signals
things
Like Hook up, Hold your brakes!! Spill your flaps,
Now fold your wings!!
Yes, carrier life is something, something dangerous
and hard

Your wings will all turn green, and your ass will turn
to lard.
Oh, take us back to "Dago" and give us stateside duty,
Where once a month we'll fly four hours, or maybe
strop a beauty!!

Passed around the wardroom, the poem was greeted with jeers and laughter. Sanderson was acclaimed as the poet laureate of the *Gambier Bay*, and the poem was saved.

Not all the officers and men of the squadron could take it quite that easy. Commander Huxtable and Chief Montgomery went to the beach with Commander Borries to get some planes to replace the weary ones. Borries managed to negotiate one new FM-2 but the old tired ones he thought should be dumped had to serve again. They did better with the torpedo bombers, unloading three of the worst ones and getting six new TBMs in return, to make up for Pyzdrowski's lost photo plane, Holleman's and Shroyer's.

Buzz Borries looked at all the brand new fighters sitting there on the flight line. But to get one you had to present the aircraft log book that was given out when a pilot showed up to claim a plane. They walked into the operations office, and saw that the desk was piled high with log books. Commander Borries reached over and selected a log book and slipped it to Chief Montgomery. They all marched over to the flight line then, and took over the planes listed in the log books. Commander Borries signed for all of them, including the purloined plane. When they saw it, they were in for a surprise. It had been obviously prepared to be a night fighter and the color scheme was much darker than the legal VC-10 planes. Borries got it aboard in a hurry. But the Lord punished him for such perfidy: the stolen plane became the supreme "Hangar Queen" of the *Gambier Bay*, spending most of its time down on the hangar deck with a mechanic or two trying to make it run properly. It never did.

That day the off-duty men went fishing. The cooks provided them with some shrimp, and they baited their hooks and threw them over the side. They caught a mess of yellowtail, enough for a real feast for the fish-lovers.

But that was the end of the recreation. Next day, July 12, they were at sea again, once more a part of Admiral Salada's Task Unit—52.14 in naval parlance. They were going back to war. Captain Goodwin was concerned that even these few days out of action may have dulled the perceptions of his crew, so the call to General Quarters was sounded at mid-morning and the gunners were set to practicing anti-aircraft fire as the ship steamed west, back to cover the Tinian invasion.

One morning Ensign Zeola was assigned to predawn combat air patrol in a fighter he had flown often before. He remembered this plane because each time he went up it seemed to be running more scratchily. On this day he had a particularly hard time getting the engine started, and then it ran rougher than ever. In take off, the pilot of a Wildcat sets the throttle for full automatic rich mixture, but the only way he could get the plane to run smoothly that morning was in the automatic lean position. He should have downed the plane and aborted, but he wanted to make the mission, so he took off anyhow. The mission went normally. When the combat air patrol returned to the carrier, Zeola still had the throttle in the automatic lean position. For landing control he moved it to full rich mixture, as usual. Immediately the engine began cutting out, and he lost power. He fiddled with the mixture control, but he could not get the Wildcat to run more than intermittently. He was fourth in the landing pattern, but he called "May Day" on the radio, and his shipmates moved out of the pattern so he could come in. But when Zeola approached, the flight deck was not ready to receive him, and Lieutenant McClendon gave him a wave-off, to come around again. He came around again, engine missing, but McClendon would not chance landing the plane in that condition so he gave him the red flag. Four times Zeola came around. On the fourth time, he got a white flag, but as he came in, coached by McClendon, the engine quit entirely, and the Wildcat nosed over and headed for the bottom of the sea. It was so close to the carrier that it hit stack wash from the flight deck and flipped completely over. The plane sank, righted itself and came to the surface. Zeola unbuckled his safety harness and dove over the side. He had been carrying a wing tank which was empty, and it had broken loose from the plane and was floating. He swam to that as the Wildcat went to the bottom. He floated for what seemed to be forever, unable to pull himself out of the water onto the wing tank. A destroyer picked him up, and he went back to the carrier. Captain Goodwin, who was fond of this hot pilot met him on the flight deck and told him how glad he was to have him back aboard, then Zeola went into sick bay for several days—victim of the gas fumes he had inhaled from the wing tank and of a mild concussion.

He spent the next week in sick bay, but at the end of it he demanded to be allowed to fly again. Actually the squadron was flying more antisubmarine patrols than anything else, but pilots were needed for combat air patrols, as well. They were not yet flying strike missions in support of troops, but Zeola felt guilty. He also felt terrible, but he did not tell Flight Surgeon Stewart that. His head ached constantly from the concussion of the water crash. But he was determined not to let it show.

On July 22, Zeola got himself on the roster for combat air patrol. That morning the antisubmarine patrol was launched first, as usual. The patrol consisted of four planes, each carrying four 250-pound depth charges. But five planes and five pilots were always assigned to their planes, so that in case one of the first four planes failed to perform before launch, its mission could be scratched and the fifth pilot assigned. Lieutenant Sanderson, the poet, was in the number five position that morning. He was sleepy and he did not expect to be up in the air, for all four planes ahead of him were brand new TBMs acquired at Eniwetok. But the number four TBM was unable to achieve maximum power on the catapult, so it was pulled off, and Sanderson was told to taxi up and get ready. Hurry was the key word. Captain Goodwin was irritable, for the ship had been pulled off its base course to launch planes. To get the wind at her bow, she was heading directly away from the formation all the while they were having the trouble with that fourth TBM.

Under the circumstances, the flight deck officer told Sanderson to get going, and the pilot hurried to buckle up and make his preflight check. But something malfunctioned, for when he was catapulted a few moments later, the TBM went into a sharp climb off the end of the flight deck, gained about 100 feet of altitude, and then crashed directly ahead of the ship's bow. The three depth charges exploded, disintegrating the plane and its crew, and lifting the bow of the *Gambier Bay* about ten feet. The ship came down with a crash, and Captain Goodwin ordered damage control to work. The damage control parties reported no external troubles, but below, several plates forward had buckled and some of the work of Mr. Kaiser's welders had come undone. One aviation gasoline compartment had sprung a leak, and the fuel had to be transferred from it, and inert gas pumped in.

This accident caused a commotion on the flight deck, and consternation in the heart of Ensign Zeola. He was still feeling queasy after his crash, and the death of Lieutenant Sanderson, radioman J. L. Richards, and gunner W. R. Zanon did not help. Still, he was a pilot, and he had a job. So he taxied forward and made his takeoff and flew the mission for four hours. As he knew it would be, landing was difficult. When he came back, Ensign Wickersham had just brought his Wildcat in, the hook had broken when it engaged the wire, the plane had hurtled along the deck into the barrier and turned over, fouling the deck. Captain Goodwin knew that his other combat air patrol planes were low on gas, so he sent them over to the *Kitkun Bay*. Zeola was not happy about making this landing; having McClendon down there waving the paddle made all the difference to him. Now he had to come in under the eye of an LSO whose ways he did not know. He felt like screaming.

Zeola came around to the other carrier cautiously, too cautiously, and he was waved off three times. The trouble was that he did not trust the landing signal officer, and every time the LSO told him to throttle back, Zeola looked down at the expanse of water between himself and the deck and kept on going, until he got another wave-off.

Finally, on the fourth time, the LSO gave him a cut, and he landed, very badly. He went down to the ready room and was sitting there, dejected, when he saw an officer with a very red face come in, purposefully. He knew this was the LSO and that the LSO was getting ready to chew him out for those passes. But one of VC-10's torpedo pilots, who had also been landed on the carrier, stopped the officer and spoke to him. The landing signal officer did not exactly grin, but he stopped and came over to Zeola and spoke to him sympathetically about the problem. But problem or not, he said, Zeola had to work on his landings again.

He got back to the *Gambier Bay* just in time to attend the memorial service on the hangar deck for Lieutenant Sanderson and his crew.

## CHAPTER TWENTY-ONE

# Tinian

The next American objective in the Central Pacific campaign was Tinian island. It had to be, for if the Americans were to use Saipan as a base for the operation of B-29 superfortresses, this island had to be captured and its anti-aircraft guns put out of action: Tinian lies only three miles from the tip of Saipan. On July 20, the day that the Tinian invasion plan was released, Tinian was defended by 9,000 Japanese sailors and soldiers. Vice Adm. Kakuji Kakuta was theoretically the commander of the island. But his unit was the base air force, which had been almost totally destroyed in the Battle of the Philippine Sea and by the carrier planes of Admiral Sallada's force. The real military commander of Tinian was Col. Kiyochi Ogata of the famous Kwantung Army, which had been stationed in Manchuria. He had just brought his troops to Tinian in March, when the Japanese realized that the Marianas would soon be under attack.

*Gambier Bay*'s role in the battle for Tinian began on July 23. That day she and *Kitkun Bay* sent fifty sorties against the island; the *Gambier Bay*'s share was twenty-three. The TBMs were armed with 100-pound bombs, rockets, and incendiary clusters and sent to the canefields and a village at the northern end of the island. The next day they were up again, but on July 24, VC-10 flew only nineteen sorties against the island. One reason for this was the delicate condition of most of the aircraft after the Saipan action. The pilots would have welcomed a whole new fleet of planes, but they knew they weren't going to get them and must depend on Chiefs Montgomery and Flanders and their crews to keep the old ones flying.

After the patrols and the strike were launched in the morning, the remaining operational aircraft were spotted in ready position on the after end of the flight deck. But as the aircraft from the *Gambier Bay* and the other carriers reached the target and began to return, the flight deck was respotted. Sallada's two small carriers were operating with the *Essex* and *Langley*, and it was conceivable that a plane from any one of those other carriers might land on the *Gambier Bay* in an emergency. So Commander Borries ordered respotting, and Chief Montgomery supervised. The quickest way to respot was to forget about the tractor and towbar, and call down to the ready room for pilots who were sitting around to come up and taxi the planes to the forward end of the carrier, behind the crash barrier. Among the pilots, Lieutenant Roby was the anathema of the flight deck for he was very fussy about the condition of any plane he touched. With considerable heat the airedales used to say that Roby never even taxied a plane that he didn't down for some deficiency. Technically, Lieutenant Roby was absolutely right. By July 24, half the planes on the flight deck were technically nonoperational. Actually, they would fly well enough, but there was no question of their deficiencies, and if it came to a matter of official cognizance, a pilot was within his rights to refuse to fly them. Captain Goodwin, Commander Borries, and Commander Huxtable all agreed that they wanted every plane in the air that could get there. So on July 24, as they were spotting planes, Commander Borries told Montgomery to call the ready room for pilots. "But leave Roby down there in the ready room," he said. He did not want any more downed planes.

The Tinian operation was the smoothest yet carried out by the American amphibious forces. For weeks before the landings, observers in the air and aboard the battleships had begun charting the points from which gunfire emanated, so that by the time the invasion began, they knew where most guns were located. The ships and the planes could be directed to the positions by coordinates, and the attacks were swift and effective. VC-10 flew many more missions with rockets, 100-pound and 500-pound bombs, and the fighters strafed known enemy positions to soften them up for ground attack.

At the end of July, Tinian was secured. Actually, stubborn little groups of Japanese defenders kept the marines busy for three months, but these brave men had few weapons and could not affect the outcome. On August 1, the *Gambier Bay* was on her way to Guam, which had been invaded ten days earlier by U.S. Marines and troops of the 77th Army Division. The Guam operation was well in hand, and *Gambier Bay*'s role was to fly patrol for the ships of the invasion fleet. At the end of the first week of this operation, the ship was in Eniwetok for provisions.

One night Admiral Sallada came to the *Gambier Bay* to dine with Captain Goodwin. The two had been close friends for many years. They talked about the battles they had just been through. Admiral Sallada was more than a little complimentary about the performance of the *Gambier Bay* and VC-10, and Captain Goodwin was proud of his ship and crew that night. Then, almost as an aside, Admiral Sallada changed the subject. He had just been promoted to be commander of Carrier Division F-Six, and he needed a chief of staff.

"Oh hell, Slats," said Goodwin, "I've got a good ship, and we're doing a good job, and I think it would be a mistake to leave it."

"That's right," said Admiral Sallada. "But I really need someone who knows something about ships to work with me as a fast carrier task force commander. I can't think of anybody I'd rather have than you. You'd be doing me a great personal favor and contributing to the war effort. The Navy Department can put someone in here who can run your ship. You've got it on the right road. I think your contribution would be better with me."

"Let me sleep on it."

So they parted. The next day Captain Goodwin thought it over. He was happy with the *Gambier Bay*, but there was a war to be won, and the prospects of promotion would be brighter for someone who had broadened his experience. The *Gambier Bay* had proved her merit in the Marianas. Perhaps it was time for a change. He dined with Sallada that night on the *Kitkun Bay* and agreed to make the change. The admiral would leave the force on August 10, and Rear Adm. Ralph Ofstie, who had been Admiral

Nimitz's air officer, would take over as commander of Carrier Division 26.

Captain Goodwin would take the *Gambier Bay* down to Espiritu Santo island in the New Hebrides. This area had been turned into a major supply base during the South Pacific campaign. Here, the crew would have a little recreation, and Captain Goodwin would turn over the ship to a new commander.

On August 11, they sailed with the *Kitkun Bay, White Plains,* and four destroyers. The destroyers seemed hardly necessary, so quiet were the waters through which they passed. The area was deemed safe enough that Captain Goodwin decided he could allow the traditional crossing-of-the-line ceremonies when they came to the equator. Of the entire ship's company and squadron, which totaled nearly a thousand men, only five percent were "shellbacks" who had been initiated into the Kingdom of Neptunus Rex on previous voyages. For several days before they reached the line those creatures of privilege regaled the uninitiated with gruesome tales of the tortures heaped upon "pollywogs" as they were taken into the kingdom. Some of the tougher members of the crew threatened to "mutiny" and have no part of the ceremony. If anyone tried to push them around, they were willing to fight. The shellbacks, led by the chiefs, then agreed to compromise. They needed help anyhow, so they bought off the potential mutineers with promises to initiate them first and then let them wreak havoc with their shipmates.

At eight o'clock on the morning of August 13, the *Gambier Bay* reached the equator at 162° 21′ 30″ east longitude. The fun began. The forward elevator was lowered ten feet below the flight deck and, with tarpaulins, converted into a swimming pool. The flight deck crew pumped in three feet of sea water, and the cooks, who had been saving garbage for two days to be sure it was slimy and adequately odoriferous, brought it forth and heaved it into the pool. A metal chair was placed on the flight deck alongside the pool and connected to a low-voltage battery. The first pollywog came forth, and was immediately surrounded by a gang of shellbacks dressed in surgeon's smocks, pirate garb, and the robes of the court of Neptune. He was laid down on an "operating table" and fed a draught of an obnoxious mixture whose secret formula would never be revealed by the shellback priests. He was then placed on the metal chair, shocked, and pushed into the tank of garbage-filled water. Some officers were put in the stocks. The pilots were treated almost as roughly as the swabbies. The first initiate, and most of those after him, also "ran the gauntlet" and shellbacks with staves smacked at them hard and true, so hard and so true indeed that several pilots reported in at sick bay for the next few days, where the diagnosis was "unfit for flight operations" because of severe bruises to the seats of their pants. As the intent and practice of the initiation came home to the cluster of pollywogs who had been herded onto the flight deck to await their punishment, a group rebelled, seized fire hoses, and began attacking the royal policemen with streams of water. The captain watched with very good humor and forbearance, especially for him, until a stream struck one of the TBMs on the flight deck. Then he was on the bullhorn, calling a halt to the fire hose operations: Aircraft and sea water did not mix.

Finally, the last pollywog was greased and dosed and bathed and smacked satisfactorily, and the ceremonies came to an end. But the pilots were not the only members of the crew of the *Gambier Bay* who limped around the decks for the next few days.

On August 16, the *Gambier Bay* approached Espiritu Santo, which was protected by a mine field. A pilot boat came out and a pilot boarded the ship to take them through. While he was navigating, the ship's gyrocompass went out, and the pilot asked Lieutenant Commander Gellhorn, the navigator, if he had a Napier Diagram. Gellhorn called for Ensign Beisang, who brought it out promptly. The pilot used the diagram to steer the *Gambier Bay* in, and when he brought the ship to her mooring, he congratulated the captain and Navigator Gellhorn on their care and skill. Goodwin congratulated the navigator, who was properly modest about his fine accomplishment. Later, as Captain Goodwin was preparing to leave the ship, he prepared all his fitness reports on the officers and went over the division heads' reports on their juniors. He discovered that Gellhorn had given Beisang an "average" report, which was the equivalent to a college C, and which never won any officer a promotion.

The captain called Beisang into his cabin and told him about the report. "Don't worry," he said, "I'm rewriting it. I know you were the one who produced the Napier Diagram."

Beisang was sorry to see the captain go. The same could not be said for many of the officers, and particularly the aviators, who felt that Captain Goodwin's demands on them had been unusual and heartless. Their complaints went as far back as that initial shakedown cruise for VC-10 when he could have sent the squadron planes to land ashore and instead insisted that they land on the carrier under the most difficult conditions. Lieutenant Commander Waring, the assistant air officer, referred to the captain as Sir Hugh. Commander Huxtable, the squadron skipper, heaved a sign of relief when he heard the captain was going. Now, if only they could get a more sympathetic commanding officer. . . .

## CHAPTER TWENTY-TWO

# The New Captain

Almost as soon as they reached Espiritu Santo, Captain Goodwin left the ship, turning over temporary command to Commander Ballinger. Admiral Sallada was in a hurry, so the new captain would not have the benefit of Goodwin's views, or perhaps the disadvantage of his prejudices. But Capt. W. V. R. Vieweg, who joined the ship a few days later, was an entirely different sort of man. He came aboard, went through the transfer of command ceremony, and then as his first act, he called on the pilots of VC-10 to report to the ready room. Given the background of the ship, the order produced considerable tension. Were they to have another "sundowner?" When the captain came in all hands stood up.

"Carry on," he said, and he sat down on a box which was used for stowing plotting boards. He then crossed his legs under him, and the pilots began to relax.

"Gentlemen," he said, "I just want to tell you that as far as I am concerned, this ship has one primary mission: to get you safely to the point where you can accomplish yours."

There was more, but in that opening gesture and opening statement, Captain Vieweg had won the hearts of the aviators of the *Gambier Bay*. "You could almost hear and certainly feel the great sigh of relief go up in the ready room," wrote Commander Huxtable. "Here was a skipper that was *for* us."

To underline his commitment, Captain Vieweg went ashore to the airstrip at Espiritu Santo. The squadron had flown some of its planes there for checkup and parts replacement, and the hope that they could trade them in on new aircraft. VC-10 was lucky this time: Engineering Officer Pyzdrowski was sent ashore to inspect and test six TBMs! With the new bombers they had acquired at Eniwetok, that meant they had gone through one complete cycle of aircraft. The same was virtually true of the fighter contingent. But there was a rub. Just as Commander Borries had hijacked a fighter at Eniwetok, there were other rapacious airmen on the prowl, prepared to commit larceny on behalf of their squadrons. So Pyzdrowski secured permission to remain ashore until the aircraft could be flown aboard the *Gambier Bay*, and he literally stood guard over the planes. Thus, Pyzdrowski was not aboard ship on the day that Captain Vieweg took command, and he had not heard the good news. While he stood guard, a big, tall flyer came by and sat in one of his TBMs. In a moment Pyzdrowski was standing by the cockpit. Pyzdrowski did not see any insignia on the officer's lapels and assumed that he must be an air officer or commander of another squadron. He decided to protect his planes.

"Sir, these planes are set aside for VC-10 of the *Gambier Bay*. If you want to check out in one of them I will have to have an order from the captain."

The big man looked down at him. There was something about his face that reminded Pyzdrowski of a big friendly dog.

"I am Bowser Vieweg," said the big man, "the new captain of the *Gambier Bay*.

"Oh," said a very lowly Lieutenant Pyzdrowski. "That's fine."

The captain then borrowed Pyzdrowski's helmet and goggles. He had become a naval aviator two years after graduation from the Naval Academy in 1924. He had flown every sort of naval aircraft, including torpedo bombers, but his major experience had been in fighters and multi-engine patrol bombers. He had not flown a TBM before, although he had just come from the *Hornet*, where he was chief of staff to Jocko Clark, commander of Task Group 58.1. If Captain Vieweg was going to run the *Gambier Bay* and its squadron, he wanted to show his crew that he knew what he, and they, had to do. He would land a

TBM on the carrier's deck, but first he wanted to check it out.

Pyzdrowski was impressed when the captain showed mastery of the TBM without an hour of instruction in it. Later that day, other pilots came from the ship, and together they all flew the six TBMs to safety from hijackers. Since the captain had Pyzdrowski's helmet and goggles, the lieutenant had to fly aboard without them, although this was a breach of air regulations. When they had landed, the captain called the pilots to the ready room again. He had a few things to say about air safety, because the *Gambier Bay* had a high rate of operational accidents, several of which had cost American lives. He made his remarks, and then looked straight at Pyzdrowski.

"Oh, yes, gentlemen. One other thing. You will remember that it is against the code of good carrier airmanship to fly aboard without a helmet and goggles. Now in the future I shall hold Commander Borries responsible for any such violations." He was still looking at Pyzdrowski, who was beginning to turn red. The whole squadron knew that he had come aboard without his helmet and goggles. "Lieutenant Pyzdrowski did just that today. Rightfully, I should put him on probation and ground him next time he breaks a rule. But that wouldn't be quite fair, would it, since I am the character who walked off with his helmet and goggles." He grinned, that big "Bowser" grin that had gained him the nickname at the Naval Academy, and he handed the goggles and helmet back to Pyzdrowski. At that moment, the pilots of VC-10 would have done anything for their new captain.

They remained in the South Pacific. At Espiritu Santo they took on supplies and ammunition. The captain announced that swimming from the ship would be permitted while they were at anchor here. The men had liberty parties ashore, which included chilled beer from the *Gambier Bay*'s padlocked supply. But the officers were not as lucky as they had hoped to be. They had chipped in $1,200 just before the carrier left San Diego for a wine fund and had paid this money over to a dealer with instructions to send the wine to the ship, c/o Fleet Post Office, San Francisco. Now they had put into port at Roi, and twice at Eniwetok, and here at Espiritu Santo. And although mail had been received dated long past the time when the wine was supposed to leave California, the wine had never arrived. It seemed quite obvious that it would not, and the officers of the *Gambier Bay* moodily discussed punishments for the thieving "liberators" as they looked into their glasses of 3.2 beer in the Espiritu Santo Officers' Club. They were no better off than the swabbies in the potato locker, and probably not as well off as the chiefs, whose ways were dark, but who always looked quite satisfied when in port. Pyzdrowski was an exception. Back at Holtville, he had received a case of Scotch whiskey, highly camouflaged, from his family in Pittsburgh, and he had managed to smuggle it aboard the *Gambier Bay*. Pyzdrowski and his friends, then, were happier than most of the officers during the Espiritu Santo stay.

Captain Goodwin had left the ship on August 18, and Captain Vieweg had arrived two days later. That gave him just five days to familiarize himself with ship and crew before sailing for Tulagi on August 25. They were busy days. The motor whaleboat was in use to move supplies, so Captain Vieweg secured a speed boat from the boat pool. The boat was operated by Coxswain Jack C. Butler, who now had the impressive title of Coxswain of the Captain's Gig. Vieweg liked to ride in the cockpit, rather than aft in the usual military splendor. When he was aboard, he never let Coxswain Butler fly the captain's flag as was usually done. Several times they were hailed by junior officers who noted the absence of a flag, and of any officers in the stern, where officers were supposed to be, and tried to commandeer the boat. Captain Vieweg would stand up then and show the eagles on his collar, and the abashed juniors would slink away. Such encounters did Coxswain Butler's heart good, and when related to the crew, endeared Bowser Vieweg as much to the potato locker as to the ready room.

The new captain was also a favorite with the chiefs, and Chief Montgomery in particular. Early in the voyage, the plane captains had asked if they could not decorate the airplanes, and Skipper Huxtable had agreed. He secretly hoped decoration would persuade the airedales to keep the planes cleaner than they might otherwise. He had approached Captain Goodwin, who agreed to the idea in the abstract. But when the TBM and FM-2s suddenly began to sprout drawings of scantily clad girls, Captain Goodwin's regulation soul was upset, and he growled at Commander Huxtable. He wanted those pictures removed. But

Huxtable, when he conferred with Chief Montgomery, agreed that the blow to crew morale would be deadly if the paintings had to be washed off. Finally, they found a solution to the problem: They washed them off the starboard side of the aircraft, which was the side that faced the bridge as the planes took off and landed. They left them on the port side, which the captain never saw. With Bowser Vieweg there was none of this official disapproval, or "chicken shit" as the enlisted men termed it. The greatest compliment was probably from the junior officers who found it hard to remember that their new captain was a "professional."

So, generally speaking, in the week of layover in Espiritu Santo, morale aboard the *Gambier Bay* improved. Just before it was time to leave, there was a last beer bust at "Duffy's Tavern," a picnic area and ballpark created by the Seabees from an old cow pasture. Chief Montgomery had the duty that day of escorting the contingent from the *Gambier Bay* and VC-10 and looking after them. That meant he put on an S.P. armband and strapped a .45 automatic around his waist.

Espiritu Santo, located just fifteen degrees south of the equator, enjoyed plenty of sunshine. Anyone who liked a tropical climate would love the place. On this particular day, the *Gambier Bay* and VC-10 boys were whooping it up, and the beer flowed rapidly. Chief Montgomery's major concern was to prevent fights between the "brown shoe" aviators of the squadron and the "black shoe" sailors of the ship. But before the afternoon was over another element entered his considerations. They were sharing the recreation area, as was usual. Today they shared it with a unit of Seabees, most of them very unprofessional nonnaval types who had come out of the construction business back in America. Generally speaking, sailors were not very fond of the Shore Patrol, and Seabees were no exception. Chief Montgomery had a certain clout with his own contingent, because they would have to live with him back aboard the ship, but the Seabees did not give a damn for carrier swabs or chiefs, and particularly chiefs wearing the S.P. label. About mid-afternoon, Chief Montgomery got a little worried. For some reason, the Seabees had not provided any Shore Patrol, so Chief Montgomery and a handful of S.P.s from the *Gambier Bay* were the only evidence of authority. The beer had begun to go to the heads of the men, and several arguments started. Soon it became apparent that Chief Montgomery faced an incipient three-way brawl among Seabees, airedales, and swabs. He succeeded in stopping an argument between a pair from the carrier and was turning away, when a red-faced Seabee picked up a half-dried cow dropping and rubbed it down the front of Montgomery's khaki shirt.

Navy chiefs did not usually take kindly to such treatment. Chief Montgomery's first impulse was to knock the Seabee into next week. But, not being burdened with beer, the chief also realized that to do so would be to inaugurate a brawl that might send half the men of the *Gambier Bay* to captain's mast. For as the Seabee finished his smear, the park grew silent, and every eye was on the pair. Chief Montgomery unclenched his fist, and looked at his assailant.

"Hey, sailor, you must be from Texas if you know how to do that." The chief put his arm around the Seabee, pulled him to his chest, rubbed cowdung on his front, and laughed. When the others saw him laugh and saw what he had done to the Seabee, they began laughing, too, and the crisis was over. Even if the Seabee leader had wanted to pick a fight, he could not have done it by this time. In those next few minutes, while all the men were "buddies," Chief Montgomery began moving his sailors back to the ship.

Back on the *Gambier Bay* the watch was sweating out the last loads of fresh provisions. On the work detail was AMM3c Potochniak, who had been assigned this task by his pal, AMlc Olaf Emblem. Moving from warehouse to ship, the work detail gorged themselves on fresh apples and drank them down with pineapple juice from cans knocked open with a combat knife. They loaded several landing craft with provisions and moved them out to the ship. The boom from the flight deck was lowered, and the provisions were moved aboard. Since the galleys were aft, the provisions were loaded onto the after elevator and taken down to the hangar deck, and then carried to the mess area. To get there they had to pass the last light lock, in the elevator. And who should have a shop in that last light lock—Tony Potochniak, the oxygen man. Before the loading got very far, he arranged for a blow-out panel to be removed from the light lock, and as the elevator came down, he passed goodies through to eager waiting hands.

Fresh eggs were purloined, and butter and apples and fruit juices, all of them supplies originally intended for the officers' mess. It was a contented gang of swabbies from the hangar deck work detail who closed down their unofficial operations that night. Had they been caught it would have been a different matter, at least a captain's mast, but since they were not, it was a wonderful joke to be enjoyed as long as the eggs and fruit juice lasted.

CHAPTER TWENTY-THREE

# The Palaus

On August 24, Carrier Division 26 raised anchor at Espiritu Santo and sailed for the Florida Islands, which to most of the men was not as meaningful a term as the Solomons, of which this small chain was a part. This was all new territory to the men of the *Gambier Bay* and not very comfortable country to be in. The heat drenched them constantly, and most of the carrier was not air-conditioned. The wardroom was, and so was the ready room, but the staterooms and the crew spaces were very hot. Seaman Quinn at his potato locker dice game and Lieutenant Bell at his typewriter both stripped down and tried to keep cool. It was difficult. In the evening the bow was the most pleasant part of the ship, but almost all the time, day and night, the heat was oppressive.

The *Gambier Bay* traveled on this voyage with the *Kitkun Bay*, the flagship, the *White Plains*, and four destroyers. Their first port of call would be Tulagi, but they were then moving on to strike Yap and the Palau Islands in the Western Carolines. Everyone in Carrier Division 26 knew this much by the end of the day. They were told to expect tough going in the Palaus, which were close to the Philippines. But those islands were also the key to the invasion of the Philippines, and on the flight deck of the *Gambier Bay* it was assumed that they would move toward Manila next.

All these developments marked a major change of plan. Since 1942 the navy's Central Pacific offensive and the army's South Pacific offensive had been headed on a collision course. Admirals King and Nimitz wanted to lead the show; so did MacArthur.

MacArthur held that they must retake the Philippines for political reasons, and that he, MacArthur, must lead the forces back there because he had promised to return. This change would mean that the navy, which had been hoping to drive on to Formosa, perhaps to the China coast, and then to Japan, was going to take a back seat. One factor in this major policy debate was certainly the army's alarm and worry about serving under the navy after the relief of Gen. Ralph Smith by Gen. Holland Smith of the marines at Saipan.

As the argument over direction and overall command simmered, Admiral King wanted an invasion of Truk, the big Japanese naval base in the Carolines. But in the spring, the fast carriers had attacked, and their planes had knocked out so much of Japan's naval and air power at Truk, that the base could be bypassed as unworthy of the effort. On June 15, as the *Gambier Bay* went into action in the Marianas, Adm. William F. Halsey was detached from his South Pacific command and put to planning the occupation of the Western Carolines. On July 26, as the *Gambier Bay* attacked Tinian, General MacArthur, Admiral Nimitz, and President Roosevelt began meeting at Pearl Harbor to decide the future. MacArthur was a better politician than Nimitz, and he told the president there of his plan for moving into the Philippines, largely on political grounds. Nimitz argued the King plan, to move from the Marshalls and Marianas directly to Formosa. But in the end MacArthur carried the day. It would be the Philippines, and MacArthur in charge.

But because of wheels that were already in motion, two major military operations would come first. General MacArthur would assault Morotai, which lies 500 miles southeast of Mindanao island of the Philippines, on the edge of the Celebes Sea. Halsey would attack the Palau Islands, 400 miles due east of Mindanao. By this time MacArthur had his own naval force under Vice Adm. Thomas Kinkaid. "MacArthur's Navy," as it was called at Pearl Harbor, had its own amphibious command, under Rear Adm. Daniel E. Barbey. The only thing it did not have was ships, and this was a serious bone of contention between Brisbane and Pearl Harbor. In the end, the bristling atmosphere of competition would have a direct effect on the lives of the men of the *Gambier Bay*.

The carriers and their escorts arrived at Tulagi on the morning of August 26. That afternoon they moved out for an exercise in amphibious landing, a twenty-four-hour rehearsal. Then they returned to Tulagi to load ammunition and bombs and torpedoes, for the invasion of Peleliu Island. For ten days the men of the *Gambier Bay* enjoyed almost unlimited liberty, and all the beer they could drink. At least it began that way. The beer stored in the brig was chilled and made ready for liberty parties. It was soon discovered, however, that a certain amount of the beer had disappeared between the loading dock at Espiritu Santo and the brig. The willing hands that moved the cases had not been idle. The system called for the men who wanted to drink beer (not all did) to buy a chit for each bottle while aboard ship. Then, when ashore, the beer was dispensed. Seaman Heinl and Seaman Harry Ray Cunningham bought enough chits for a case of beer. When they were taken by boat over to the recreation island and they got their beer, they settled down to enjoy it. Then they discovered someone aboard the *Gambier Bay*, somehow, had gotten into the beer, and that they had a case of bottled water.

As usual, the men on liberty separated. The ship's complement stuck together and so did the squadron. In fact, the officers and enlisted men of the squadron were closer to each other than either group was to their opposite numbers of the ship. But this harmony was seriously threatened within the squadron at Tulagi when one of the fighter pilots who had bought some liquor in the officers' club, sold a bottle of whiskey to some air crewmen. He charged them $40 for a bottle that had cost him $3.50. Eventually the matter came to the attention of Commander Huxtable, and he was more furious than the chiefs and the victimized enlisted men. The fighter pilot was virtually ostracized by his brother officers until it blew over. On the other hand, torpedo pilot Pyzdrowski became the more popular man aboard the ship for he still had most of the case of Scotch whiskey under lock and key.

During the action in the Marianas, the *Gambier Bay* had expended thousands of rounds of 40-mm ammunition. In the easy days since, the ship's metalsmiths had taken the brass casings to make ashtrays and pencil holders and paperweights. Olaf Emblem, a sturdy member of Chaplain

Carlsen's flock, had decided to make something even more elaborate, a set of etched wine cups for communion. He polished the shells and lacquered them. He lined them with zinc and weighted the bottoms so they would not tip. On the first Sunday that they were to be used, the chaplain put them on the altar, a hundred strong, placed in handsome trays made in the metal shop. With special thanks that day Chaplain Carlsen began the communion service. All went well until the moment when the faithful knelt to take the wafer and the wine. It was then that the men of the *Gambier Bay* learned of the effects of metal on wine. Each quaffer puckered up as if he had sucked on a lemon.

When the crew of the *Gambier Bay* had time for such frivolity as this, it meant they were at ease. But that condition changed on September 8, when the ship sailed with the *Kitkun Bay, White Plains,* and their four escorts. They headed north toward the Palaus and soon joined up with the invasion force, taking station between two convoys of transports that were loaded with marines.

Earlier in the week, planes from the fast carrier force had hit the Palaus for the third time. Besides those attacks, the islands had been struck by numerous raids of heavy bombers based in Dutch New Guinea. So Peleliu and Babelthuap and the other islands seemed to be almost totally clear of Japanese aircraft. In the six days of the voyage, the *Gambier Bay* worried more about the effects of a small typhoon than of attack from any of the nearby islands. Admiral Halsey was already convinced that the Palau assault was a waste of time, and he had argued in favor of bypassing the islands. But once launched into planning, an invasion was nearly impossible to stop, and so the attack went on. On September 15, the First Marines landed without much opposition. The Japanese of Peleliu had recognized that they could not stop the landings, so they concentrated their defenses on higher ground above the beaches. They had built a strong network of fortifications here. Their artillery was concealed in concrete pillboxes, came forth to fire, and then retracted so that the guns were virtually invisible from the air.

On the voyage to Peleliu, VC-10 had flown combat air patrol and antisubmarine patrol missions, but they had been so unexciting as to be mere exercises. On September 15, a strike of four fighters strafed ahead of the marines in response to a request from the ground, but the pilots saw no enemy troops and had no idea of the effectiveness of their fire. Rear Adm. J. B. Oldendorf, commander of the bombardment forces, was so pleased at the lack of resistance that he pointed with pride to the job done by his ships in a three-day barrage and predicted that the capture of Peleliu would be completed in a few days. But within a matter of hours the marines discovered that the Japanese were deeply entrenched in a web of caves and tunnels and would have to be dug out, position by position.

VC-10 had an inkling of the problem that day. Commander Huxtable had drawn additional duty as part time Air Coordinator of the attacks of the escort carriers. He took off at one o'clock that afternoon and circled above the island. At 3:45 a strike group composed of twelve planes from the three carriers assembled on station, and he sent them in to strafe. He moved about, bombing and strafing, too. At five o'clock, he was running low on gas and went down to fire his last rockets, so he could return to the carrier and land empty. At Tinian, Lieutenant (jg) Pyzdrowski had returned from a mission with several rockets, and on landing he had gone into the barrier, one rocket had come loose and skittered across the deck, breaking the leg of aircrewman Ketcham. "Hux" wanted to be sure that sort of accident did not occur again. Just as he was ready to turn for the ship, Burt Bassett appeared on station with six TBMs and called out that he could see many vehicles down below. Huxtable asked where Bassett was, and Bassett replied that he was on the east side of Peleliu's spinal ridge, a position the marines had already discovered to be so difficult it had been christened Bloody Nose Ridge that day. The TBMs were at 4,000 feet, Bassett said. Huxtable was down "on the deck" at that moment, and he made a pass along the side of the ridge and saw a number of two-man tanks heading down from the height to the road that led to the airfield. Obviously the Japanese were heading for a dusk attack on the beachhead, where most of the troops were still located, just south of the airfield.

The elaborate plans for management of the air traffic by the flight coordinator were suddenly thrown out the window. Those tanks had to be stopped and stopped in a hurry. So Huxtable got on the radio, and described what he had seen and the position of the enemy. "Everybody go," he said, signaling a general attack. By this time a number of fighters had joined the TBMs, but there was no way they could be separated into orderly patterns, and do the job in time. Everybody had to take his chances in the traffic.

Huxtable then swung west over Bloody Nose Ridge and turned to the east which lined him up on a causeway that crossed a marshy area just before the point where the road reached the airfield. The first enemy tank was moving onto the bridge as he came, and he flashed in, firing the only weapons he had left, the 50-caliber machine-guns. Huxtable was so intent on his shooting that he did not realize he had moved down into a depression, until out of the corner of his right eye, he saw palm trees flashing by *at eye level.* Huxtable yanked the stick—pulling back as hard as he could—and just managed to lift the TBM over the line of trees at the far end of the marsh. "The adrenaline was flowing full blast from fright," he said, so he pulled out over the ocean and relaxed for a moment to regain control. Several tanks were ashore at the east end of the beach, and one of the fighters asked if he should take a run on them. Huxtable looked and shouted over the radio: "Hell no, that's one of ours. Can't you see the white star?" Then the squadron commander moved inland to watch the action. The fighters and TBMs plastered the Japanese tanks as they headed for the airfield and the beach, and not one tank got more than halfway across the airfield. Huxtable gave Bassett full credit for stopping the attack, because he had spotted the tanks in time. Five white-starred tanks came up and finished the job the aviators had started.

On September 16, the carrier planes launched more strikes. While the ship was in Espiritu Santo, one of the chiefs observed to Landing Signal Officer McClendon that if the wind ever stopped blowing in battle and they hit a dead calm as they had in the Tulagi area, they would have a difficult time operating. "The trouble with Mr. Kaiser's coffins," he said, "is that they are fifteen-knot ships and this is a twenty-five-knot war." It was not quite as bad as that, of course, but they did have a ship that could make only sixteen to nineteen knots in a dead calm, and on September 16, the wind stopped. When it came time to recover aircraft, Captain Vieweg began maneuvering for wind, and turned the ship in a doodlebug pattern to try to find it. Commander Huxtable came back from his mission and saw this maneuvering. He started to laugh, but eventually he got "the old turkey" aboard.

The other pilots had much the same experience. Their missions were successful; they were called upon to help expose and destroy those hidden artillery pieces, and they did finish several of them on that second afternoon. Lieutenant Bassett, who had put on a virtuoso performance on September 15, with a single-handed rocket attack that knocked out a tank, came home with two depth charges after antisubmarine patrol and asked the air-ground coordinator where he might unload them. He was directed to a 90-mm coastal gun, and he destroyed it with the second charge.

On return to the carrier, Bassett found the ship still maneuvering for non-existent wind. He landed too fast to compensate and put his left landing gear in the catwalk, but the damage was only moderate. Next day he was flying again. That day, September 17, four *Gambier Bay* fighters took off at five o'clock in the morning to help the troops. The marines had encountered stiff resistance as they moved into the rough ridge and gulley country of Peleliu. Bombing and strafing helped, and all the carriers provided strikes.

The island of Anguar had also been invaded, and the marines were having trouble there with pillboxes and blockhouses. VC-10 sent a flight of eight fighters which carried 250-pound bombs, and the air-ground coordinator reported hits on pillboxes. The fighters had plenty of time for strafing and bombing because Japanese air opposition was non-existent. Only one Japanese plane gave them any trouble, and this was an observation seaplane that came over the area at night. They called it "Washing Machine Charlie" (after the original which had operated at Guadalcanal in 1942) and some of the nervous worried. But the principal effect of "Washing Machine Charlie" was to cost honest men good sleep since every time he came around it meant another call to General Quarters.

By the third day, the men of the *Gambier Bay* realized there was something unusual about this invasion: no attempt by the Japanese to reinforce or strengthen their garrison or to provide any sort of air support. On September 18, it also became apparent that the ground troops were having a rough time, and more strikes went after pillboxes and gun emplacements. For the first time in four days Lieutenant Bassett found anti-aircraft fire bursting all about him as he attacked. So the Japanese did have anti-aircraft defenses! They also had some air power remaining, for, on the nights of September 19 and 20, planes bombed the troops on Peleliu, and on September 21, the *Gambier Bay* sent twelve fighters on a sweep to locate and destroy what were believed to be seaplanes hidden on Babelthuap island's shore. They found some boathouses and shacks along the waterline that might have housed seaplanes, and worked them over, but they never did see a plane.

VC-10 also went on a mission to Yap. Lieutenant Stewart would lead seven fighters. The purpose was to hit Japanese aircraft either on the ground or in the air and prevent them from getting anywhere near the task force. It was going to be a long mission—300 miles to Yap and then return, and the FM-2 was not a long-range aircraft. The night before, when the pilots learned the details, a good deal of concern was registered in the ready room. It was a long flight, and they were supposed to carry two 250-pound bombs each; they were to fly off at 3:30 A.M. an hour and a half before daylight, and they were to be catapulted. They did not like any part of this mission. Finally, after discussion, Lieutenant Stewart went to Commander Huxtable and Commander Borries, and they all conferred with Captain Vieweg. The pilots wanted to carry only one bomb, and a wing tank of gasoline, Stewart said. If the purpose was to knock out Japanese fighters, and they ran into them in the air, they would have dogfights, which would use up enormous amounts of fuel.

Captain Vieweg sat in his chair, face impassive. The fighter leader was a little worried about the reaction, for if Captain Goodwin had been in charge, there would have been no argument with the orders. But Vieweg nodded sympathetically, so Lieutenant Stewart went on. Furthermore, the fighter pilots did not want to be catapulted. The catapult was for turkeys (TBMs) not for fighters. Everyone knew how the fighter pilots hated the "turkey shooter."

When Stewart had finished, Vieweg smiled. "All right," he said, "about the wing tank. You've got a point there. But no on the catapult. That's how you'll go. Too much weight to risk an accident in the dark."

So they were catapulted, with one wing tank and one bomb each. The mission turned out to be tame; they found nothing on the Japanese airfields but burned out planes and no sign at all of a Japanese military presence. There were no dogfights, and the VC-10 fighters had a very pleasant flight home with plenty of gas. They came in safely, and in the ready room they had to admit that it had been a little hairy getting off in the dark, and that the captain had been quite right to send them off the "turkey machine."

Vieweg was thorough, and so was Lieutenant Bell, who spent his time asking questions. Captain Vieweg decided they ought to take a look at Ulithi, which had a protected harbor that Admiral Nimitz wanted to use for a staging base. Commander Huxtable flew to Ulithi and found no sign of a military presence there. A second mission to Babelthuap encountered heavy but inaccurate anti-aircraft fire. All this puzzling information was transmitted to Admiral Halsey, commander of the Third Fleet, and he concluded that he had been right in the beginning. The Palaus had seemed important because the Japanese could have used them as an air base to strike the Philippine invaders. But it was obvious that the Japanese had nothing here with which to strike, although the ground troops could be expected to resist to the end. Admiral Ofstie was directed to take Carrier Division 26 into Ulithi and anchor in the harbor. They entered and anchored and met no resistance at all.

Meanwhile, a small infantry unit invaded Ulithi and met no one but natives. The Japanese were all gone. When this information had been sent off the troops were put to constructive effort: building Duffy's Tavern No. 2, which would serve as a recreation base for the men of the ships. Liberty was scheduled to begin ashore on D-Day + 2, but not for the men of the *Gambier Bay*. On September 25, the carrier sailed for Hollandia. The observations of Commander Huxtable and his pilots had been added up with similar findings by pilots from other carriers of the Third Fleet, and Admiral Halsey had recommended that the Philippines attack be set forward. There was no need to hold back, and to wait might give the enemy a chance to recover and resupply some of the areas hard hit by the fast carrier forces in recent weeks. So in a moderate way the pilots of the *Gambier Bay* had contributed to a major tactical change in the conduct of the war. The scuttlebutt had it that the *Gambier Bay* was going home to San Diego for repair of that structural damage forward. But the fact was that her destination was Manus Island, and from there she would join the stepped-up invasion of the Philippines.

## CHAPTER TWENTY-FOUR

# Invasion

Hollandia was hot. The *Gambier Bay* arrived on October 1, 1944, having crossed the equator for the third time. The old salts paid no attention to that crossing but were hoping for liberty when they hit the shore. They had the liberty, or most of them did. But in anticipation Quartermaster Bell had decided to do a little premature celebrating. On the dull trip down to New Guinea, he had gotten hold of some alcohol more prosaically used to fill the compass box, and he spent the next three days in sick bay, a very unhappy sailor. As his shipmates went on leave to walk the beach and do very little else, Quartermaster Bell was aboard. When the ship went on to Manus Island, the staging point for the Philippine invasion, Quartermaster Bell was still so sick that he had to be sent ashore to a military hospital.

Many of Quartermaster Bell's shipmates had the same impulses as he, but were luckier. At Manus, AMM3c Potochniak again fell into good luck, courtesy of his friend Olaf Emblem, the wizard of the work details. Acting Boatswain's Mate Emblem offered Potochniak a berth on a work detail. "Doing what?" asked Potochniak. "Shore Patrol," said Emblem. "Are you kidding?" asked Potochniak. "No," said Emblem. "Here's the scoop. . . ."

He explained then that the procedure was to don the Shore Patrol armband (which automatically made its wearer the enemy of every beer-thirsty sailor) and go ashore. "Then," said the knowledgeable Emblem, "you take off the armband and put it in your pocket and join the party."

Such virtuosity was not to be denied, and Potochniak was persuaded. He took a shower, trying to stay cool in a hot climate, and they went ashore with a gang of the flight deck crowd. About thirty of them showed up at the beer stores depot, to discover that some smart "black-shoe" from the ship had drawn all the beer for the *Gambier Bay* and gone off with it half an hour earlier. One of the VC-10 officers showed up then, and asked for the beer for a non-existing ship, giving the boys a big wink. Behind the counter a harassed enlisted man looked over the list and did not find the ship. He could not issue any beer, he said.

In righteous indignation, the officer exploded. He read the poor swabbie recollections from the Blue Jackets' manual, the articles of war, and perhaps Commodore Farragut's orders to his men at New Orleans—he talked so fast and so explosively that no one remembered precisely what he said. The ploy was successful; the swab behind the counter was cowed and the beer issued, and the Shore Patrolmen and their charges went off for a day of festivity.

The provisions taken aboard at Espiritu Santo had been exhausted, partially through the pilferage of Potochniak and his friends, and in the wardroom the officers felt it had been months since they had tasted any fresh fruit or vegetables. Then came the word that they were in for a treat. The base at Manus had acquired some brand new milk powder, so they were to have fresh milk one night. Everyone who heard gathered early in the wardroom for the treat and looked at the tables, where the stewards were decanting cold glasses of beautiful white milk. Commander Ballinger came in, and they rushed for their chairs. Then almost to a man, they reached for the milk glasses and took a mouthful. The room was suddenly filled with sputtering, coughing officers reaching for their handkerchiefs. The liquid tasted like essence of chalk. So the milk treat was a disaster; not for several days did the chief wardroom steward learn that one must mix the milk twenty-four hours in advance.

For two weeks the ship lay at anchor in Manus harbor. The officers and men of the *Gambier Bay* were busy loading supplies. The officers and flight crews of VC-10 had almost no duty and spent their time reading and writing. Mail came, and Lieutenant Bassett had an answer to a letter he had written to Louise in Florida, to tell her about the death of Sandy Sanderson. He had sent her a picture of himself, and she had wept over it because he looked so weary and thin. The war was taking its toll, she knew; she could only hope that the toll would not include the life of her husband. But of course, that could not be put down in the letters. What Lieutenant Bassett—and all the rest—wanted were letters that reeked of home and happiness and the way things were going to be when the war ended. There was a good deal of tension in the men of the *Gambier Bay* these days. Pilot Lischer wrote home chiding his family for indicating that the defeat of Hitler would mean the whole war was virtually over. "I can tell you that the war against Japan is just beginning," he said. All one had to do at Manus to be convinced was to look out at the armada of hundreds of vessels assembled in that harbor, named Seeadler for the German raider that Count Von Luckner had sailed across the Pacific in World War I. For this operation, the *Gambier Bay* was assigned to Vice Adm. Thomas Kinkaid's Seventh Fleet, or "MacArthur's Navy." In the command quarrel between MacArthur and Admiral Nimitz, the control of the Third Fleet, the major striking force, remained with Admiral Nimitz. Halsey's orders were to support the invasion of the Philippines, which he intended to do by ranging the waters around the islands, knocking out all shipping and air power the Japanese might try to send. Admiral Halsey's battleships would not bombard Leyte, nor would Admiral Mitscher's fast carriers support the landings with air attacks on the beaches. The old battleships of Admiral Oldendorf's Pacific invasion force would be off the beaches, and the air strikes would be flown by planes of the *Gambier Bay* and seventeen other escort carriers. The escort carriers, designed to accompany convoys and track down submarines, were now to be used in the manner that ancient fleet doctrine had prescribed for carriers of all sorts. It was understood that the escort carriers were slow and would be easy targets for enemy capital ships. But no one had any intention of letting an enemy cruiser or battleship within a hundred miles of the jeep carriers. As for enemy air attack, modern American carrier doctrine held that the carrier's own fighter planes were its best line of defense. Of course, MacArthur wanted those big fast carriers offshore to support his invasion, but Halsey and Nimitz were gunning for the Japanese fleet, and Halsey was sure that this Philippine operation would bring that fleet out.

Admiral Halsey's hunch was completely accurate. Or, one might say, the Americans made sure the Japanese would react by inadvertently giving away their own plan. Somewhere in diplomatic circles there was a bad leak. Early in October, the Japanese ambassador in Moscow learned that the American 14th and 20th Air Forces were planning major attacks to isolate the Philippines. The Japanese high command needed no more information. SHO, the victory plan, had been drawn shortly after the disaster in the Philippine Sea. All that had remained to be decided was where the Americans would attack next in force, so the SHO plan could be achieved in that area.

Admiral Toyoda and his staff in Tokyo had decided to risk all in one major battle. It would be complicated because the shortage of fuel oil had brought about a split in the Japanese fleet. The carrier force, accompanied by its cruisers and destroyers, was stationed in the Inland Sea, under the command of Admiral Ozawa, who had fought so unhappily in the "Marianas Turkey Shoot." The battle force, including the *Yamato* and *Musashi*—the most powerful surface ships in the world—was stationed at Lingga Roads, just across the strait from Singapore. These two forces would be brought together from the north and south to strike the Americans when they landed in the Philippines.

On October 7, as the *Gambier Bay* loaded ammunition and supplies at Manus, Admiral Halsey had begun a new air offensive against Marcus island, Okinawa, and the Ryukyus. Admiral Toyoda put SHO-1, the plan of attack in the Philippines, into motion. He was not deceived by this feint.

The first step in SHO-1 was to transfer almost all operational aircraft to land bases. The carriers *Zuikaku, Zuiho, Chitose, Chivoda, Ise,* and *Hyuga* flew off most of their planes, which were then sent south, island hopping, to Formosa and the Philippines. Many of them were unfortunate enough to arrive at Formosa airfields just hours before Admiral Mitscher's task force began a three-day strike against the island. When one realized that Mitscher could put up 1,400 sorties a day, the difficulties of the Japanese became apparent. In the Formosa air attacks, Admiral Toyoda lost 500 planes he had counted on to help in the SHO operation.

In the first week of October, Quartermaster Bell was still very sick. The doctors were not quite sure how ill he was, and they took many tests, including a spinal tap. But in the second week he began to mend, and, on October 13, he was supposed to be released and sent back to his ship. But the release form was misplaced and Quartermaster Bell was kept one more day. When he went down to the harbor to find the ship, she was gone, as were most of the others that had clogged the anchorage for the past few weeks. She had sailed with Task Group 78.2 for the Philippines. Next day they joined ships from Hollandia, and the *Gambier Bay* and *Kitkun Bay* supplied air cover for a segment of the armada, largely consisting of LSTs and other transports.

In Tokyo, Admiral Toyoda was waiting to see where the Americans planned to strike before he dispatched the fleet. The Philippine islands covered so much sea front that to send the ships to the wrong place might be fatal. On October 17, scout planes identified minesweepers in Leyte Gulf, and since the only reason minesweepers would appear would be to prepare for other ships, Admiral Toyoda knew, and the sailing orders were issued. They were already late; the Japanese could not possibly reach Leyte before the Americans had landed. And that meant more difficulty in dislodging the attackers. The southern Japanese force went to Brunei in the East Indies, to fuel and wait to sortie. Admiral Kurita then would move to attack the American forces in Leyte Gulf. He chose to come by way of San Bernardino Strait.

On October 20, the Americans had landed on the Leyte beaches, and the escort carriers had moved out into Leyte Gulf to provide air cover. The carriers were divided into three groups: Taffy 1, Taffy 2, and Taffy 3, names selected for their easy enunciation and understanding in even half-garbled radio broadcasts. Taffy 3 was under Rear Adm. Clifton Sprague. The force consisted of the carriers *Fanshaw Bay, Gambier Bay, Kitkun Bay, White Plains, St. Lo,* and *Kalinin Bay,* plus the destroyers *Hoel, Johnston,* and *Heermann,* and the destroyer escorts *Samuel B. Roberts, Dennis, John Butler,* and *Raymond.* The whole Escort Carrier Group (TG 77.4) was under command of the "other Sprague," Rear Adm. Thomas L. Sprague. Admiral

Ofstie, commander of Carrier Division 26, continued in that command, but was superseded for this operation by Adm. Clifton Sprague aboard *Fanshaw Bay*.

The pilots of VC-10 were detailed to support the landings that day by bombing and strafing. Lieutenant Stewart, the leader of the fighter section, was ordered to take eight fighters on an attack against the south end of Samar island, which abuts Leyte. The Japanese had brought up artillery here to overlook Leyte Gulf, plus a concentration of troops who might move to Leyte. The fighters were to strafe and to use a weapon with which they had begun experimenting: napalm. The ordnance people made napalm bombs by pouring the napalm into a wing tank with the detonator inside. These tanks were fastened to the wings of the fighters, and once armed they could not be disarmed. When a pilot reached his objective he pulled the wing tank release and away went the bomb, to strike, break, and splatter the burning sticky substance over every object near the explosion. Lieutenant Cordner, the ordnance officer, warned them that wing tanks and wing tank releases were not precisely bomb-oriented. Therefore, they were to drop their wing tank bombs in level flight and their speed at drop point was not to exceed 200 knots. In other words: no dives. But the pilots found this a distinctly unappealing prospect, since a Japanese rifle bullet could explode the napalm and turn an aircraft into a flaming torch. Lieutenant Stewart had been shot down at Saipan by a single fluke bullet that struck an oil line. No one wanted to take that sort of chance. So that day when the fighters came in on the Samar concentration, they dived down from 6,000 feet, pulled out at 500 to 300 feet, spraying .50-caliber machine-gun bullets, and then dropped the tanks. Lieutenant Steward went back for a look. The result was awesome, the whole area was alive with flame, and he could see vehicles burning. The napalm was a great success—except with Lt. E. H. Courtney. When he pulled the wing tank release, nothing happened. It was jammed, and the wing tank bomb hung there, quite capable of falling off at any time, fully armed. The fighters looked about for Japanese aircraft, found none, and headed back to the carrier. Stewart expected Captain Vieweg to tell Courtney to roll over, bail out, and be picked up, letting the Wildcat go down with its bomb. But Vieweg cleared the deck, put the fire-fighting personnel above deck, brought in all the other planes and had them stowed, and then brought Courtney down. Lieutenant McClendon might have been sweating as he watched that plane, but the tank held, and one Wildcat was saved to fight another day.

For three days the war went easily for the *Gambier Bay*. There were no air attacks against the carrier. The missions were carried out efficiently and without incident until October 23, when Commander Huxtable and five TBMs attacked a small town west of the landing beaches to lend air support to the troops below. When they returned to the carrier it was nearly dark, and Lieutenant McClendon was in a hurry to get them aboard. Commander Huxtable turned downwind on his approach, he came around, put the wheels down, flaps down, and hook down, and shifted into low pitch on the propeller. The prop began windmilling, and he began pulling switches to find the trouble. But there was no time. He was crosswind, and it was apparent that the TBM was going into the water. He was so busy concentrating on making a three-point landing that he forgot to pull up the landing gear. Probably they would not have retracted anyhow since he had lost hydraulic pressure. Nor did he have time to grab the microphone and announce to gunner Martin and radio operator Blaney that they were going to make a water landing. But they sensed it before the plane struck. The wheels struck, and dragged the plane over, and it turned completely turtle. In the cockpit, Huxtable's straps caught, and he had a moment of panic before he was able to disengage and swim under the wing and pop to the surface. He saw "the old bird floating upside down." Blaney, in the tunnel, did not know the plane had flipped over, and he was looking for the escape lever for the tunnel door at the bottom. Finally, he found it on top of him. Instead of pulling up, he pulled down, and stepped out, on to the fuselage, quite dry. He saw Commander Huxtable sitting on the wing, bleeding from a cut on his forehead. Martin still had not appeared, but as Blaney looked down under at the turret, he came up on the other side.

They all pulled the toggles of their life jackets and held hands to stay together. But since the plane was floating nicely, Huxtable climbed up on the belly and waved at the *Gambier Bay* that all was fine with them.

"Get off there or she will suck you down," shouted Blaney. Huxtable heard and jumped back into the water with them. A few minutes later the plane sank, but then the destroyer *Heermann* came along and brought the ship up so close that the landing net alongside was there to touch. They crawled up, Blaney nearly exhausted. He threw himself on the deck and lay there panting. Commander Huxtable could not get up without assistance. Two sailors came down and helped him. When he reached the deck he saw why: he still had on his pistol belt, the .45 automatic in its holster, and his canteen. The ship's doctor came up and asked whether they wanted rye or brandy, which proved a remarkable restorative. *Heermann's* captain, Cdr. A. T. Hathaway, was talking about Huxtable making a fourth for bridge that night—when the word came to put them back aboard the *Gambier Bay* immediately. A line was passed, and they came home in a breeches buoy, one by one.

After they were safely aboard, Commander Huxtable reported to Captain Vieweg, and he remarked ruefully that when the power failed he had forgotten to pull up the wheels, or at least to try.

"Well, you can't think of everything in one day," said Vieweg cheerfully, and the captain's stock went up another notch with his squadron commander. For VC-10 the Leyte operation was going very well indeed.

CHAPTER TWENTY-FIVE

# October 24, 1944

On the morning of October 24, the Japanese made a major air attack against the Americans in Leyte Gulf. Admiral Halsey's strikes against the Philippine airfields in the early days of October had reduced the Japanese air force in the islands to about thirty fighters and fifty bombers, but, on October 23, more than 350 planes from the Japanese Second Air Force were sent to reinforce the defenders. The next morning they sent 250 planes to attack.

Adm. Thomas Sprague had the word, and, at five o'clock on the morning of October 24, *Gambier Bay* launched a double combat air patrol—eight fighters—to protect the ships and the troops on the ground. When they took off and gained altitude the fighter pilots discovered that they were a small part of a large American force. At least sixteen of Admiral Sprague's carriers were in action, and each had sent up a reinforced combat air patrol that morning. So more than a hundred fighters were in the air, circling over the scene of operations. The weather in the Philippines was spotty that day, and the Japanese had considerable difficulty in finding their way to Leyte Gulf. When they did reach the area, they discovered the defenses.

*Gambier Bay*'s planes were operating in two divisions. The first division consisted of Lieutenant Roby, Lieutenant (jg) Phillips, Lieutenant (jg) Courtney, and Lieutenant (jg) Hunting. The second division included Lieutenant Seitz, Lieutenant (jg) Dugan, Lieutenant Ellwood, and

Lieutenant (jg) McGraw. The two divisions were sent to orbit over the Tacloban area, where the troops were fighting on the ground. For two and a half hours nothing happened; then the Japanese arrived, coming from the west and northwest, heading toward the ships in Leyte Gulf. The first Japanese plane to appear was a lone Sally.

Lieutenant Roby and Lieutenant (jg) Courtney had been investigating two friendly planes that were dropping propaganda leaflets along Carigara Bay. They knew what that was all about, for, earlier in the week, VC-10 had been given the same mission, to announce the arrival of General MacArthur and the "Liberation forces." So the leaflet planes aroused no suspicions, but at 8 o'clock Lieutenant Roby spotted a Sally coming in from the west, above them. "Tallyhoo," he shouted, and he began to climb. At the same time his wingman, Lieutenant (jg) Courtney, saw another Sally off to the right and claimed it as his victim. But the first Sally was too far away, and Roby was ahead of Courtney, so he fired the first burst into the Japanese bomber. The plane caught fire. Courtney moved in and shot off the right wing. The Sally rolled over and went into a spin, flaming, until it hit the ground and exploded. No Japanese parachutes were seen.

Meanwhile, Lieutenant Seitz's division had seen four Sallys a little further off. Seitz made a high-side run on the starboard quarter of one, pressed his gun release for four seconds, and saw the port wing fall off. The plane went down in flames. Behind him, Lieutenant Dugan was at 7,000 feet, and he saw several Sallys at 10,000 feet. The Sally had an altitude advantage, and he had to chase it all the way to the eastern side of the island. He got into range just west of the town of Tacloban and shot down the plane. Dugan pulled up then and joined a large flight of American fighters heading back to the northwest. He had scarcely joined when they spotted a large formation of two-engine Japanese bombers coming in. These were Lilys, moving in an attack pattern that involved an even-angled glide of fifteen degrees without deviation. Dugan fired a deflection shot and missed, then got on the tail of one bomber, and shot it down. The Lily crashed five miles north of Tacloban airfield.

By this time the *Gambier Bay* fighters were very low on fuel. Dugan looked at his gauges and announced that he was going home. He joined up with Lieutenant Ellwood, but then spotted a bogey and chased it until it turned out to be another FM-2. He had used up precious fuel in the chase, and his tanks were empty. Just then he spotted a carrier force below and landed on a strange carrier (whose name he did not know). He refueled and was in the air again and flew back to the *Gambier Bay*.

Lieutenant Ellwood had mixed it up with a Zero that morning. He had been climbing for altitude when he was attacked from above and astern. He turned. The Zero began firing, and Ellwood moved around to try to get a head-on shot. But he could not and ran the danger of crossing directly in front of the enemy, which could have been fatal. He put the stick down into what was in essence an outside loop, blacked out, and then came out of it on a course that should have put him behind the Zero and chasing. But the Zero had disappeared. He started home, found Dugan, then lost him, and then flew back to the *Gambier Bay*, arriving on deck at 9:30 after four and a half hours in the air.

Lieutenant (jg) McGraw was Ellwood's wingman, but they became separated in the first melee, and McGraw joined up with Lieutenant Seitz. At 8:30, Seitz left him because he was short of gas, but McGraw still had sixty-five gallons left so he stayed on in orbit. Ten minutes later a group of twenty-one Lilys appeared at about 15,000 feet. McGraw was flying at 13,000 feet and he began to climb. He caught up and fired a long burst at one plane. He could see the tracers hitting, but the Lily did not fall. He turned to the next in formation and fired at the wing roots. The bullets hit the gas tank and engine, and the Lily burst into flame. All this while the Japanese had held formation; now this Lily fell out, dropped, and the starboard wing came off as it spiraled down.

McGraw found another Lily flying below the formation and attacked. He flamed the port engine then rolled to the left. As he did so, the Lily's rear hatch gunner fired at the FM-2 and scored several hits. The Lily turned off on one wing and crashed. McGraw's plane was not damaged seriously, and he recovered to find himself on the left side of the bombers. Their number was now down to six. He joined a group of American fighters in the chase, but his fire did not damage any more planes. He saw three more bombers shot down by others, then they were over the gulf, and the last three Lilys dived down through thin layers of clouds toward the ships. The anti-aircraft guns began firing, and McGraw pulled up and turned back toward his patrol point. He saw two of the Lily's shot down by anti-aircraft fire. As he last looked, a single bomber, all that was left of the twenty-one, was heading toward a large transport just off shore. He returned to the *Gambier Bay* then, landing with eight gallons of gas in his tanks.

In the interrogations that followed the return of the fighters, Lieutenant Bell put together the picture of the mission. Lieutenant Hunting had credit for destroying one Lily. McGraw had shot down two Lilys and damaged a third. Roby had shot down one Sally, one Lily, and damaged another Lily. Courtney had a probable, Dugan had two kills, Seitz had a kill, and Phillips a probable.

In the afternoon, Commander Huxtable was assigned a mission against the enemy on Leyte. Meanwhile, planes of Admiral Halsey had warned that the Japanese fleet was on the move. That morning a plane from the carrier *Intrepid* had found a large force led by four battleships off the southern tip of Mindoro Island which butts into the Sulu Sea. Then came a report from a *Franklin* plane about a force—but it was a different force and at a different location. The first of these was Admiral Nishimura's force; the second was Admiral Shima's force of two heavy cruisers, a light cruiser, and four destroyers. Adm. Clifton Sprague, commander of Taffy 3, wanted more information as at 4:45 P.M. two of the small carriers of Taffy 1, the *Chenango* and *Saginaw Bay* with the destroyer escorts *Edmonds* and *Oberrender* under command of Rear Adm. G. R. Henderson were being dispatched south to Morotai to engage in submarine reconnaisance.

Huxtable selected TBM pilots Bassett, Dahlen, Weatherholt, Bisbee, and Pyzdrowski to accompany him on the mission. Six fighters were also to go, piloted by Seitz, Roby, Courtney, Dugan, Phillips, and McGraw. They were to head for Mt. Guinhandang on Leyte, to drop 500-pound bombs on several points of strong resistance, and strafe and attack with wing rockets. They had not been informed about the Japanese naval movement, and it seemed like another routine day of troop support.

But when Huxtable's group reported on station, Huxtable was told to separate from his fighters. The fighters would proceed as planned, but Huxtable and the TBMs would go into the Sulu Sea to look for an enemy naval force. They would be accompanied by a flight of F6Fs from Taffy 1, fighters chosen because they had longer range than the FM-2s. The planes would go to Surigao Strait and search for as long as their fuel would permit. The reports were garbled, but there seemed to be a cruiser force loose in that area.

Huxtable led the flight all the way down to the tip of Mindanao, but they missed Admiral Shima's force, which was coming down from the northwest, and Admiral Nishimura's force, which was heading into the Mindanao Sea between Negros and Mindanao. The F6Fs flew at 12,000 feet, and the TBMs at 8,000 feet. They saw nothing on the water. On their return, Lieutenant Bassett did see a float plane about 500 feet off the water, and the four F6Fs wanted to attack. Commander Huxtable was reluctant to let them go, because he had a long way to go home, and the Japanese fighters might try to keep him from getting there. But they had not seen any planes either, so Huxtable relented and told them to go get the float plane, which was obviously a cruiser's scout. The fighter leader swooped down, too fast as it turned out, and opened his guns. He missed. "Shit," he shouted, and the word was quite audible in the earphones of the TBMs. But just then his wingman yelled, "I got him!" And indeed he had. A single burst had flamed the float plane, which was hitting the water as the bomber pilots looked down.

They went home then, the F6Fs to their carrier down south, and the TBM pilots of VC-10 flew east of Samar to find the *Gambier Bay*. As they reached Bugho Point on Leyte, they saw a striking sight below: a whole flotilla of PT boats deployed, speeding along, their long white wakes making a linear pattern in the sea.

They found the *Gambier Bay* easily enough, Fox flag flying and the blinker flashing, which meant "come in and land." They were low on fuel, but Huxtable made an orderly approach. He told any pilot who wanted to jettison those unused bombs to do so; it might be dangerous to land with a bomb load. Lieutenant Dahlen decided he would save his bombs, and he prepared to land with them. As he came into the pattern, he made his turn, dropped his flaps and landing gear, and the tail hook. But the unaccustomed weight of the plane caused him to undershoot, and he got a wave-off from Landing Signal Officer McClendon. He opened the throttle, and the tail hook caught on a wire, and the TBM chose that moment to sputter. The plane went into the water, flat, and the ship sailed past. The standby destroyer was *Heermann* again. She came alongside, and picked Dahlen and his crew out of the water. Commander Hathaway had his fourth for bridge that night.

The last pilot to land on the *Gambier Bay* was Ensign Zeola. He had been one of the pilots assigned to the afternoon mission, and when Huxtable's TBMs were diverted to the Sulu Sea search, Zeola and the others had been ordered to take the place of those F6Fs from Taffy 1 and to cover Leyte. At one point the air controller vectored Zeola out to intercept a bogey and in his eagerness to attain full speed in the chase, Zeola jettisoned his wing tank, although it still had gas in it. The bogey turned out to be an American TBM, but when Zeola returned from the investigation he was so low on gas that he could not join the rest of the flight when it was sent down to Cebu to strafe Japanese-held airfields. By the time the others returned, Zeola was so low on fuel that he did not have fuel to make the carrier, which was 100 miles northeast of Leyte. He announced the fact to Lieutenant Stewart, and was told to land at Tacloban, the airfield now held by the Americans on Leyte, to refuel, then come home. Zeola was flying on the wing of Wickersham, and the latter volunteered to stay with him, so they headed for the field. As they came to Tacloban, Zeola could see that the runway was dirt and the whole area was covered with equipment brought in from the ships in Leyte Gulf. He headed downwind, rocking his wings, and was surprised, when he saw puffs of antiaircraft fire rising around him. The FM-2 was hit, and he was beginning to wonder who was friend and who was foe. Just then out of the corner of his eye he saw a Japanese Betty bomber in a dive off his starboard quarter. He made a snap roll to the right, and the Japanese plane pulled up to escape him, thus presenting itself as a perfect target for the anti-aircraft gunners of the invasion fleet in Leyte Gulf. So, in a way, Zeola could take at least moral credit for having helped knock down a Japanese plane that day.

At that moment, however, Zeola was not thinking about taking any credit. He looked at his port wing and saw that it had several holes in it as large as platters, and he knew he was going to have trouble landing the plane without crashing it. One pass, and that was all; the FM-2 would never climb up for another. So he came around and ran in, flaps down and holding the landing gear up until the last moment. He had throttled the engine down to sixty-two knots, although as the General Motors engineers had warned them, the FM-2 stalled out at sixty-seven. Finally, in the midst of all the equipment on the field, he found a clear spot of several hundred yards and landed. Then he sat in the cockpit for several minutes, shaking. The engine had quit just as he hit the ground.

Zeola's plane was surrounded by soldiers. A medic came up and stood on the wing, and when Zeola released the "greenhouse" canopy, the medic began mopping his head with alcohol and asking where he was hit. The plane looked as though it had been in a dogfight. Zeola was so scared he had not turned off the ignition, and the plane's guns were still armed. Eventually he gathered enough presence of mind to attend to these vital details, and he got out of the cockpit. He was taken to a command post where he met several generals, and they asked him how things were going. It was all a blur to him; he never remembered the names of the generals after that hour. Then he was taken to a tent, fed an enormous sardine sandwich and a huge mug of coffee and told to take it easy. He asked about his plane. He was lucky, one of the sergeants told him. This field was being made ready for Maj. Richard Bong's P-38 squadron, and the men around him were the squadron ground crews. They could patch up the FM-2 to get him back to the carrier.

So the air corps mechanics put the navy fighter back together again, and late in the day Wickersham and Ensign Zeola took off once more and headed for the *Gambier Bay*. When Zeola had landed and told his story to Commander Huxtable, the squadron leader patted him on the shoulder and commiserated.

"Take the day off tomorrow. I'll put someone else on the morning combat air patrol. Relax. Take it easy."

And that was what Ensign Zeola planned to do on October 25.

## CHAPTER TWENTY-SIX

# Night of Tension

When Lieutenant Roby returned to the *Gambier Bay* on October 24, after his encounter with the Japanese planes over Leyte, he did two barrel rolls across the deck at 100 feet before landing. That maneuver was a signal: He had shot down two enemy planes. When Roby was on the flight deck, he was surrounded by a band of officers and men congratulating him on his victories. This was what the men of the *Gambier Bay* had come to do, and it was satisfying to be doing it.

The failure of Lieutenant Dahlen's TBM brought a moment of concern, as did that of Huxtable's. But Huxtable was down safe and Dahlen was expected to be decanted the next day from the *Heermann,* so there was no tragedy at the moment to give the shipmates cause for concern. They were alert but unworried and unafraid. The greatest tension was on the bridge, where Captain Vieweg knew that something important was brewing. All afternoon messages from the flagship and intercepts from various other commands indicated that the Japanese were moving a number of ships into Philippine waters. The messages were incomplete and apparently conflicting. Three different forces were identified, and many of the *Gambier Bay* officers wondered how much was truth and how much error in the reports. But, no matter what, it was apparent that October 25 promised to be a busy day, with plenty of action for the fighters and the torpedo bombers. Every aircraft on the flight deck and the hangar deck was checked over. Those sent up to the flight deck were fueled and armed with general-purpose bombs, for use against troops and military installations on the ground. In the wardroom at dinner the talk was about the action of the day, and the unexpected appearance of so many Japanese bombers over Leyte, and the long but negative search conducted by Commander Huxtable's planes that afternoon.

At eight o'clock that evening of October 24, Captain Vieweg called a conference in the Combat Information Center. Commander Ballinger was there, Commander Borries, Lieutenant Commander Waring, and Lieutenants Elliot, Buderus, and Odum were there. The captain discussed the ship's readiness to continue its assigned mission of supporting the troops. Captain Vieweg spoke to these officers about the increasing number of Japanese aircraft that had been observed that day, and warned them to expect more planes on the 25th. Some of those planes would certainly be sent to attack the carriers, particularly in view of the known Japanese attitude that carriers were always primary targets. Vieweg then asked each of his senior officers for their assessment of the situation. All agreed that on the 25th they must expect maximum air effort from the enemy, and that the ship must be prepared for any eventuality. Vieweg closed that meeting with a warning: "Well, anyway you look at it, we are in for a fight tomorrow and we'll be lucky to escape heavy damage."

Lieutenant Odum and the other junior officers were dismissed then, and Odum went to his cabin. He wrote a letter to his wife, then got into his bunk to get some sleep before the call to General Quarters that always came too early in the morning. He drifted off with the captain's words in his mind. "Let the Japanese planes come," he said to himself, recalling the Marianas days. "We'll shoot them down one at a time or in bunches as we have before."

Chaplain Carlsen had a call from the captain that evening. He had been giving evening prayers over the public address system before taps. The captain told the chaplain to please ask that night not that the ship and crew be preserved from danger but that they might have what it took to see them through. The chaplain left the captain with the feeling that something was going to happen next morning.

Captain Vieweg called in Commander Huxtable and Lieutenant Cordner, the ordnance officer. The senior officers then discussed a new matter: the possibility of action against enemy fleet units. Were they ready to make a torpedo attack if necessary? That was the major question in Captain Vieweg's mind. Since he had come aboard the ship there had been no occasion for torpedo activity, and he was not familiar with the degree of the squadron's readiness. How good were the torpedo pilots of VC-10?

Commander Huxtable assured the captain that they were all competent. Further, he assured them, and Lieutenant Bell verified the fact: The pilots had all been thoroughly briefed in enemy ship identification. These assurances gratified Captain Vieweg, and he dismissed the meeting with a reminder to Lieutenant Cordner and Commanders Borries and Huxtable that they must be prepared to load torpedoes on short notice.

As that meeting was taking place aboard the *Gambier Bay*, Admiral Kurita with the main Japanese attack force of battleships and cruisers had turned around in the Sibuyan Sea after having suffered major damage from Halsey's air attacks all day long. Kurita had already been torpedoed out of his flagship, the cruiser *Akagi* and had spent half a day in a destroyer before moving to the battleship *Yamato*, where he was unhappy because half his communication experts had been lost with the cruiser. During the day the *Yamato* had been hit by the Americans and hurt, and her sister ship, the *Musashi*, one of the most powerful vessels in the world, had been hit by no fewer than nineteen aerial torpedoes and seventeen bombs. Kurita passed her as she fell behind, then he reversed course when he decided to give up the attack, and passed her again going back toward Brunei. When Admiral Toyoda in Tokyo heard that Admiral Kurita was abandoning the SHO plan, he was furious and told Kurita to go back and fight. So Kurita once more passed the *Musashi* as her captain and crew struggled to save her, and just as he passed the third time, the *Musashi* rolled over and sank—an unlucky harbinger of things to come, it seemed. But there was no alternative in the face of a direct order from Tokyo, so Kurita and his battleships and cruisers continued on toward Leyte. They would thread the narrow passage at the end of the Sibuyan Sea called the San Bernardino Strait, and come down on the Americans from the north.

As Captain Vieweg talked about the possibility that the *Gambier Bay*'s TBMs next day would have to strike capital ships with torpedoes, those capital ships were bearing down on him in the darkness.

When the actual word of warning about Japanese warships came to Captain Vieweg late that night, the message did not refer to the Kurita force, but to the Nishimura force of two battleships, one cruiser, and four destroyers that had moved into the Surigao Strait after Commander Huxtable and his TBM scouts had missed them the day before. Nishimura planned to reach a point off the entrance to Leyte Gulf at 4 o'clock on the morning of October 25.

Coming up behind, several hours behind in fact, was Admiral Shima's force. At 11:30 that night of October 24, American PT boats in the Surigao Strait spotted the advance elements of the Nishimura force and attacked. The Japanese destroyer *Shigure* began firing on the PT boats, and the cat was out of the bag; the Americans knew that the enemy was there. By midnight, Admiral Oldendorf had the message and was lying in wait for the Japanese. At 2:30 in the morning, Captain Vieweg was awakened by the communications watch officer, who brought a message that the Battle of Surigao Strait had begun. Sleepily, Captain Vieweg took the message and then snapped awake. His next word was to order the TBMs of the *Gambier Bay* to be loaded. The morning flight was already loaded, he was told, with bombs. Then load the rest, he said, with torpedoes. The missions preplanned would be flown, but the *Gambier Bay* would be ready to strike the enemy's big ships, too. It would not be much of an effort at first; VC-10 was obligated to send six of the TBMs on other chores. But those last four torpedo bombers would be ready. Two planes were loaded with torpedoes immediately, and two more torpedoes were placed in the fully ready condition on the hangar deck and could be loaded in a matter of minutes.

On the flight deck and in the hangar there was trouble. One of the airedales, spotting planes for the next morning's operations, pulled up to the bow elevator in a tow tractor, and jumped off, not setting the brake. At that moment the ship hit a heavy swell and lifted, and the tractor dropped down. The elevator at the moment was at the bottom of the shaft, where a fighter plane had just been loaded for transport to the flight deck. The tow tractor hit hard enough to damage the engine of the FM-2, and the fighter had to be taken back into the hangar for an engine change.

Some members of the crew, sleeping near the hangar deck heard the crash and thought the ship had been torpedoed. It took half an hour to settle them down. Then came word to the hangar deck that the remaining torpedo planes were to be loaded with torpedoes. That message caused one of the airedales to wake up chief ordnance man Andy Andrews, and he awakened Chief Montgomery who slept in a bunk nearby. The planes would have to be defueled and brought down to the hangar deck, loaded with torpedoes and then brought up again and fueled. It was going to take some time.

At 4:30 came the call to General Quarters. The pilots of the fighters selected for the combat air patrol got ready to man their planes. Lieutenant Odum and the other ship's officers dressed, donned sidearms, with knife and life belt, and hurried to their action stations. Before dawn, the fighters were launched and the ship secured from General Quarters. Lieutenant Odum went into his Aerology office to check the weather signs: The sea was calm with a long rolling swell; there was virtually no wind; the current was moving west. Lieutenant Odum reported to the bridge, then went to the wardroom to breakfast. He returned in fifteen minutes so Lieutenant Commander Waring could go to eat; his battle station was Air Plot and when the *Gambier Bay* planes were in the air they maintained a constant watch. Lieutenant Buderus also returned to the Combat Information Center to watch. They kept an eye on the big plexiglass board where the CIC men plotted the results of the radar search.

When the ship was secured, the enlisted men headed for the mess deck. The line was always long in the mornings, and AMM3c Potochniak did not feel like facing it. He decided to take a little nap in the oxygen shop. As he was lying down in the storage section he experienced a most peculiar sensation: He felt he was in two worlds at the same time, there in the oxygen shop, and also disembodied. He saw the image of his dead grandmother, and she spoke to him in Ukrainian. She said, "Don't stay here. This is why." And before Potochniak's eyes, the oxygen shop seemed to explode, and the corrugated bulkhead that separated Potochniak's shop from the fire fighters next door blew up in a shower of metal. Potochniak was so upset that he got up and left the shop, and went topside. Usually, he was careless about obeying the order to keep his life jacket on during General Quarters. Now he made sure he had all his equipment laid out.

Shortly after midnight, Admiral Kurita's ships were safely through the narrow San Bernardino Strait. All during the passage Kurita had braced himslf, lest the Americans be waiting there at the narrow bottleneck to blow his vessels out of the water (as they were just then doing to Admiral Nishimura at the Surigao Strait). But Kurita saw nothing; there was no guard on the San Bernardino Strait. Admiral Kinkaid *assumed* that Admiral Halsey was guarding the strait, but Admiral Halsey had discovered the whereabouts of a fourth Japanese force—the carriers—and as Admiral Toyoda in Tokyo had confidently predicted, Halsey would jump at a chance to destroy the carriers. Halsey might not have been quite so eager had he known that the Japanese carriers had been stripped of nearly all their planes, and so were scarcely more dangerous at the moment than transport ships. But this whole Pacific war had turned into a carrier war, and Admiral Nimitz quite agreed that Halsey was to go after the carriers if the chance was offered. The Japanese strategy of decoying Halsey was absolutely brilliant; but it was also totally futile, given the forces available to the Japanese. Admiral Kurita had recognized the futility from the beginning. To be sure, with luck, they could steal down on the Americans off Leyte like wolves in a sheep pen and raise havoc for a few hours. But, without question, the vengeful Americans would destroy them before they could ever get back to Japan or Brunei. So the whole SHO plan could be nothing but an exercise to prove Japanese bravery and willingness to die in the defense of the homeland. No senior staff officers publicly admitted that the SHO plan was a cynical sacrifice of the whole fleet to try to gain some time, but it could be regarded in no other way by an objective observer. In the Battle of the Philippine Sea the fate of the Imperial Navy was sealed; everything that was happening at Leyte and would happen from this point in the war on to the end was equally futile, aimed at such grandiloquent self-destruction that the Americans would back away from their demand for unconditional surrender and grant Japan a peace under which the militarists could still claim national honor.

Admiral Kurita knew that his one chance of achieving the limited success of destroying *before* being destroyed was to surprise the Americans at dawn. Shortly after debouching the strait, he formed his force on a broad thirteen-mile front, and then turned south down the coast of Samar. An hour before sunrise, the Japanese ships assumed the circular pattern they used in defense against enemy aircraft. Their intelligence told them that a number of fleet carriers were located off Leyte, and they expected to run the gauntlet of Halsey's power.

Kurita had very little information about the enemy other than that, and this was faulty. Shortly after the Kurita force came through the San Bernardino Strait, he had a message from Admiral Nishimura saying he was then entering Surigao Strait, and there was nothing in sight except a handful of torpedo boats. An hour later came a report that Nishimura had sighted three American ships, what sort of ships Nishimura had not said. At that point where Kurita had turned south and committed himself, he heard last from Nishimura. Then, about an hour before sun-up he had a message from Admiral Shima, traveling to Surigao Strait behind Nishimura: The Nishimura force *had been destroyed!* The battleship *Yamashiro* blew up and took Admiral Nishimura with it. The battleship *Fuso* had broken in half. The cruiser *Mogami* had been sorely hit, turned about and ran into Admiral Shima's flagship the *Nachi,* and then sank. The attack from the south had been a total failure, and the destroyers that were left were scrabbling for safety.

Admiral Kurita continued southward. He expected to come out among the American ships of Leyte just after sunrise. Then the Kurita force at least would do its assigned duty.

## CHAPTER TWENTY-SEVEN

# "Kee-rist, Look at Those Pagodas . . ."

It was 6:30 when Adm. C. A. F. Sprague sent a signal by TBS that the ships of Taffy 3 could secure from General Quarters if they wished and go to Condition Three—which meant that only the ordinary watches would be manned. Captain Vieweg passed the order and then remained on his bridge with Lieutenant Commander Gellhorn, who was working up his morning position. Lieutenant Stewart and seven other fighter pilots had been up above Taffy 3 for an hour and a half, and they had nothing to report, although the sun had come up ten minutes earlier. So it was easy enough to assume that there was nothing around to see that could be considered unusual.

Of course the visibility was bad. "It is the rainy season," wrote Admiral Ugaki, chief of staff to Admiral Kurita, in his diary that morning, "and the weather on the east coast is particularly unfavorable. It is almost impossible to determine when day breaks, and scattered dark clouds accompanied by squalls hang low. . . ."

At 6:44, Admiral Ugaki's reverie was sharply interrupted by a lookout aboard the *Yamato*. There on the horizon, twenty-two miles off to the southwest and bearing north were masts. They seemed to belong to three carriers, three cruisers, and two destroyers (the *Gambier Bay, White Plains,* and *Kitkun Bay* closest to the Japanese, and the

*Fanshaw Bay, St. Lo,* and *Kalinin Bay* nearby, with the destroyers *Hoel, Heermann,* and *Johnston,* and the destroyer escorts *Samuel B. Roberts, Dennis, Raymond,* and *John C. Butler*).

About a minute later, on the bridge of the *Gambier Bay* Captain Vieweg heard an intercepted voice transmission from a plane of another force, frantically announcing that the Japanese fleet was down there below him, forty miles from Taffy 2 and a good ten miles closer to Taffy 3. A moment later a TBM on antisubmarine patrol for Taffy 3 announced the sighting: four Japanese battleships, eight cruisers, thirteen destroyers.

Then came a report from Lieutenant Cuming in radar. He had heard that first voice transmission and turned the search radar in the direction indicated. At first he could see nothing on the screen—the distance was too great. But then the blips began to appear. It could be nothing but enemy, everyone knew that; there was no American force that could have gotten into a position twenty-five miles northwest of Taffy 3. And soon radar plot confirmed the size of the force. It was *big*.

With that initial report of radar sighting the alarm for General Quarters began to sound. It was 6:45. A minute later came a message from Admiral Sprague to change course to a heading that would let the carriers launch planes into the wind, and make maximum speed. Captain Vieweg ordered the planes launched.

Commander Huxtable was in the wardroom, when he heard the general alarm. "Another hop to the Sulu Sea," he said to himself, "and no lunch." So he stayed put in his chair, determined at least to get a glass of juice and a piece of toast before going to the ready room. All other officers scrambled, and in two minutes the ship was at General Quarters, all stations manned, and Commander Huxtable had the wardroom to himself. Just then Lt. John Holland rushed in. "You'd better get up to the ready room in a hurry," he panted. "They are already launching the planes."

Huxtable knew then that this was an emergency. Captain Vieweg would never have started this kind of air activity unless something had happened. He and Holland began running for the ready room.

"What's going on," asked Huxtable.

"I don't know, but all hell must be busting loose."

As they entered the ready room, Huxtable saw Lt. Vereen Bell putting on a flight harness. He grabbed his own harness. It must be another sweep to the Sulu Sea. "You stay here," he said to Bell. He grabbed his plotting Board and ran for the flight deck.

Gunner Charlie Westbrook was just sitting down to a breakfast of baked beans when the alarm went off. He hurried through the crew compartment, woke radioman Lee McDaniel, who had replaced Larry Austin after the shooting accident, and hurried to the flight deck. Ensign Crocker's plane was the third in line, and the pilot was already aboard, running the engine. McDaniel never showed up, so Westbrook persuaded radioman Lock to go with them. His pilot's plane was down in the hangar deck and would not make it up for this emergency.

On the bridge, Captain Vieweg and Commander Borries were getting ready to launch. There were three napalm bombs sitting on the No. 5 sponson for the operations of the day had called for troop support. These were jettisoned over the side. Nine minutes after the call to General Quarters, Vieweg saw the first sign of the enemy, large-caliber salvo splashes near the small ships on the northern edge of the formation. Ten fighters were on deck and seven TBMs were also ready, although they were not loaded with bombs or torpedoes.

When General Quarters sounded, Chief Montgomery and Chief Horton, the maintenance chief, were on the flight deck testing out the engine that had been installed in the fighter hit by the falling tractor the night before. Chief Martin got into the cockpit and tried to run up the engine. Chief Montgomery stood by with a $CO_2$ bottle to put out any fire. The engine fuel pump would not function, and they were working on it when the pilots ran to man the planes.

Ensign Zeola and Ensign Tetz were in the wardroom when the alarm sounded. Zeola had just given an order for his eggs, when the call came: "Pilots man your planes." He and Tetz ran to the ready room, grabbed their parachute harnesses and ran for the flight deck. On top Zeola saw all fighters but one with their engines running. He went to the last fighter and threw his leg onto the step and began to hoist himself up—only to come into the grinning face of Lt. (jg) Joseph Dennis McGraw, who was in the cockpit and had possession. So a disappointed Zeola stepped back down, and joined Ensign Tetz and Lieutenant Courtney, who also had missed out.

Seaman Quinn was in the spud locker peeling potatoes for the noon meal when General Quarters sounded. He left his watch, money, and all his other belongings in the spud locker and went to his 20-mm gun. He saw flashes on the horizon and swung the gun around, looking for planes. He did not see any.

Fred DiSipio, the youngest man aboard the ship, was assigned to damage control. When the call came to General Quarters he was asleep on the flight deck under a plane, to escape the heat below. He rubbed his eyes and ran to his battle station. And there he waited.

Down below decks Lieutenant (jg) Mallgrave was in the after engine room with Chief Engineer Sanders and seventeen enlisted men, who were the regular crew assigned to this battle station. When the call came to General Quarters, the ship was making 127 rpm and all boilers were steaming. Then the bridge called down, ringing up "flank" (top speed) on the engine order telegraph. In two minutes the engines were making 177 rpm. The bridge called down. "Are you making all possible speed."

"Affirmative."

"Enemy ships are closing. Don't mind about smoke."

"Permission requested to light off smoke screen burners," said Lieutenant Mallgrave.

"Permission granted."

The *Gambier Bay* began to make smoke.

The *Gambier Bay, Kitkun Bay,* and *Fanshaw Bay* were in the same sort of disposition that the Japanese favored for defense against air attack: The three carriers lay inside a screen composed of the three destroyers and four destroyer escorts as they launched planes. As the *Gambier Bay* began making smoke, so did all the other ships.

Admiral Kurita was pleased for almost the first time since he had the SHO plan orders back at Lingga Roads. "By heaven-sent opportunity we are dashing to attack the enemy carriers," he radioed Admiral Toyoda. Poor Kurita had no conception of the vast resources of the American fleet at this point, and he believed the half dozen carriers he saw before him were Halsey's southern task group. If he could knock these off, he would indeed have established a place for himself in the Japanese pantheon, no matter what happened.

The Japanese battleships opened fire from 35,000 yards—not quite twenty miles. Soon geysers were rising around the carriers. Several salvos straddled the *White Plains* and *Fanshaw Bay*. The *Gambier Bay* still seemed safely unnoticed, and Captain Vieweg was concentrating on getting off all his planes. At the helm was QM Birger Dahlstrom, who had taken Quartermaster Bell's place when Bell went into the hospital. Vieweg was on the deck above, talking down through the speaking tube.

AMM3c Potochniak heard the bugle blow and the bell clang, and he went to his shop and put on the bulky kapok life jacket, for the first time in months. He also strapped on a belt with the ten-inch bayonet his friend, the marine Andy Horvot, had given him months earlier. He put on two canteens, a diamond ring, and other valuables he had for safekeeping, and picked up a contraband .22-caliber pistol he had acquired from Al Kubichek, one of his shipmates. This was one call to General Quarters that Potochniak was taking seriously. He left the oxygen shop then, went through the light lock and onto the port catwalk.

Seaman Heinl had been in the messhall that morning, too, and he had a spoonful of beans poised about two inches from his mouth when the bell began to ring. He jumped up and ran to the ship's magazine on the port side of the *Gambier Bay*, which was his battle station. He could see the black smoke trailing aft of their ship and the smoke from the others.

When Commander Huxtable reached his plane, he asked AMM3c Gutzweiler, his plane captain, what sort of load he had. "None," said the plane captain, so Huxtable told him to run and call Commander Borries over the voice tube and ask about a load. He could see no use in going out without weapons. He watched the bridge. Borries moved forward and said something to Captain Vieweg. The captain made a sweeping gesture with his arm, as if to say, "Get 'em off." Just then, Huxtable heard what sounded like a rifle shot. He turned his head and saw a salvo of heavy-caliber shells splashing alongside the carrier *White Plains*. Until that moment he had no idea that they were actually in contact with the enemy.

There was no time to waste. Three TBMs were ahead of Huxtable, and he went in turn. As he took off, the lead plane had started his 180-degree turn for a regular carrier join-up. When Huxtable was launched, he took the lead and called Admiral Sprague's ship for instructions. The code name was Bendix. In a moment an excited voice from Bendix answered: "Attack immediately." Huxtable headed aft into the overcast at 1,200 feet to comply.

Pyzdrowski was in his stateroom when the alarm bell rang. A pilot who was not flying had no particular battle station aboard a carrier. He was supposed to go to the ready room, more to keep him out of the way than anything else. So Pyzdrowski was in no hurry, for he was not scheduled for takeoff that morning. He walked casually out to the catwalk to see what, if anything, there was to be seen. At about this time Ensign Zeola and Ensign Tetz came back down from the flight deck, nursing their disappointment at not getting off in the scramble for planes. They all looked out across the water, and there they saw the tall black tripod masts that were characteristic of Japanese battleships. Zeola blew out his breath.

"Kee-rist," he said, "look at those pagodas . . ."

## CHAPTER TWENTY-EIGHT

# First Blood

When they saw what the ship faced, the three pilots on the catwalk rushed to their staterooms and found their life preservers, their guns, knives, canteens, and other survival gear that they had chosen for emergency. They hurried to the ready room. It was empty but the blackboard had a message from Commander Huxtable:

"Bisbee, take charge. Weatherholt, Gallagher, and Pyzdrowski, fly off with torpedoes when ready." The four extra TBMs were still on the hangar deck, where the crews were loading and arming torpedoes. Bisbee came in, saw the message, ran to the hangar deck and came back. They would have to launch individually, as the planes came up in the elevator. Bisbee turned to the others. "Gallagher, you go first. Weatherholt, you team up with him if you can. Pyzdrowski, you go third. Don't wait for me. I'll wait for the last plane."

The time was 7:05. It was just twenty minutes since the sighting of the enemy had been confirmed and the *Gambier Bay* had gone to General Quarters.

Lieutenant Bisbee grabbed Pyzdrowski's arm. "Pyz," he said, "give me the combination to your locker. We need a drink around here." Suddenly Pyzdrowski realized that he was about to take off, and that most of these pilots in the ready room, and Lt. Vereen Bell, would be stuck to ride the ship to whatever destiny she might have. He recited the combination to his liquor locker twice to Bisbee, and then followed Gallagher and Weatherholt up to the flight deck. Bisbee, Vereen Bell, John Holland, Joe Phipps, Ernie Courtney, Leo Zeola, John Tetz, Joe McCabe, Owen Wheeler, and Tuffy Barrows would not be launched. There were no planes. So if they needed a drink to conceal their disappointment, they were welcome to it. Bisbee took off for the Pyzdrowski stateroom, and the three pilots with planes moved toward the flight deck. They passed the upper first aid station, and Pyzdrowski saw Dr. Wayne Stewart, the flight surgeon, setting up his surgical shop. It reminded him of what he had read of the old days in sailing ships, when the surgeons got ready their saws and burning irons, and strewed sawdust on the deck to soak up the blood that would flow.

Almost at the moment the pilots reached the flight deck, Gallagher's TBM came up the elevator, with its torpedo in place. Gallagher and his air crewmen leaped aboard. Immediately the plane was rolled to the catapult to be yoked for launching. The plane captain ran along behind, yelling and waving his hands. "It's got no gas. It's got to be gassed. Wait." It was 7:08. As the airedales hesitated, a voice came over the TBS from Bendix, the command ship:

"All carriers launch all aircraft."

The captain signalled. Launch. Gallagher nodded and waved his hand. He knew by that time that he had only forty-five gallons of gas in the TBM, perhaps enough to keep him flying for five minutes after takeoff. He also had a one-ton torpedo that should be delivered. As soon as the torpedo bomber was airborne, Gallagher turned left and headed for the first big ship he saw.

The next plane up the elevator was Bob Weatherholt's TBM. There had been no forgetting with this one, it was loaded already with a full tank of gas. Weatherholt got into the plane calmly, smoking a cigarette, and just before the catapult operated, he flicked it over the side, grinned, and took off.

The third plane came up, loaded with gas and a torpedo. Jerry Fauls the gunner, Bob Jensen, the radioman, and Pyzdrowski shook hands, stepped up to the TBM, and took their places. The plane was taxied to the catapult. Pyzdrowski's eyes were glued to the deck-edge controller who watched the catapult light console. He used his fingers to signal the catapult launch officer the status of the catapult charge and the instructions of the bridge. The clenched fist meant hold. One finger up meant get ready. Two fingers up meant clear to fire. The controller's fist was clenched as the plane was hooked up. Then he raised one finger and Pyzdrowski turned to face the launch officer. He waited. And he waited. And he waited.

It was 7:30. For fifteen minutes a squall had lain between the ships of Taffy 3 and Admiral Kurita's force, and only a few salvo splashes had come in, remarkably near the *White Plains* and *Fanshaw Bay* given the circumstances and the absence of Japanese spotter planes. Admiral Sprague used this respite to ask Admiral Kinkaid down south if he might move the whole protective carrier force toward the safety of the battleship fleet. The answer was no. So Admiral Sprague knew that the escort carriers were regarded as expendable. If they had to be sacrificed to save the main body of Kinkaid's fleet, then that was how it was going to be. They could maneuver east or west, but they could not head south to safety. Whether or not they could have achieved safety was questionable anyhow. The small carriers had been operating for many weeks without dockyard attention and seventeen knots was regarded as a good speed for them. *Yamato,* the Japanese superbattleship, had a flank speed almost twice that of the Kaiser carriers.

The controller held one finger up waiting on the bridge command. Pyzdrowski could not understand it. "She's charged. Let 'er go," he shouted. He looked at Commander Borries and called to him. "Let me go." Borries pointed silently to the ensign atop the ship's mast. The captain had headed downwind to try to escape the enemy. One Japanese cruiser was moving around the northeast flank of the carriers, and salvos were beginning to fall close. The Japanese radar was not nearly so advanced as the American, so Admiral Kurita's gunners relied on an old device: Their various salvoes were color-coded so that the gunners could correct their aim. A green series of splashes would be followed by a red series, then yellow. And each series came closer to the *Fanshaw Bay, White Plains,* and *Gambier Bay.* The cruiser was coming at thirty knots, and soon would have a square shot at the *Gambier Bay.* The salvoes increased in concentration.

Captain Vieweg was busily "chasing salvoes." On the principle that lightning does not strike twice in the same place, as soon as one salvo of shells plunked into the water, the captain turned in that direction. Then came another salvo and he turned again. As Weatherholt was launched salvoes straddled the ship. It was 7:25. The range was close enough now that Admiral Sprague ordered the carriers to "open fire with the pea shooters," and in a moment the five-inch gun on the fantail began shooting.

Pyzdrowski got the "cut" signal. He shut off the engine of the TBM, jumped out and ran for the bridge. "What's the matter?" he shouted. "The catapult is charged." Commander Borries held up his fist. "Wait." Pyzdrowski ran back to the plane and ordered Fauls and Jensen out. He intended to fly this one himself, alone. The signal was to hold up. He jumped out and again ran to the bridge, calling to Borries. "We can take off without wind." It was true. While the ship was in harbor at Espiritu Santo, the torpedo bombers had been fitted with new twin-barrel Honeywell carburetors which were promised to increase engine efficiency. Carrier doctrine, however, said you must not take off except into the wind, and with salvoes falling all around the ship, Commander Borries was not about to argue with the captain.

"Sure, sure," he said to Pyzdrowski, and then he pointed at the catapult. The TBM was just then being shot off, pilotless. It took off beautifully, just as Pyzdrowski had said it would.

It climbed for a moment, then flipped over on its left side and went into the water. The last plane had left the *Gambier Bay*. It was 7:50 A.M.

Lieutenant Stewart, in charge of the first eight fighters that had left the *Gambier Bay* before dawn, was totally unaware of what was happening in the beginning. His mission was to support the ground troops on Leyte with strafing, bombing, and rocket attacks. This activity consumed a large amount of fuel, and so about 7:30 he was considering a return to the *Gambier Bay* for fuel. When he called the air controller, he learned that the Japanese had arrived in force off Samar, and that his carrier was under attack and could not land any planes. The same was true of all the other carriers of Taffy 1, 2, and 3; they were running from destruction and their planes had to take care of themselves. The alternative was Tacloban airfield, which was in worse shape on the 25th than it had been the day before when Zeola landed there. The night's rain had made a sticky mess of the dirt runway. But what else was there to do? By the time Stewart brought his flight of eight over Tacloban, a hundred planes were orbiting. They came from the sixteen escort carriers of Admiral Sprague's command and from Halsey's fleet carriers offshore; and they shared a common plight: They had no place else to go. The first fighter in the pattern made a pass over the field, then came into land. His gear caught in the mud, and the plane nosed over in the middle of the runway, blocking it. The next plane, desperate, landed in the sand on the seaward side of the runway. He bumped down and bounced along, but he was down safe and so was his plane, and that was what counted. Thereafter, planes began landing on sand and runway every few seconds. Some nosed over. Some came in hard, and the landing gear crumbled beneath them. Some caught fire, but the planes continued to land. Hundreds of soldiers appeared to help pull and drag planes off the runways and the clear spots, so more planes could land. The Tacloban field was like a giant beehive, with the worker bees coming to carry off the injured to make room for more to land.

After Commander Huxtable had the order from the flagship to "attack" he led his six fellow torpedo pilots toward the enemy. As long as the planes were under 1,000 feet they could see the Japanese ships below, but to make an attack they had to gain altitude and come down through the clouds. The weather was so bad, however, that it seemed unlikely a high-altitude attack could be successful, and the flagship had ordered immediate action. Below, he could see the four cruisers and four battleships in the gloom; at least that is what he thought he saw. Without doubt he could also see the American destroyers and destroyer escorts running in to make torpedo attacks on the big Japanese ships to stop the punishment of the escort carriers.

Huxtable did not even know what loads the other TBMs were carrying. His own plane had only ammunition for the guns, but at least, he said to himself, he could give the enemy a scare. So he headed down in a shallow dive on the starboard side of the line of cruisers. He could see the red balls of anti-aircraft tracer coming up as he dived at 190 knots. Huxtable came in to about 2,500 yards. The anti-aircraft fire was growing more intense, and he pulled up in a wide circle. The Japanese kept shooting with five-inch shells, and he flew through the smoke of the bursts, they were so close.

Not knowing what Admiral Kinkaid had said to Admiral Sprague that morning, Huxtable volunteered the information to Bendix that the best course for the carrier force was due south. There was no comment.

Lieutenant Bassett was right behind Commander Huxtable when they took off from the carrier. As Huxtable dove for the cruisers, Bassett was on his wing; Huxtable took the second ship in the column and Bassett peeled off to attack the lead ship, a *Mogami*-class cruiser. Bassett had two bombs. As he dropped the first at 2,000 feet the antiaircraft fire became intense, and the TBM was hit and began to shudder. Immediately he dropped the second bomb and pulled out of the thirty-five-degree dive at 1,000 feet and turned into the clouds ahead of the cruiser. So he did not see the results of his bombing, but he heard no explosions and was inclined to believe that his two 500-pound bombs had not been fused, and that they did not explode even if they struck the target. Just then, he did not much care; his mind was totally occupied with the shuddering TBM. How badly was it damaged? He climbed to 8,000 feet on instruments, deep in the clouds. When he emerged his crewmen could check the damage to the tail. The starboard horizontal stabilizer had been hit from below and a hole ten inches wide had been blown in the bottom side, with the shell emerging to make a hole 18 inches wide at the top. When Bassett pulled back the stick, he felt a binding, but that was all. The instruments responded properly. The question was how much structural damage had been suffered, and could the plane fly to a landing place? Radioman Houlihan found a piece of shrapnel in his compartment and a hole in the port window. But that was all the damage. Bassett flew toward Tacloban field, but when he got there so many planes were stacked up in the sky that the field was accepting emergency landings only. He circled for an hour; meanwhile the others of his group came up, and he joined them to land at Dulag airfield shortly after 11 A.M.

Ensign Crocker had also joined up with Commander Huxtable. His plane, like Huxtable's, had no bomb load, so the commander told Crocker to hang back and not go in on the first pass. But Crocker felt he had to do something, so he flew in low alongside the cruisers to divert their anti-aircraft fire. The Japanese five-inch guns fired on him, and one burst came so close it knocked out his instruments and his radio. He saw a TBM smoking, and tried to lead it to Tacloban. It was apparent, however, that the TBM was not going to make it, and in a few seconds it nosed down, and landed in the water about a mile ahead of the American ships, nosed over, and soon sank. Crocker saw the three crewmen get out. He dropped several dye markers and a float light. Then he made another pass and dropped his seat boat pack to the men in the water. He then circled, waiting for another plane to come along to join up with, but none came. He made an attack on the Japanese destroyers at the edge of the formation then, firing his guns and rockets. In the turret, gunner Charlie Westbrooke fired his single .50-caliber gun. The Japanese anti-aircraft gunners were good shots; they put a 20-mm shell into his port wing and engine, but there was no loss of power. When Crocker ran out of ammunition on his third run, he headed for Dulag to land. When he came in, and was taxiing off the strip a fighter ran into the TBM and damaged the propeller.

Ensign Shroyer had also joined Commander Huxtable. When Huxtable attacked the cruisers, Shroyer went after one of the battleships. He had two 500-pound bombs, but on his first run he strafed only because the cloud cover restricted the visibility so badly as he attacked. He came out of the attack at 2,000 feet right over the cruisers, and for a moment the air all around him was filled with anti-aircraft bursts. But he dived for the deck and escaped. He climbed then to 10,000 feet and attacked a *Tone*-class cruiser, following a dozen FM-2s that were strafing. He dropped his two bombs, and they hit the fantail of the cruiser. He did not see that, but Lieutenant Lischer, piloting one of the fighters, and Lt. Paul Garrison, a *Kitkun Bay* pilot, both saw the bombs hit. Half an hour later Shroyer flew over the cruiser and saw it was dead in the water. He headed for the escort carriers, but was ordered to Tacloban. There he was diverted to Dulag and landed.

Lieutenant Gallagher had taken off with that first plane of the TBM group that were loaded with torpedoes. Knowing that his gas supply was severely limited he headed straight for the enemy ships and dropped his torpedo against a cruiser. No one saw the results, but in a moment

Gallagher joined up with Commander Huxtable, seeking instructions. His plane had been hit in the attack, and the engine was smoking. Huxtable told him to head for the beach, and Gallagher obeyed and turned.

The engine sputtered and died. Gallagher headed for the water and landed. His was the plane that Crocker saw go into the water. The three men got out, into a rubber boat, and waved. Crocker flew off, and no one else reported them. They were never seen again.

Lieutenant Weatherholt had taken off just behind Gallagher, but fortunately his plane had been gassed. He circled the *Gambier Bay*, waiting for Pyzdrowski and Bisbee, but they did not come. After half an hour of circling, Weatherholt went off to find other planes to join for an attack. He found one other torpedo plane, and went in with that plane to attack a battleship. They attacked from the two sides of the bow. The other plane dropped first and the battleship turned toward the torpedo and then straightened out. Weatherholt dropped and sped for the deck to avoid the anti-aircraft fire. He did not see any hits.

Lieutenant Roby was one of the first to rush from the ready room to the flight deck when the captain called on the pilots to man all planes as the Japanese fleet approached. Roby launched at 6:55, circled and joined six of the carrier's other fighters. They climbed toward the Japanese fleet. Twenty minutes after taking off, they saw Japanese destroyers below, and dived down to strafe. Roby made three runs. He got separated from the other VC-10 fighters and joined another group to make more passes. Again he was separated and joined a third group. By 8:00 his guns were empty, but he continued to make dry runs on cruisers to harry them and draw fire. Just before 10:00 he flew to Tacloban, circled for nearly an hour, and then landed.

Ensign Bennett, flying a TBM, got separated from Huxtable in the clouds and joined up with one VC-10 fighter. Together they attacked the Japanese cruisers. The fighter went in first on a cruiser and the TBM followed. Bennett had no bomb load nor any rockets. He strafed with the wing guns and his gunner and radioman strafed. They came out and saw the battleships and attacked. Bennett did not believe his attacks did any damage, but they did divert anti-aircraft fire from other attacking planes. He headed for the beach hoping to find some bombs, but was diverted to the carrier *Manila Bay*, and landed on the flight deck at 10 o'clock.

Lt. (jg) Joe McGraw was one of the escorts for Huxtable's little group of torpedo planes. He made eleven strafing runs on a *Fuso*-class battleship. He saw one Japanese cruiser listing and apparently badly damaged. He also saw one escort carrier dropping far behind the others and smoking badly. He did not know it was the *Gambier Bay*.

Lieutenant Phillips was with a group of VC-10 fighters that attacked the destroyer disposition. On his first strafing run all but one of his guns jammed. He kept on attacking with that one gun, until it ceased firing. Then he went to Tacloban. Ensign Wallace and Lieutenant Hunting both joined attack groups that went in to strafe either battleships or cruisers. They attacked until their ammunition was gone, and then they went to Tacloban.

Ensign Osterkorn, in a TBM, did not find any planes of VC-10 when he took off from the carrier. He headed for the enemy fleet and attacked alone. As he came out of the run, he saw a group of fighters and joined up on them for his second attack. He dropped his two bombs on a cruiser but saw no results. Then he went to Tacloban and was diverted to Dulag.

Lieutenant Seitz made eight or nine runs on carriers and destroyers, and before he left the battle area he saw one Japanese cruiser and two destroyers dead in the water.

Lieutenant Ellwood made repeated runs on the cruisers to help the bombers unload without being smothered in anti-aircraft fire. His guns gave him trouble and finally quit altogether, whereupon he made dummy runs. He saw one bomb hit the bow of a cruiser and apparently knock out the forward turret. When he was down to forty gallons of gas he turned toward Tacloban.

Lieutenant Dugan's experience was almost the same, although he concentrated on the destroyers. The results, as with others, were impossible to ascertain from the air, and, of course, in the melee, with planes from all the sixteen carriers involved in the action, it was impossible to tell whose attacks produced results. Ensign Shroyer's hit on the after section of a cruiser was an exception. That ship may have been the *Chokai* or it may have been the *Chikuma*, although the Japanese believed the tremendous explosion aft on that ship was caused by a torpedo. No matter, the Japanese accounts credited the American planes with an effective effort on the whole. The cruiser *Suzuya* was badly damaged. The *Tone* was damaged and her captain was badly wounded by strafing fighters. It would have been poetic justice had the fighter been one of VC-10's, for *Tone* was the cruiser that attacked the *Gambier Bay* most effectively that day. The *Chikuma, Haguro,* and *Chokai,* proud cruisers, were all damaged by air attacks. Several of the cruisers sank on their way back to safety later in the day. Not all this damage was done by the aviators, of course. For another battle story was being told that morning on the surface, by the destroyers and destroyer escorts.

As Admiral Kurita's force swooped down that morning all that stood between the carriers and disaster were the little ships of the destroyer screen. They turned like foxes to fight, and just before seven o'clock they came under fire from the Japanese ships. They began to attack. The destroyer *Johnston* went in first with torpedoes, fired and ducked into a rain squall. Destroyers *Hoel* and *Heermann* and the destroyer escort *Roberts* followed. The *Johnston* kept nipping at the heels of the Japanese until she was sunk. *Hoel* went in, attacked, scored hits on Japanese ships and came under heavy fire. She, too, was sunk. The *Heermann* also went into action. The men of the *Gambier Bay* knew the *Heermann* well. Indeed, Lt. Bucky Dahlen was aboard her that day, with his air crewmen.

Two air crewmen had been assigned to a repair party, and Lieutenant Dahlen, who had volunteered to help, was sent to the gunnery officer to spot Japanese planes. When no Japanese planes appeared, he returned to the bridge to ask Commander Hathaway for another assignment. He arrived at the same moment as a Japanese shell, which killed him and three others. Captain Hathaway was not at that moment on the bridge, having gone to the fire control tower where he could see better. Captain Hathaway survived, and so did his ship, but Bucky Dahlen's second lease on life had lasted less than twenty-four hours.

The destroyers and the destroyer escorts most certainly saved the carriers that day, or most of them. The cost was the loss of the *Johnston* and *Hoel* and *Samuel B. Roberts,* and the carriers did not remain unhurt. But the fact that half of them were not destroyed was attributable to the fierce attack from air and sea that the Japanese encountered off Samar.

The first carrier to be hit was the *Kalinin Bay*. At 7:10, when Captain Vieweg first started chasing salvoes, the *Kalinin Bay* took the first of fifteen shells. *White Plains,* with salvoes falling around her and obscuring her from view, was not hit at all. The *Kitkun Bay* was straddled and straddled again, but never hit. The *St. Lo,* the starboard ship in the second line of carriers, was also nearly hit half a dozen times, but she was saved for another fate. (She was hit by a kamikaze plane later in the day with such force that the fires could not be put out and she sank.) But the principal honor as sacrificial victim that day belonged to the *Gambier Bay*. When Admiral Sprague began maneuvering to try to put water between his force and the enemy, the change of course put the *Gambier Bay* at the end of the line, nearest the enemy. The course change came at 8 o'clock. Ten minutes later the Japanese drew first blood from the *Gambier Bay*. A shell struck the after end of the flight deck on the starboard side, starting fires on the flight deck and down on the hangar deck. Several men were killed or wounded. In damage control, Seaman DiSipio was sent to fight fire, but the fires were so many that he gave up, and instead began carrying wounded men down to flight surgeon Stewart's aid station. It was 8:11.

## CHAPTER TWENTY-NINE

# Under Fire

For the first time in history, a group of escort aircraft carriers was under fire from a vastly superior force of capital ships, although the Japanese paid an unconscious tribute to the fighting spirit of the pilots and the men of the destroyers and escort carriers; the official Japanese reports called the destroyers "cruisers" and upgraded the escort carriers to fleet class. But given a continuation of what was occurring off Samar that morning, the fleet should have lost three or four small carriers. The *Gambier Bay* and *Kalinin Bay* were the most obvious choices for destruction after the formation turned southeast, leaving them on the exposed flank with their smoke blowing back over their heads. From 15,000 yards these two carriers were sitting ducks for the cruisers and battleships. The salvoes were coming about a minute and a half apart for the first half hour, and Captain Vieweg had been able to forecast the shooting pattern. But that shell on the flight deck was just the beginning. The cruisers had come up within 10,000 yards, and the tempo of their firing increased.

Pyzdrowski was on the flight deck then. He walked over to the elevator well and looked down. The last TBM was down there with its full load of gas and a live torpedo. And it was afire. He headed for the bridge tower to Air Plot to see what was going on. He saw several men slumped against a bulkhead. One of them had no head. He turned and went back to the flight deck, to watch the enemy come down on them like foxes in the henhouse. He saw the battleship *Yamato* firing, the largest ship he had ever seen in his life.

Suddenly another salvo dropped very near the ship, and almost immediately Pyzdrowski felt the engines slowing. He looked up and saw the battle ensign beginning to droop. The ship had been traveling at more than seventeen knots. Suddenly the speed dropped to eleven knots. No shells from that salvo had actually struck the *Gambier Bay*, but one had missed so nearly that it had smashed a hole in the plates just by the forward engine room. It was 8:20. Oiler John Lemirande was on duty in the after engine room with Commander Sanders, Lt. (jg) Mallgrave, Fireman Richard Person, and Chief Walter Kalbe. Lemirande had stood the 12-to-4 watch that morning and had cleaned out the filters in the hours of darkness as was their habit in order to pump the sludge while leaving no trace by daylight. When the call came to battle stations and he rushed below, Commander Sanders warned him that they were under attack. For the first hour all they knew of the attack was the account piped down from the bridge, where Chaplain Carlsen was reporting, and the orders given to Person, who had the earphones. Person adjusted the throttles every time a change in speed was ordered, and Lemirande adjusted the condensers. The first real feeling of war was when that shell had come through the flight deck and knocked out one of the engine room's ventblowers. Then came the shell that blew in the plates, next to No. 1 boiler. In a few moments the water was coming in.

"Let's get the hell out of here!" shouted Commander Sanders. They secured the boilers so they would not blow up. By this time they were waist deep in water and the ship was listing to port. Lemirande headed for the hangar deck and crawled under one of the planes that had not gotten off. Just before they left, Commander Sanders called from the after engine room and reported that they had secured. Then communications went out, and he climbed the ladder.

Since the forward engine room supplied power to the forward part of the ship, for a time there was no power forward. Then the whole load was switched to the No. 3 generator aft. On the bridge, the equipment was working, but when they slowed to eleven knots, the range between the ship and the enemy began closing with a frightening speed. The American aircraft above the Japanese were attacking all this time, and the destroyers and destroyer escorts were launching their torpedoes, but the Japanese seemed hardly to notice as far as the men of the *Gambier Bay* could tell. The tempo of fire became furious, and the ship was hit by nearly every salvo. Two portable electric bilge pumps had been placed in operation in the engine room by the damage control party a minute after the plates caved in, but soon came a report that bulkhead 100 had split—and that meant the machine shop forward was flooding.

Up the ladder from the damage control center came Robert Platner, one of the oldest warrant officers, with twenty-one years of naval service, with a young machinist mate slung across his shoulders. He reached the hangar deck when the force of an explosion blew the injured youngster off his shoulder but slowed the flying shrapnel which penetrated and immobilized Platner's neck.

At 9:00, Lt. Al Martin, the Skinner uniflow-engine specialist, and warrant machinist James Buford abandoned the pumps in the forward engine room, and found their way to the hangar deck when still another shell exploded. Engineer Hartin suffered a broken upper arm and a broken knee when he noticed at his side Buford with a hole in his head. He managed to drag him to the sponson where he could tell that the injury was fatal. Unable to inflate the life jackets. Hartin clung onto Buford, slipped into the water, and found a life raft.

On the flight deck, Seaman DiSipio was hit by shrapnel in the back and leg, and the force of the blow blew off one shoe and his shirt. He saw his friend Gene Murray a little further along and ran to him. Just as he reached Murray a shell blew off his friend's head and fractured two of DiSipio's ribs. He watched for what seemed two or three minutes as Murray's headless body continued to move and then slowly slumped to the deck and was still.

The salvoes were coming in every other minute, and at least one shell per salve was doing damage. Those shells that hit the superstructure did very little damage, for they were armor piercing, and they went right through without exploding. The damage was done by shells that hit just short of the ship or at the waterline, and went in to explode below.

Seaman Heinl felt one shell come through the ship as

he was walking from the port magazine to the starboard to check on the men there since the ship was listing. As he came onto the catwalk under the flight deck, he saw the hole through both sides of the ship. He could look right through where the shell had passed.

When Heinl reached the starboard magazine, he found Seaman Mike Williams, who had been telling him a few days before that he was about to be returned to the United States for duty. His two elder brothers had both been killed in action, and his mother had asked the Red Cross to bring him home. The navy had acquiesced, and Mike Williams's orders were being cut. As soon as this engagement ended, Williams was to be flown back to the U.S. Heinl spent a few moments talking to Williams and to Seaman Klotkowski, who was also on duty there. Then he went back to his own post. As he reached the magazine, the ship shuddered from the impact of another shell, and the lights went out. That shell also killed Mike Williams at his post. Heinl went out onto the catwalk again since he could not see inside, and as he came out he saw another shell strike and Klotkowski's left arm disappear. He got to a phone and called for a corpsman, but the corpsman never appeared, and in a minute or two, Klotkowski was dead. (The corpsman was killed en route to the catwalk.)

AAM3c Potochniak was on the catwalk when an explosion behind him knocked him down. As he scrambled to his feet he saw that this first shell had knocked out his oxygen room, just as he had seen it happen in his vision. Where his oxygen room had been was now a large, smoldering hole. He moved up the port catwalk, forward, and his head was tumbling with thoughts. What about his tombstone, with the inscription: "Lost at sea, age 19 years." And what would his family say when they learned he had been killed?

Potochniak reached the flight deck. He saw bodies lying on the bloodstained wooden deck. He headed for the parachute packing light lock. When he arrived, he saw that it had been turned into a first aid station. Just behind him came the flight surgeon, Commander Stewart, followed by two enlisted men, one of whom was AMM3c Marty Showers. Lying on a stretcher was a badly injured enlisted man. Commander Stewart asked Potochniak to move over, since he needed that space to work on the wounded man. Potochniak stepped back and the surgeon stepped up and knelt down by the stretcher. Just then a shell fragment burst through the flight deck, and killed surgeon Stewart. Potochniak saw other men fall. He heard aircrewman G. C. Phillips shout, "I'm hit." Potochniak was hit, too, by small fragments in the hand and legs. He looked at the stretcher. Surgeon Stewart's body was lying across that of the injured sailor, in a pool of blood. The compartment began to get hot, and Potochniak went out the port side of the light lock to the catwalk.

Photographer's Mate 2c Johnson remained at his battle station on the catwalk aft of the landing signal officer's platform. He leaned over the side just as one shell hit the motor whale boat and blew it apart. He watched, fascinated, as shells continued to go completely through the ship and then explode 300 yards further along. He also saw shells ricocheting off the flight deck without exploding, which, of course, indicated the close range from which the approaching cruisers were firing. He saw Aerographer 1c John Ammon clamber up onto the flight deck from the catwalk, and begin to sprint toward the island. When he was halfway across, an explosion below caused the flight deck to undulate like a wave, and Ammon fell flat on his face, lay there, jumped up and hobbled into the island structure. The whole performance had probably consumed ten seconds, but it seemed like an hour.

Johnson decided to go down to the photo lab and pick up his dress blues. He had them made up in a tight package with a white hat in the center. Months earlier he had been impressed by the tale of one old timer who described his woes after he lost his ship: Because he had no dress blues he could not go ashore on liberty for months until they reached port and he could get re-outfitted. Johnson had determined this would never happen to him, and now, with shells exploding all around, his dress blues were foremost in his mind.

He worked his way back to the passageway that led onto the gallery deck and the photo lab. He encountered heavy black smoke but held the door to the light lock open and let the breeze clear the air so that he could see. It was lucky that he had, for eight feet in front of him was a gaping hole through the passageway deck down to the hangar deck. There was no way to get past. He turned back toward his station, saying good-bye to his dress blues. This time, on the catwalk he encountered Seaman 1c Gilman, one of the fire rescue team. Gilman was slumped against the bulkhead, crying and holding his arms in front of him. Johnson came up and saw why: Gilman's abdomen was ripped open and he was trying to hold his intestines in.

"I'm ruined," he kept crying, "I'm ruined, I'm ruined." And he did not look up as Johnson went by.

Johnson went by one of the 40-mm sponsons and saw one of the ammunition passers he knew, a real "tough guy" who had been complaining since they left port, "When are we gonna see some *real* action?" Now the ammunition passer was standing at the gun, just gazing off into the distance, eyes glassy, a string of slobber hanging from his jaw.

"Well, buddy," said Johnson. "Is this enough action for you?"

The ammunition passer looked right through him, and did not recognize him or answer. He was blowing little bubbles, Johnson noted.

Johnson walked back to the very end of the catwalk where he saw a lookout in a chair, his glasses turned out. He was sitting there, as calm as if he was in his back yard listening to the Yankees playing the Red Sox, humming a little tune. "How ya doin'?" he asked.

"Fine. How're *you* doing?"

"Okay. Pardon me." The lookout spoke into his chest microphone. "*Tone*-class cruiser bearing 060 now 3,000 yards." He turned back to Johnson. "What were you saying, pal?"

Lieutenant Lynch's battle station, after he was relieved by Lieutenant Commander Gellhorn as officer of the deck, was at the five-inch gun on the fantail. He had received orders to begin firing at 7:45 and had been firing steadily since. On the sixth round they had hit a cruiser, and about three rounds later they made a hit on another one. Then they were told to stop firing because somebody in gunnery control believed the five-inch was drawing fire to the ship, and that it might stop if they quit irritating the Japanese!

When the fires started the five-inch gun crew broke out two hoses and put several fires out. Then came that shell that knocked out the forward engine room, and a few moments later, orders from the bridge to flood the magazines. Gunner F. S. Hughes supervised the flooding, then Lynch reported to the bridge. The bridge gave him orders to begin firing again, but when they tried to fire the gun, they discovered the power was out. Switching to manual, they discovered that the rammer had been jammed by one of those shaking near misses. They were working with the gun when several men from the hangar deck appeared, wounded. Worst hurt was Machinist's Mate 3c McMillan, with a mutilated arm. Lieutenant Lynch broke out the first aid kit and began patching up the wounded.

Yeoman 1c J. V. Hammond was the talker on the bridge, and he was aware of everything that was going on as various divisions reported in to state damage and the remedies that were being taken. Then, just below him, he felt a tremendous explosion. "There goes the pilot house," he said to himself. And it was true. On the deck below, helmsman Birger Dahlstrom was having serious difficulty with the steering. Several times the power had failed and the helm had not responded to his attempts to turn. Then, the power went out altogether, and the captain ordered the after manual steering manned.

"Dahlstrom," called the captain, "do you still have any control?"

"Some, sir."

"Then . . . hard left rudder. . . ."

Just then came that big explosion that had jolted talker Hammond. Most of the pilothouse, directly behind Dahlstrom, was blasted to pieces, with the men in it. Dahlstrom felt something hit his foot, and he lost all feeling in it, as if the foot was gone. All the instruments were knocked out.

From the bridge came the captain's voice.

"Helsman, have you any more control?"

"No, sir. Everything is dead."

In that after steering compartment, Quartermaster Hagerty and three others were in water a foot deep. The water was seeping in through the hatch that led to the five-inch gun's ammunition locker. After gunner Hughes had flooded the locker, another eight-inch shell from a Japanese cruiser had sprung open the hatch, and the water was now pouring in. They were wondering just how long they could last, when a hit somewhere amidships knocked out all power.

Lieutenant Odum was in his Aerology office, listening to Chaplain Carlsen's account of the battle over the public address system, when suddenly the box gave a squawk and quit working. The public address system was knocked out.

Odum had been smelling the acrid cordite mixed with the smoke from the ship's stacks for an hour and was as used to it as he would ever be. Suddenly the odor changed; the cordite became predominant, and the stink of burning diesel fuel fell off. At the same time he felt the motion of the ship stopping. He began stuffing his classified materials into weighted bags. Aerographer's Mate John Ammon was back down at his station after running that dangerous message to the captain. Odum told Ammon he was going to Air Plot to check if the abandon ship order had been given.

"If I don't get back here and you hear that the captain has ordered abandon ship, then be sure you get these bags off and get the men off," Odum said. Then he headed for Air Plot.

Chief Montgomery was on the flight deck, moving from one fire to another as the eight-inch shells from the Japanese cruisers and a few twelve- and fourteen-inch shells from the battleships hit the ship or nearby, sending white-hot fragments onto the wooden deck. He saw Chief Flanders running down the catwalk with an armload of fire hoses. Flanders came to that point where Johnson had nearly fallen through, looked, and leaped across the enormous hole; without a pause he kept on running forward.

Suddenly Montgomery remembered that he had forgotten to put the flame cover over his bunk that morning. He went below to the CPO quarters. He found that a medical crew had taken over the writing table and were operating, as their emergency lights blinked on and off. They were standing in water ankle deep. Montgomery went to his bunk. He reached under his pillow and pulled out a pocket copy of the New Testament, where he kept his wife's picture. He put it in his shirt pocket, spread the flame cover over the bunk, and went back to the flight deck to join the damage control parties. He was sent with three men to officer country on the deck below, but when they arrived, the officer in charge said he had plenty of help and told them to go further forward, where the ship had just been hit. Montgomery led his men forward along the catwalk, following another group. Suddenly another eight-inch shell struck the ship. The group of men in front of him seemed to disintegrate, and he was knocked down. He picked himself up. He was the only one alive. He began walking along the catwalk, back to officers' country.

RM3c McCollum was standing on the catwalk outside the radio shack, watching the battle. He had no duty since he had stood the morning watch. The shell that stopped the ship knocked McCollum off his feet, and when he got up he saw that one end of the passageway had been hit squarely, and many of his shipmates were dead or wounded. The cries began. "Corpsman . . . Corpsman. . . ." After the loudspeaker system went out, some of the men around McCollum began seeking other parts of the ship, on the theory that lightning did not strike twice in the same place, just as the captain had reasoned. An officer appeared and directed them to get out of the passageways, go below to the officers' staterooms if they did not have a battle station. A half dozen of them went, McCollum among them. They had no sooner crowded into the six-bunk room than a shell hit nearby and the room was filled with flying shrapnel. Several men were killed. Others were wounded. A bit of shrapnel banged against McCollum's helmet but did not penetrate. "Oh, God, please save me," he prayed. Then someone yelled, "Let's get the hell out of here!"

Lieutenant Cuming had been watching the battle on radar in the Combat Information Center, and informing the bridge. But when the Japanese ships closed on the carrier, the radar was ineffective. It did not make any difference. The lookouts on the edges of the flight deck had a better view, and they could tell Captain Vieweg all he needed to know. Still, Cuming stayed at his post, giving what assistance he could, as the battle continued.

Lieutenant McClendon had very little to do as landing signal officer, but as flight deck officer, he supervised the fighting of fires and the cleanup of debris as the battle continued. He saw men fall, dead and wounded. He saw one man pick up a red-hot nose cap from a shell that was burning into the deck, walk over and heave it overboard. He did not see the man's hands, but he knew how badly they must have been burned.

Lieutenant Mallgrave was in the after engine room when that crippling shell struck at 8:40. The salvo was the same that hit the island and knocked out the steering. The shell in the engine room came through the port side, pierced the No. 3 boiler and went into the generating tubes. It knocked the quick-closing valve off boiler No. 3. WT3c Boren had to use the fuel oil throttle valve to close off the oil supply. When Lieutenant Mallgrave saw the size of the hole in the ship's skin, he knew there was no way of closing it. He ordered the engine room secured and abandoned before they all drowned. Chief Heald lifted the safety valves before they left, and then all men went up the ladders to the second deck and, another set of ladders to the hangar deck, and there they scattered. No one was injured.

After Pyzdrowski's TBM had been jettisoned, he had stood on the flight deck, looking at the Japanese ships for quite a while. The idea crossed his mind that perhaps the Japanese would come alongside and board. (Pyzdrowski had read many tales of the age of fighting sail as a boy.) He touched his .38-caliber revolver and the survival knife at his belt. He looked at those ships as they grew bigger and bigger. Then, having no place to go, Pyzdrowski automatically headed for his stateroom. When he got there, he saw that his locker was open and the whiskey was all gone. He took off his helmet and goggles, tossed them on the bunk and sat down to collect his wits.

Just then Lieutenant Bisbee appeared in the doorway with an opened bottle of that Scotch in his hand. "Need a drink?" he asked and offered the bottle.

Pyzdrowski took a drink and then followed Bisbee into the adjoining stateroom. There he saw a pile of VC-10 pilots, huddled beneath a huge tepee formed by stacking all the mattresses that could be collected from nearby staterooms. From the tepee came noise, the discordant sounds of drunken voices trying to harmonize. Pyzdrowski looked at his friends.

Most of the bottles were empty, and the pilots were all pie-eyed.

Just then the shell struck in the after engine room, and the ship went dead in the water in less than a minute. "Better get these guys ready to go," said Pyzdrowski.

"They'll be all right," said Bisbee.

Pyzdrowski headed for the catwalk. Two of the officers were missing. He encountered Lieutenant McClendon. "Where are Bell and Holland?" McClendon asked. "They're coming," said Pyzdrowski. Bell and Holland were outside, getting the enlisted men moving.

It was 8:45. Captain Vieweg surveyed his ship hopelessly. The steering was gone, and the power was gone even if the steering had functioned. The final blow was the shutdown of the after engine room, for that single shell had sealed the fate of the *Gambier Bay*. The ship was dead in the water, and there were no more chances. The captain ordered all classified materials thrown overboard in those weighted bags. On the port side he could see the approaching division of Japanese cruisers, now scarcely a mile away. On the starboard came a division of destroyers, and back of them the battleships. The *Gambier Bay* was being hit by shells from both sides, every few seconds. There was only one order, and he gave it.

"Abandon ship," he called. It was 8:50.

CHAPTER THIRTY

# Abandon Ship!

When Lieutenant Mallgrave reached the hangar deck from the engine room, he saw that it was covered with oil from broken lines. He heard the fire alarm bell ringing, and when a seaman came running by, he called to him.

"Why's the bell ringing?"

"Abandon ship!" shouted the seaman, and then he sped away.

Mallgrave went to the quarterdeck behind the ventilation trunk. Just then an explosion blew behind him, and he saw sparks and flame in the air. He did not even turn around to see the damage but hurried to No. 3 sponson. He inflated his life belt, and got MM2c Topczewski to help him cut loose the cargo net.

He and Topczewski climbed down the net and then had to jump four feet into the water. Behind him, the other men of the engine room did not bother with the net but jumped overboard from the sponson. Even with the ship's list it was a long jump. But the flames were right behind them.

RM3c McCollum responded, when someone said "Let's get the hell out," and he moved toward the radio shack to see what had happened to his buddies. He found a huge hole blown in the passageway to the room; there was no way for him to reach it. He fumbled his way through smoke to the side of the ship and found a life line that someone had hung over the edge and went down hand over hand, dropped into the water and began swimming.

Photographer's Mate Johnson heard the order "Abandon ship," but he heard it only once. He asked his lookout friend to call and verify the order. The talker called.

"No answer."

The phones were dead.

Johnson saw rafts being cut loose on the deck and life lines being thrown over by the gun crews. A boatswain's mate on the after 40-mm gun lined up his crew and gave the word to go over the side. The first man balked. The second man balked. Johnson stepped up. "If you guys don't want to go, by God, I'm going." And he slid down the rope at a good clip. About halfway down, he looked outboard, and saw another shell hit the water. But not only the water. As Johnson watched, a man who had just jumped was caught up in the spout that arose from the shell, and his figure was raised forty feet above the surface of the water.

Just then Johnson's feet touched the water, and he dropped in and sank like a stone. He struggled upward. Only then did he realize he was wearing his steel helmet and his shoes, and he was carrying a canvas bag loaded with film magazines over his shoulder. He shucked off the the bag and helmet and struggled to the surface. Then he inflated his life belt by blowing. It seemed to take forever.

Lieutenant Cuming heard the order and left the Combat Information Center with several of the others. They went to the adjacent catwalk and found a rope. Cuming slid down the rope, hand over hand, scraping off some skin. He was wearing a kapok life preserver, which did not have to be inflated. Just after he hit the water, he remembered the old story about the suction of a sinking ship dragging men under, so he swam rapidly away from the *Gambier Bay*. He bumped into a man and then saw that the man was dead. He felt around for identification but found none. He stripped off the dead man's kapok life jacket. Someone else could use it better.

Most were abandoning from the port side, where the heavy list made the distance to the water shorter than on the starboard, and the drop straight down. Seaman Heinl went to the starboard side, cut down a raft and dropped it into the water. He clambered down the line then, but by the time he reached the bottom he saw that the raft was filled with other men who had been swimming and was on its way. He waited for another raft to come by from the forward part of the ship and climbed aboard. He took off his shoes and helmet and threw them overboard, then joined the others to paddle away from the ship.

Chief Montgomery picked himself up from the fatal blast on the catwalk and headed back for officers' country. He met Lieutenant Bell and Lieutenant Holland in the companion way. Bell said they were getting ready to abandon ship. "Wait a minute, chief," he added, and he ducked into his stateroom. He emerged with a half-filled bottle of Scotch. "Have a drink."

They all had a drink, and Bell put the bottle carefully back in the room. Then they started toward the port railing on the bow. Montgomery went over the side and came up near Lieutenant Courtney, who was riding a mattress.

"Come on aboard," said Lieutenant Courtney, waving genially. That seemed an eminently sensible idea, so Montgomery joined him on the mattress. Bell and Holland had disappeared.

Lieutenant McClendon and Lieutenant Pyzdrowski made their way to the port rail, too. McClendon looked back. "Let's go. I'll go first and you follow me." He loosened his helmet, took one look back at the bridge, saw that it was empty, and went down the rope hand over hand. Pyzdrowski started down when McClendon was a third of the way to the bottom. The man behind Pyzdrowski slid down with his feet onto Pyzdrowski's hands and knocked his grip loose. Pyzdrowski fell on McClendon and knocked him into the water. McClendon went down, and came up sputtering. "You stupe, you," he shouted at Pyzdrowski, and then tried to get his helmet off before it dragged him down. Then he looked up. They were under the overhang of the flight deck, certainly no place to be. He turned back to Pyzdrowski. "Get as far away as you can in case she blows up." Then McClendon began to swim. He looked at his Mae West and decided not to inflate it just then. Not until he had cleared the ship. He swam on, and Pyzdrowski swam after him.

When Lieutenant Odum heard the call to abandon ship, he was on the starboard catwalk. He did not relish the idea of going off the high side so he worked around through the passageway in the center of the ship down the stairs to his room, heading for the port side. Near his stateroom he was thrown against the bulkhead by an explosion in the forward elevator machine room. Shell fragments ricocheted along the space, but he was not hit. He decided to stop at the stateroom, and there he found Lieutenant Bell, his bunkmate, who had brought Holland back after seeing Chief Montgomery. Bell was collecting survival gear: a pilot's raft, a Very pistol and dyes, a chart of the area and a compass, and several Mae West life jackets. Odum pocketed a palm-sized mirror and stuck an unopened package of cigarettes in his shirt pocket. Then he joined the others to move out. Bell remembered the bottle of whiskey. "This isn't going to do anybody else any good. So let's drink it." He took a swig and passed the bottle. All the others drank, and the "dead soldier" was tossed aside. "Good luck fellows," said Lieutenant Bell, and he led the way, carrying a mattress. The pilots and Holland followed behind, but Odum was cut off by a charging group of men from below decks who were determined to get out and get out in a hurry. By the time they had passed him, he had decided that his original idea of going out the port side was sounder, even though Bell and the others had gone back to the starboard. Odum went to the side, unlaced his shoes, dropped his helmet and his sidearm and holster, and slid down a heavy rope. The list, he estimated, was forty degrees. His shoes helped drag him under when he hit the water, and he kicked them off, and then swam away from the ship.

When Quartermaster Hagerty and his three shipmates heard the call to abandon ship, they headed for the fantail. Fires were everywhere. They could see them burning in the living spaces, but they did not have to go that way. They hurried on. Just as they began climbing the last ladder an armor-piercing shell went through the port side, not twenty feet behind them, through the tailor shop and the barber shop. When they reached the fantail, they did not hesitate, in taking the thirty-foot jump to the water. Hagerty came up and inflated his life belt immediately. He saw Quartermaster Dugan about forty feet away with a life ring. He swam over and grabbed onto it. Together they began swimming away, as far from the ship as they could get. They had swum sixty feet when a Japanese shell hit close by and forced them both under water with the effect of the explosion. They came up covered with red dye but otherwise unhurt. They were lucky: The marker shell had been the easy one. One of the three others of the salvo struck a loaded raft and blew the men apart. The others killed many swimmers with concussion, and Hagerty and Dugan saw many "swimmers" who were floating face down and not moving.

Ensign Zeola had left the drinking crowd in the middle of a song and gone to the ready room. He was there when the word came to abandon ship. The ready room talker on duty was Seaman Kopecky. Zeola watched in awe as Kopecky carefully took off his headphones, coiled them in the prescribed manner for stowing headphones, wrapped the cord around them, and stowed them in the headset receptacle, just as if he was coming back in half an hour.

Zeola watched him and then hurried out to the electric winch motor on the bow, which, in better days, had been used to hoist aircraft aboard. Zeola remembered that the last time he had been dunked he had nearly drowned because he was wearing a .45-caliber automatic, a Very pistol, two knives, and two canteens. They had kept him scrabbling around that wing tank, never able to pull himself up, until he was exhausted. This time he stopped and leisurely took off his shoes and threw them over the side. Then he took off his helmet and threw it over the side. Ensign Keith Cruse came up as Zeola was looking into the water thirty feet down.

"What are you waiting for, Leo?" asked Cruse, and he simply walked off the edge. Zeola started then jumped out over Cruse, toward the water. He hit hard, went down, and came up sputtering and swimming. He did not stop until he was exhausted. Then and only then he began to tread water and pulled the $CO_2$ cartridge on his Mae West. As it inflated, he took a moment to look around, thinking he must be half a mile from the ship. Then he looked up. There she was, right over him; he was under the catwalk. He realized then that he had gone off downwind, and with the current, and the ship had drifted right along with him, still burning as brightly as ever. Now Zeola did a nice easy breast stroke to take him back to the stern, and he watched the ship drift away from him. He had never been so glad to see the end of anything in his life.

Lt. Cdr. Elmo Waring left Air Plot with the order to abandon ship and headed for the starboard catwalk. He remembered vividly that other day, in September 1942, when the *Wasp* had gone down in the South Pacific to a Japanese torpedo, and how he had burned the fingertips on both hands in sliding down an unknotted rope with a 200-pound lieutenant who was knocked out hanging between his legs. This time he was alone, and he went down slowly, carefully, hand over hand.

In the water he soon found a raft, and on it one of the young ship's ensigns with a cigar in his mouth. The ensign smoked and led the men in songs. You would have thought they were going to an Elks picnic.

Chief Flanders was on the flight deck on the starboard side. He saw a mess attendant Lovett sitting on the edge of the deck, seemingly dazed. He looked down. The catwalk beneath had been shot away. The man must have been standing there when it happened. Flanders made sure the man's life jacket was fastened. He looked around. Most men had already left the ship. This man had to go, too, but he showed no indication of movement. Flanders pushed him over the side and then jumped. He came up near the man, who was now swimming and saying, "I can't swim" with every breath. Flanders inflated his own Mae West. It went up when the $CO_2$ bottle hissed out its gas, but then it deflated. He looked at it. A piece of shrapnel had cut a slice across the front. There he was, in the creek without a paddle. He began to swim.

Talker McCollum passed the word over all his circuits to abandon ship, then did it again, and then a third time. Not waiting for acknowledgments he did not expect, he tossed aside the headset and his helmet. The other talker, Vogan, did the same. Just then they heard a tinkling and saw that a Japanese shell had passed through the glass windshield a few feet from their heads. McCollum went down the escape hatch on the outboard side of the open bridge. He waited at the catwalk for the crowd to thin out and stopped to light a cigarette. He saw an abandoned .45 automatic on the deck, picked it up and fired two clips of cartridges at the nearest Japanese ship. He saw a kapok life jacket nearby and picked it up. He adjusted his own Mae West and grasped the line. He saw a life raft out in front of him in the water. Just then that red-dye salvo struck, and what had been a raft with ten men aboard became a bundle of wreckage with chunks of bodies oozing blood onto the sea. A shell struck the ship near him and he felt a stabbing pain in his left leg. At the same time the wind was knocked out of him by two pieces of shrapnel that struck the kapok life vest against his chest. He saw the kapok smoking and knocked a piece of red hot shrapnel out of it. Then he swung down the line and into the sea, and swam away from the ship.

Helmsman Dahlstrom heard the captain shout, "Abandon ship," and he looked around. The ladders and catwalks around the pilothouse were all blown away. He climbed down the bulkheads like a monkey. All that was in his mind was that he was walking on a bomb. Down on the flight deck he saw men he knew, dead. He headed to the hangar deck, reasoning that it would not be so long a jump. He saw sailors running in all directions shouting, "Let's get out of here. Let's go." He saw that some of them were badly hurt, and he panicked. "Help, help," he shouted, and he ran for the side. He found a rope and hurled himself down it. Just then an ammunition locker topside exploded and blew up half a dozen men. Sheets of steel were tumbling over the side all around helmsman Dahlstrom. "Here I go," he said. "This is it," and flashes of his mother and father and home raced through his head. Then he prayed that God would not let anything happen to him. He began to swim.

Lieutenant Lynch's talker on the five-inch gun heard talker McCollum give the word to abandon ship, and he passed it along. The men cut the floater net away from the side of the ship and jumped after it. All the five-inch gun crew and the magazine crew made it safely. After Lieutenant Lynch finished bandaging McMillan's arm he helped the injured man over the side, then went back to check the port side for stragglers, but found none. He returned to the starboard side just as an eight-inch shell hit the fantail. The Japanese were not a mile off now, firing at point blank range at the carrier, and hitting her every few seconds. Lynch turned the corner and found Lieutenant Edmondson lying on deck with his right leg nearly torn off. AOM1c Cain and Lynch bandaged the wound and lifted Edmondson over the life lines and threw him into the water. Cain then jumped after the lieutenant. Lynch started to take off his shoes. Just then a whole salvo hit the ship and rocked the fantail so badly it nearly threw Lynch overboard. He forgot the shoes, grabbed the rest of the first aid supplies, and jumped.

When AMM3c Potochniak heard the bell ringing on the

bridge above him, he assumed it was the abandon ship signal. Already he could see men strung out in the water behind the ship for 300 yards. He went to a life raft and pulled out his bayonet to cut the ropes. But some bright lad had also wired the life rafts—that was why so few of them were put in the water. But he was going to have a life raft, so he began hacking at the wire with his bayonet. He releasd two life rafts and part of another—the rest of it had been shot away. Then he jumped and began swimming for the rafts. By the time he reached them, they were nearly full of men. Adrift alone nearby was Robert Guelich in shock. Gripping him, Potochniak latched onto a raft and for the better part of two days and two nights the two shipmates endured.

Fred DiSipio never heard the abandon ship order. One moment he was standing on the flight deck. Then came a tremendous explosion and the next thing he knew he was in the water, forty feet from the ship. He had been hit again by shrapnel, in the head and right shoulder, but he could swim. He swan to some flotsam, which had lines attached, and began lashing together a makeshift raft. Another swimmer joined him. When he tried to climb up on the raft, DiSipio discovered that the explosion that had thrown him into the water had also blown off all his clothes but his shirt.

Seaman Quinn was serving as talker at his 20-mm gun on the port side, when suddenly the phones went dead. He never heard the order to abandon ship. He stripped off the earphones, passed the word that they were out, and ran across the flight deck to find his buddy, Bud Dickerson, who was serving on gun No. 4. All he could see at the gun was a pile of dead men. The ship was listing very badly, and he decided against trying to make it on the starboard side and ran to the fantail. He jumped, and when he came up, he saw one screw was completely out of the water. He also saw a shell hit a raft and blow one man thirty feet into the air. He swam away from the ship until he came to a life raft.

Oiler Lemirande had hidden under a plane on the hangar deck when he came up from the forward engine room. He lay there, listening to the shells come in, until suddenly one hit the plane under which he was lying and exploded. He came to in the water, and swam "straight for the Japanese fleet." Twice he was dazed by shells striking the water nearby, but he managed to maintain consciousness, and after a long time he reached a floating life net.

When the captain saw that it was all over and the ship was nearly ready to capsize, he gave the abandon ship order and then told Ensign Beisang to go to the code room and destroy the files. Vieweg said he would go to the hangar deck and be sure everyone was off the ship. Beisang followed his instructions, threading his way through the bodies of the dead. He threw the weighted bags over the side then went back to the bridge. It was empty, except for one man, the second talker, who had been dazed by a shell and was huddled in the corner. Beisang tried to push him overboard, but the man was too big. He tried to reason with him. But the man was beyond reason. He had to leave him there. Beisang then jumped to starboard, believing he would hit the water, but the list of the ship was so pronounced that he landed in the flag box, cutting his leg severely from ankle to groin. Bleeding, he lifted himself up and dived over again from the flagbox; one leg caught in a lanyard as he went over, trailing a string of signal flags behind him. When he reached the water, the Japanese ships were almost alongside, and they were aiming their six-inch guns at the bridge and pounding it mercilessly. The talker had no chance in that hail of shells.

Commander Ballinger had made sure that the men who could make it were up from below to abandon ship and then he slid over the side and found a life raft.

Captain Vieweg went from the bridge down toward the hangar deck. As he left the bridge, another salvo smashed through the superstructure. He tried to go down the interior island ladders, but when he reached the hangar deck level, the smoke became so thick he could not see. For a moment he was overcome. Then he recovered and staggered up the stairs to the flight deck and aft, to go over the starboard side. He looked back. There were no moving men left aboard the ship. She was smoking and from her interior gouts of flame occasionally burst forth. The Japanese were alongside, firing.

CHAPTER THIRTY-ONE

# In the Water

When Captain Vieweg reached the safety of a life raft, he took time to look back at the *Gambier Bay*. She was listing heavily, and a Japanese cruiser was standing just about a mile off her beam. The captain noted that the Japanese were still firing and still missing. He did not have a very high regard for the quality of Japanese gunnery. He watched as the ship shuddered, then began to move, and capsized to port. The keel came up, she rolled and settled in the water, then at 9:11 by Executive Officer Ballinger's watch, the *Gambier Bay* went to the bottom of the Philippine Trench, one of the deepest valleys of the sea. As she slid down, men on several of the lift rafts gave three cheers for the old ship. Oiler Lemirande noticed that the starboard screw had been shot off.

For months Commander Ballinger had nagged at the men of the crew to take care of their life jackets and to be sure that they were always available and always in good condition. Lemirande was one of those who paid little heed. He came to regret this inattention just a few minutes after the ship sank. He had the belt folded around his middle but had not tried to inflate the $CO_2$ bottles. Now he tried and found that the rubber was rotten and the belt was useless. If he did not succeed in hanging onto the life net, he had no chance at all.

By 9:30 that morning Captain Vieweg and Commander Ballinger had begun organizing the survivors in their areas, and other officers had followed suit. Seven separate groups of men lashed together life rafts and collected sections of flight deck planking that had been blown off the ship. The men worst off, by far, were the wounded; the salt water got into their wounds and exacerbated their suffering. A few rubber rafts had survived, and the most seriously wounded men were loaded into these, while the unhurt clung to the lifelines around the sides. The wood and metal life rafts were found to be far less efficient than they had been expected to be. They were provided with water breakers, which had been checked and refilled just two days earlier. But the spigots were knocked loose as the rafts were cut loose and fell into the sea, or the men kicked them out as they climbed in. Not one keg of fresh water was available for the men in these rafts. Nor were the rafts any good for the wounded, for the canvas lines holding the grating to the bottom gave way almost immediately, rotted out. The lines were replaced by other pieces of line, and the gratings could be replaced.

Lieutenant Mallgrave swam to a raft off the fantail and found Lieutenant Lynch and a number of men on the raft and hanging to the lifelines around it. Mallgrave was exhausted so he climbed into the raft and rested for a few minutes. Then he climbed out again and clung to a line. There were so many wounded that they needed the support of the bottom of the raft if they were to have a chance of survival. From their raft, these men watched the ship sink, then Mallgrave and Lynch began bringing all the nearby rafts together and lashing them so they would not drift apart. Their chance of survival was greatest, they knew, if they could increase the size of the group. The medicos and the officers used the first aid kits in the rafts to treat the wounded. Most valuable was the morphine to keep down pain. The bandages tended to get wet and slide off. One man, WT2c Muntz, kept groaning and vomiting that morning. Mallgrave asked what was the matter. He had been hit in the stomach, Muntz said. That was the sort of wound about which nothing could be done, even if the tale were true. All Mallgrave could see were superficial wounds in the man's hand, but Muntz kept falling off the raft and had to be rescued several times. Finally Mallgrave examined him and found no evidence of a wound. But in the afternoon suddenly he looked at Muntz, and he was dead.

By this time Mallgrave's raft had joined the group under

Commander Ballinger. The executive officer looked Muntz over, pronounced him dead, and they buried him at sea.

MM3c Cowles was one of the wounded who suffered most. His arm had been nearly severed at the bicep. They put a tourniquet on the arm, but it kept slipping and he lost more and more blood. That afternoon Cowles died.

Commander Ballinger was everywhere. He swam out twice to bring lone survivors to the rafts. Ensign Barrows helped him go to get a lone survivor in a rubber raft. "Tuffy" Barrows, one of the pilots who did not get off this last day, was the strongest swimmer in the group. Ensign Zeola was also on that raft, and in his way he made a sort of game of saving men. He and Lynch and others would spot a head bobbing somewhere in the sea. "Okay, Tuffy, go get him," they would call, and Ensign Barrows would swim to the man and bring him back to the raft cluster.

One of those saved was S2c Earl Fetkenhier, who had been hit in the legs. One foot was hanging in shreds, so they put him in the one-man raft and kept him doped with morphine. They tried to stanch the flow of blood and managed at least to keep it down enough that he did not die. They tried to bring all the wounded aboard rafts for two reasons: to preserve the men as much as possible from exposure, and to keep them from bleeding in the water. For of all things, they feared sharks as much as any other danger.

One of the rafts in this group was captained by Commander Borries. After Chaplain Carlsen abandoned ship, he found himself aboard this raft.

"Why don't you take off your glasses, Padre?" Borries asked as he helped the chaplain into the raft.

"No, I'll keep them on. I'm so nearsighted I can't see a thing without them."

Borries chuckled. "You'll see just as well without these. The lenses are gone."

After Lieutenant McClendon and Lieutenant Pyzdrowski began swimming away from the ship to avoid the suction, they became separated. McClendon found himself in the Borries group, that joined the Lynch-Mallgrave raft and then come up with Commander Ballinger.

Pyzdrowski did not arrive for several hours; his group was picked up by Ballinger around noon.

Seaman DiSipio found himself with a group of eighteen other men, on a collection of rafts and flotsam. Somehow they were in a current that pulled them away from the others, and in a few hours they were alone. A Japanese destroyer came by, and they flinched, expecting to be strafed in the water. But the Japanese sailors lined the rails and took pictures of them, then the destroyer speeded up and was soon out of sight.

The other groups tried to draw closer together. They did not seem to be so seriously affected by the current, and the captain collected all the rafts he could find and moved to join forces with Commander Ballinger. Both groups were in view of a large *Kongo*-class battleship (they thought) which seemed to be dead in the water. A destroyer remained nearby. Finally, the big ship began to move. As the men in the water watched, TBMs and fighters arrived to attack the enemy. From his position, Potochniak watched as several TBMs launched a glide bombing attack that damaged the ship. Then one TBM was hit and mushroomed in flame. No one got out as it crashed into the sea near the Japanese ships. The cruiser stayed in the area apparently adrift, until dark.

Lieutenant Odum swam to a raft where he found thirty men. The senior officer present was Lt. Robert Foley. Lt. Sid Kimball, Odum's roommate, was also aboard, and so was Chief Boatswain's Mate Charles Polansky. Ten of the men were in the raft, and the rest were hanging around the edges. This group was close enough to the aerial action so that spent shells and bullets from strafing planes spattered around their position, as Odum came up to join. He reported to Foley and asked if there was anything he could do to help.

"Yes," said Foley. "You must take command. I'm not going to make it."

Odum could see nothing indicating any injuries, and he asked again. "Are you hurt?"

"I was trapped below," Foley said, and then he seemed suddenly to let go. His voice dribbled off into a mumble, and he sank into a stupor.

Odum took over. He moved all the uninjured men off the raft, leaving seven men aboard the rectangular ring which was four feet by six feet inside, atop the wooden latticework. He and the other uninjured men hung on the ropes outside. Soon enough, as he took stock, he realized that water was going to be a problem. The bungs of the water barrels had come out. No water. The raft contained only one cansiter of rations: three pounds of malted milk tablets. His personal stores consisted of his wristwatch (which continued to run), his billfold, which would identify him in case the worst happened; his cigarette lighter which would not work, a white handkerchief, a small pen knife, the palm-sized mirror he had picked up at his bunk, and an eight-inch, navy-issue knife in a sheath at his belt. The cigarettes he had picked up at the bunk had turned into a sodden mass. He had no head cover and he was still wearing his white socks, having kicked off his shoes. He was also covered with oil and dye from the marker shells. His condition was more or less like that of every man in the water.

The raft continued to be a disappointment as he, Kimball, and Polansky explored. It had an eight-foot tarpaulin, and one four-foot oar. But the Very pistols and flares which were supposed to be attached to every raft had disappeared. There were no long lines, but many short pieces. That was all.

Someone asked Odum what he thought of their prospects of being picked up.

"It's not a question of will we be, but when," he said. He explained that Task Force 74 would not send planes or ships out while the battle continued. There in the water ahead of them they saw the Japanese cruiser and destroyer. Until those ships had been dealt with, or moved away, they would simply have to wait. He expected to be picked up by a destroyer that evening, he said. They settled down to wait.

The battle was still very much in progress as the men of the *Gambier Bay* floated in the sea off Samar Island. *Kumano,* the flagship of the Japanese fleet, was hit by a torpedo forward early in the action. The cruisers *Suzuya, Tone, Chikuma, Chokai,* and *Haguro* were all hurt. At just about the moment that the *Gambier Bay* was sinking, Admiral Kurita had word of another force of six "fleet carriers" to the southeast (Taffy 2). How many carriers did the Americans have, and where were their battleships? These questions so disturbed Admiral Kurita that he ordered two float planes to go out and discover the disposition of the Americans. Both float planes were shot down by the fighters of the escort carriers, so he had no information at all. Then, as the *Tone* and *Haguro* closed in on the other ships of Taffy 3, one of the destroyers fired a spread of torpedoes at *Yamato,* the fleet flagship. To evade them, the *Yamato* turned about and ran seven miles from the battle before her captain was sure he was safe. Admiral Kurita then was miles from the battle, in spotty weather that allowed no accurate visual observation, with bad radar, bad radio communications because of the weather, and no spotter planes in the air. At the very beginning of the battle, when Admiral Sprague had learned that the Japanese were bearing down on him with battleships and cruisers, he had violated security: He had sent a frantic message in the clear by voice radio to Admiral Kinkaid calling for help. That message had been intercepted by Admiral Kurita's radio, and the admiral had been informed. Obviously there must be a large American force nearby. But where? And what were its components? This information worried Kurita, who was also an imaginative man. What if the Americans were tricking him? Given all these considerations, confusions, and Kurita's distaste for the entire mission, he made the decision to turn around. The combination of the heroic attack of the destroyers and destroyer escorts of Taffy 3, the beelike persistence of the planes of all the escort carriers, and the "breach of security" had saved all but one of the escort carrier fleet. For the second time in twenty-four hours, Admiral Kurita had turned back, and this time at a crucial moment.

The cruiser that the men of the *Gambier Bay* saw near them, either barely moving or dead in the water, was *Chokai*. A destroyer circled around her for several hours, and finally took off the crew, and she was abandoned before nightfall.

In that retreat just after the *Gambier Bay* was sunk, Pyzdrowski saw one of the other cruisers (*Tone* or *Haguro*) come by the raft group. The men feared that they were going to be used for "target practice," but instead they heard a signal given (they were that close by), and the men at the rail snapped to attention as the cruiser slid by. Admiral Ugaki, Kurita's chief of staff, commented very favorably on the unexpected bravery he witnessed in the behavior of his enemies:

"Sighted scattered patches of water colored by dye-loaded shells and a considerably larger area of darkish red water (probably colored by the fuel tanks of the *Gambier Bay*). Immediately beyond the latter were enemy survivors, some clinging to damaged cutters and some just drifting. I wonder what these survivors thought on seeing our fleet

. . . ? Even though they were in need of help they gave no indication of it when they saw who we were. . . ."

As the Japanese began to retire, American fighters and bombers came back into the area and began attacking the cruisers and destroyers as they headed north. These were the attacks witnessed from the water by Lieutenant Odum and other survivors of the *Gambier Bay.* "The enemy survivors who witnessed these attacks from afar must have given three cheers," said Admiral Ugaki. How right he was. The sight of the planes harassing their enemies was the only happy aspect of the plight of the men of the *Gambier Bay* that day. Among those planes were their own. Commander Huxtable had been unable to secure any bombs at Dulag, so he did not get back in the fight that day. But Lieutenant Stewart had found gas and ammunition at Tacloban, and he organized the fighter component of the squadron and kept four planes in the air most of the rest of the day. In the next three days they fought the Japanese in the air, and Stewart shot down one enemy fighter, and assisted in the destruction of another that was attacking a ship in Leyte Gulf. Ensign Turner's fighter was forced down at sea.

Ensign Bennett and Lieutenant (jg) McGraw had not followed Stewart to Tacloban. They had landed on the USS *Manila Bay,* seeking gas and ammunition. At 11:15 they joined five *Manila Bay* fighters and ten TBMs in a search for Kurita's force. They passed over the *Chokai,* dead in the water, with her destroyer circling, and over the survivors of the *Gambier Bay,* and never saw them. They found the Japanese off Samar, heading almost due north, away from the battle. Ensign Bennett joined in the attack on a cruiser with his TBM, loaded with bombs. He started his glide at 8,000 feet, and "jinked" in to avoid the heavy anti-aircraft fire. He dropped the bombs, and his crewmen reported three hits on the stern of the cruiser and one near miss. He returned to the carrier group and landed aboard the *Fanshaw Bay* at 1:30 in the afternoon.

McGraw joined that same force, led by Commander Fowler, the squadron leader of VC-5. McGraw dived on a battleship and strafed, and he saw Fowler's bombs hit the battleship amidships. McGraw then strafed a cruiser and a destroyer before he ran out of ammunition. On his way back to the *Manila Bay,* he passed over the *Chokai* and he also saw a pilot in the water in his life raft. But he completely missed the survivors of the *Gambier Bay.*

McGraw landed aboard the *Manila Bay* at 2:15. He was debriefed by the ship's air intelligence officer and reported the downed pilot and his own adventures. He was back in the air at 3 o'clock, this time as section leader of an eight-plane flight on combat air patrol. The Japanese had begun their air support of the SHO plan that morning. By mid-morning many Japanese airplanes had begun to appear in the Leyte area. This time something new had been added. Admiral Ohnishi, the commander of the Philippine defense, had decided that desperate means were all that were left to him, and he had organized the first of the kamikaze units. At 7:25 that morning, as the *Gambier Bay* was maneuvering desperately to avoid the Japanese battle force, the Shikishima unit of the new kamikaze corps took off at Mabalacat looking for the enemy. The force consisted of five kamikaze suicide divers, escorted by four Zero fighters, whose pilots were honor-bound to remain above the attackers, protect them, and then return to base to report on their successes.

As the Japanese planes had neared Leyte, Admiral Kuritas' cruisers and battleships were scoring hits on several of the escort carriers. The *Kalinin Bay* was hit repeatedly and could not land her planes. The *Fanshaw Bay* was hit by fire from two cruisers and several Japanese destroyers. The *Kitkun Bay* was damaged by one near miss. When Lt. James Murphy of the *Kalinin Bay* needed to land to refuel, he found haven on the *St. Lo,* another of the carriers of Taffy 3.

He landed at 10:40. Ten minutes later the planes of the Shikishima kamikaze unit found the *St. Lo,* and Lt. Yuko Seki made history by diving onto the flight deck of the *St. Lo* in a Zero fighter armed with two bombs under the wings. In less than an hour the *St. Lo* had been abandoned and sank. Earlier that morning, the *Santee* had been hit by a crash diving plane, or one that fell on her. The *Petrof Bay* was damaged by a near miss. The *Suwannee* was hit that day, too, but in a short time was again taking planes aboard. Before the day was over the *White Plains* was damaged by a near miss, and the *Kitkun Bay* and *Kalinin Bay* were both hit again by kamikazes. So by 3 o'clock that afternoon it was no wonder that McGraw was flying combat patrol instead of striking on the Japanese force. About an hour and fifteen minutes out, McGraw and his flight spotted eighteen Val bombers with an escort of a dozen Zero fighters. They attacked, McGraw shot down one fighter, and his wingman shot down another. He shot down one bomber. Then he ran into a flight of six planes, and when they turned out to be Zeros, he decided on discretion and went back to the carrier.

That evening a Japanese submarine attacked the force, and very nearly sank the *Petrof Bay*, although she emerged safe. All this activity made it quite certain that Lieutenant Odum's prediction would be correct. As the sun began to drop in the sky above the survivors off Samar, they were wondering just how long it would be before the ships or planes came out to get them.

The truth was that on this busy day, threatened by enormous force and an entirely new weapon, Carrier Division 26, Taffy 3, and Task Group 77.4 had no time to give to thoughts of rescue, and no one at Task Force 77 had apparently thought about it either. In a few hours, the Kurita force and the kamikazes and submarines had inflicted more damage on the American naval forces than the Japanese had managed since the Formosa battle, which after all was part of the SHO plan. The plan would not succeed—it could not—but in the execution the Americans were put to straining every resource to destroy their enemy and protect their ships. The men in the water would have to wait.

## CHAPTER THIRTY-TWO

# The Rescue

The *Gambier Bay* had sunk at 11° 31′ north latitude, 126° 12′ east longitude, which was about sixty miles east of the island of Samar and ninety miles north of San Pedro Bay in Leyte Gulf, on the island of Leyte. The general drift of the current was westward toward Samar. The sinking was observed by other ships of Taffy 3, and reported by Admiral Clifton Sprague, commander of the unit, to Admiral Kinkaid down in Leyte Gulf with a request that rescue operations begin immediately. That message, however, was but one of scores transmitted in the morning hours of October 25; others told of the sinkings of the destroyers and the escort and of the destruction of the *St. Lo* and the attacks on the other carriers. So much information produced confusion.

At noon one passing airplane did see several hundred survivors in the water, and the pilot returned to report to Admiral Felix Stump aboard the *Natoma Bay*. But as was not unusual for carrier pilots, his navigation was a little off, and he placed the survivors in position thirty miles south of their actual location. Due to error in transmission, when the word was finally given to begin search at 3:30 in the afternoon, the error was compounded. The USS *Richard S. Bull* and the USS *Eversole* were ordered by Admiral Thomas Sprague to search at another spot just as far away. They found nothing.

Meanwhile the men of the *Gambier Bay* (and those of

the *Johnston, Hoel,* and *Samuel B. Roberts*), waited hopefully for the rescue they were sure would come in a matter of hours.

AMM3c Potochniak was with a small group. Pharmacist's Mate Horace Phillips was with them, too. He had a shell casing strapped to his shoulder, and in it he carried medical supplies. He swam from raft to raft, giving first aid to those who needed it. The men wondered when they would be rescued. Toward dusk they began to pray that they *would* be rescued. After dark, the last Japanese destroyer parted from the *Chokai,* and shortly afterwards she went down with a single underwater explosion. Potochniak felt it as a blast of cold water against his hindquarters. The destroyer flashed its lights in Morse code, and then moved away. As the ship came near on its way north, Potochniak looked for his pistol. He found it, the barrel dripping water.

Oiler Lemirande was growing tired as night fell. His useless life jacket was a drag. He was about to throw it away, when he realized he could at least use it as a lifeline. He passed it through a loop of rope in the life net and tied it around his waist. It would keep him from floating away from the others. As night come down, he began to see things that were not there.

Chief Montgomery had joined a group of men who were spreading a floating life net. It was a difficult job because there were not enough of them at the beginning. Lieutenant Commander Houlihan was in charge, and Montgomery swam around the perimeter to try to spread the net. He saw a man in white, apparently a mess cook or baker. The man was not helping so he nudged him. The man was dead. Chief Montgomery took his ID cards and gave them to Houlihan.

Montgomery's group had a fine view of the aerial activity above. Each time a flight of planes came over, they cheered and pointed. "They went that away," they shouted. They were expecting rescue hourly. As darkness came, it was broken by the glow from the burning cruiser *Chokai,* and then they saw the light go out and heard the explosions under water. It grew colder in the water. They tied themselves together with the strings on their life jackets. One of the men, Ship's Cook Leonard Martin, had a large piece of shrapnel sticking out of his back. Someone went to pull it out, but one of the ship's surgeons was in the group and he stopped the man. If they pulled it loose, Martin might bleed to death. Montgomery and others took turns holding Martin's head above water and comforting him during the night. The life net did not let anyone dry out, in the center a man resting on the net would be waist deep in water. At the edges it was shallower. They were cold and constantly drenched with salt water.

Most of the men found themselves in groups where they knew at least a few of the others. Lieutenant Cuming found himself on the edge of a raft with a group of men he could never remember seeing before. The life of an officer in the Combat Information Center was a restricted one; these were men from below decks. He clung to the lifeline as did the other able-bodied men. The injured and those who were out of their heads were kept on the raft.

Chief Flanders counted thirty-seven men in his group. He did not have a life preserver nor did they have a raft, but they kept together, and he supported himself on a piece of a blown-up, doughnut-type raft. The able supported the wounded, but as night fell, the badly wounded began to die. One man from N Division had his leg shot off at the knee. When he died, Chief Flanders took his life preserver, and the body was pushed away into the sea.

Helmsman Dahlstrom was a long time in recovering from his sense of panic. He believed he could see sharks right under him as he swam away from the ship, and then he was alone. It seemed that he was by himself for hours, with only his life belt to sustain him. Then, as darkness fell, he saw a raft. He shouted.

"Is that you, Birger?" said a voice. Aboard the raft was his friend Floyd Green; they had been together since the commissioning of the ship. Green and others pulled Dahlstrom aboard the raft, and he felt that he was saved.

With Captain Vieweg's group, which joined the Ballinger group just before dusk, 140 men were together. Around 750 men had escaped the ship by sea. Fifty-one pilots and air crew members had flown off the ship in the morning, and nearly 200 men had gone down with the ship, most of them killed by the Japanese shelling. In all groups, the wounded began to die, and in the Ballinger-Vieweg group the wounded and the dead were dragging the rafts down, so in the evening Ballinger gave orders that the dead were to be cast adrift. It was done, and then it was not long before the sharks came.

At first some men said they felt some sort of fish brushing their legs. But there were no attacks. Captain Vieweg ordered the rafts strung out in a column, to slow the drift and to increase the chances of discovery. He sent Ensign Zeola into the lead raft to keep the men busy (he tried to put an officer in every raft), and Zeola tried every means he knew to keep spirits up. He swam back to the captain's raft and asked how long he thought they would have to keep this up. The captain encouraged him and sent him back. He was swimming slowly alongside the string, toward the lead raft when he passed a raft occupied by a young enlisted man who had a piece of canvas over his head.

"Mr. Zeola," said the man, "you'd better hurry."

"Why's that?" demanded Zeola.

"Because there's a big shark behind you."

Zeola had been very tired, but this announcement sent him into immediate action. He thrashed his way up onto a floater net and sat there, shaking for five minutes. Then the shark was gone, and he went back to his number one raft to try to keep up morale.

That night the men had a meal. It consisted of one biscuit about the size of a Ritz cracker, with a piece of Spam aboard. Seaman Heinl ate and vomited. The absence of fresh water was beginning to get to him.

That night some of the wounded and some who were not wounded simply drifted away and were not seen again. One man drifted off but was brought back by the blowing of a whistle to attract him.

At dawn hope returned again. Surely they would be rescued. They looked around the horizon. Nothing. The night before, as they dozed in their nets and on their rafts, destroyer escorts *Bull* and *Eversole* reached the false position and combed it for four hours. Then they had a new report and went dashing off in another wrong direction.

For some reason, the entire command of the Seventh Fleet had fouled up the search. Perhaps Adm. Thomas Sprague was too much concerned with the state of his other carriers to worry about the problem. Perhaps Admiral Kinkaid was too bemused by the attack and the kamikazes, and his anger at Admiral Halsey for leaving San Bernardino Strait uncovered and not telling him. But the fact was that the Seventh Fleet had a perfectly adequate air-search system, and it simply was not put into effect. No aircraft were sent out that first day to find the survivors and direct ships to them. The first serious attempt to find the men was ordered by Rear Adm. Daniel E. Barbey, who had no basic responsibility for the men of the *Gambier Bay*. He formed Task Group 78.12, consisting of two patrol craft (PC 623 and PC 1119) and five LCI gunboats under Lt. Cdr. J. A. Baxter. He sent a surgeon Lt. D. B. Lucas, from his own flagship the *Blue Ridge* and two pharmacists' mates. But they had orders on such short notice that they had to fuel before leaving on the search, so they did not get under way from San Pedro Bay until 6:30 on the night of October 25, and then they could make only ten knots which meant nearly ten hours to reach the point ninety miles north where the ship was supposed to have gone down.

Lieutenant Buderus, one of the CIC officers who had escaped just before the ship went down, had been injured and was bleeding from several wounds. He was told to stay on a raft but as morning came, Buderus felt he should take his turn in the water and he came down. Captain Vieweg and Commander Ballinger ordered the rations opened again, and this morning the men had a malted milk tablet and another bite of biscuit. Some could not swallow because their throats were so dry. Buderus was in the water when he got his rations, and he ate them. He was around the corner of the raft from Yeoman Hammond, and Hammond could see his white skivvy shorts. Buderus suddenly let out a yell.

"A big fish," he shouted.

Then he started screaming. The men in the raft above grabbed him and pulled him in. He was bleeding badly, and his entire buttocks had been ripped off. He had bad bites on his back and legs. He was half unconscious. There was nothing that could be done for him. The damage was too severe to remedy. He lingered for a few hours, then he died.

Looking down, Yeoman Hammond saw the huge shark that had attacked Buderus, lurking under the raft. Then sharks began to appear all around the rafts. The men beat the water with hands and paddles and drove them away. But not far away. Still, one man was badly bitten on the left hand even while he was beating to frighten away a shark. That morning a prayer was said for Lieutenant Buderus and he was consigned to the sea. Chaplain Carlsen was at his best in these hours. He led prayers several times, and there were few, if any, who did not join in them wholeheartedly.

On the second day thirst became the problem. On Hammond's raft a radioman decided all he had heard about sea water was untrue and deliberately drank a large quantity. At first he announced it was delicious, but within an hour he began to suffer and became delirious. Heinl drank sea water, too, but for some reason did not seem to suffer any ill effects from it. On DiSipio's raft a number of men decided to drink. Two of them soon began fighting. Two others said they were going to get some beer, and they dove into the sea and did not reappear. Two others said they were going to swim to islands they could see clearly a few miles away. They, too, disappeared.

Oiler Lemirande must have swallowed a good deal of sea water at some point, for on the second day he became delirious and had to be taken into the life net and watched.

In Montgomery's group, he and several other petty officers tried to police their area to prevent men from drinking sea water. Ship's Cook Martin became delirious from his wounds and died that second day. Montgomery was holding Martin as he died. He had little time for contemplation of the grisly event, however, for almost immediately he had to swim around the raft. Two of his ninety charges announced that they were going to the bar around the corner for a drink and began swimming. Montgomery caught them as they were ducking to drink sea water and forcibly restrained them until their temporary fit ceased. Everyone seemed to go out of his head from time to time. Montgomery had the same feelings; his training kept him from drinking sea water, but he saw mirages at these times, of cool mountains with sparkling streams coursing down, and green trees, and once a fleet of rescue ships that did not exist. At one point a man began pounding on Montgomery's head, berating the chief for sneaking in ahead of him in the chow line. Toward midday Montgomery spotted something on the horizon, and swam out to see what it was. (His horizon was not far away.) He and another man found Chief Storekeeper McArdle towing two wounded men who were supported by life jackets. One was Forrest Kohrt and the other was Hillard Dennard, both of them from VC-10. McArdle had a water breaker full of fresh water! They brought the wounded men in and rigged a drinking hose from one of the Mae West inflation hoses to a spigot on the breaker. A second-class storekeeper was given custody of the water and some provisions

McArdle had carried. The wounded were served first, but every man got a small drink of water and a malted milk tablet for lunch.

On the first day the weather had been a plus factor for the men in the water. The clouds kept the sun away, and several times it rained so that many men were able to get at least a little water. But on the second day the sun came out, bright, clear, and hot. By noon nearly all of the men suffered from sunburn. In Montgomery's group they were eased a little when they found a drum of oil floating nearby, and they all smeared their faces but by then it was a bit late. They were already badly burned. That day Montgomery's life jacket began to give out. One of the ship's warrant officers, Gunner Hughes, had found a gangway post and was clinging to that. He offered half of it to Montgomery, who joined him gratefully. It meant locking one arm around the post to support himself, and then, after an hour, changing arms. A bit tiresome to the arm, Montgomery said later, but it was surprising what a man could stand when his life was in jeopardy.

Early on the morning of October 26, Lieutenant Commander Waring and Slc Orville Propes decided they would try to go for help. The captain and Commander Ballinger agreed to the mission, although they had no confidence that the pair would reach Samar as they proposed to do. The two took a one-man life raft, and set out. Soon they came upon another life raft with a single man in it, dead. They hitched the raft to theirs and continued paddling; it was a measure of their befuddlement that they believed that somehow they could take the dead man with them and that when they got to shore they could identify him so they could inform his mother! Soon they were out of sight of the others. By afternoon the trailing raft was half sunk, and sharks were attacking the dead body. They continued paddling for a while, then realized that they were carrying shark bait, and cut the other raft loose. The sharks began to surround their raft, but they slashed at them with their paddles, and eventually the big fish swam away and left them.

Back in the captain's group, Leo Zeola developed a laughing jag. He swam to the head of the rafts again and tied a rope around his chest and began chanting, "Heave ho, heave ho." He soon had the men believing that by paddling they were moving closer to land. On the second day they could see the mountains of Samar and this was no mirage. But they were still many miles from safety, and the current was taking them very slowly.

In the afternoon they saw planes, overhead, and Captain Vieweg fired the Very pistol, but a red flare in bright sunlight was hardly likely to attract much attention, and the planes flew by without showing any signs of recognition.

AMM3c Potochniak's group also saw the planes and later a PBY Catalina flying boat. They flashed mirrors and fired a flare, but there was no response.

Early on the morning of October 26, Admiral Barbey's rescue ships reached the point where survivors reportedly had been seen by the airplanes on the day of the sinking. It was actually thirty miles south of the point where the *Gambier Bay* went down. They combed the area, but, of course, found nothing. The *Bull* and *Eversole* continued to charge about until the evening of October 26. They were never informed of the existence of Barbey's rescue force. Finally they were recalled to strengthen the destroyer screen.

In mid-morning, Lt. Cdr. R. E. Sargent suggested that all the reports they had received had been false and they must move further north. By noon the rescue group had reached a point eighteen miles northeast of the spot where the *Gambier Bay* had gone down, and they knew they had gone too far. They observed the current moving toward Samar, and they began working south and west. At 3 o'clock that afternoon they spotted a survivor and hurried to pick him up hoping he could lead them to the rest of the group. But the man was a Japanese pilot whose plane had been shot down, and he knew nothing about the *Gambier Bay*. They took him aboard.

Around noon, Odum's group made contact with the Borries group. That day several of the groups drifted close together as they were carried by the current toward Samar. It became increasingly apparent that they would be taken to the island in time. They were about thirty-five miles off Samar at noon. They looked forward to the landing with mixed emotions for the Japanese were still in control of Samar. But nearly all of them agreed that even the prospects of prison camp were preferable to drowning, or death from thirst. By the afternoon of October 26, the degree of faith in Admiral Kinkaid's rescue efforts was greatly reduced. There was more talk about the prospects of landing. That night, Odum and Chief Polansky decided to swim over to join Borrie's group. They wanted to confer about the prospects since the smell of land was in their nostrils. Odum bumped into a large fish, he never discovered what sort it was. In those waters it might have been a dolphin or a shark. When he reached the group, Odum told Borries that his men had no water and little food and that they were in desperate condition. So were the others, said Borries, so were they all. Odum wanted one of Borries's rafts. Borries had nothing to give him and told him so. Odum then began talking about returning to his own group.

"Commander, if I have your final word about having nothing to help my men with, I must take my leave and return to them."

This dramatic announcement did not have the desired effect.

"Ronnie," said Borries, "go over there to the raft and rest."

Odum went.

The night had brought its terrors. Lieutenant Bell had apparently drunk some sea water, for he weakened and began hallucinating. He decided he would swim to Samar, and he set out. Someone went after him and brought him back. He did it again. Once more someone brought him back. The third time, Lieutenant Bell managed to slip away without being noticed. He did not come back.

Except for a handful of men, most of the survivors had given up hope of rescue. Chaplain Carlsen had removed the silver crosses from his shirt lapels. He was anticipating their landing on the beach at Samar and capture by the Japanese. He had heard a rumor that the Japanese always killed the chaplains first, so he was taking no chances.

But Commander Borries did not share the general feeling of resignation that seemed to have seized the men. He was busy that night with his flares and Very gun. He had told Odum to wait and they would be rescued. He believed it. Every hour he sent up a flare.

At 10:30 that night he sent up another, and this one was spotted by Admiral Barbey's rescue group, who had reached a point in their combing twenty miles east of the survivors. PC 623 was detached from the formation and sent ahead to check out the flares. She came swiftly, but cautiously, for the lights might be a Japanese trap. At around one o'clock on the morning of October 27, PC 623 came up on the rafts.

"Ahoy, the raft," was the call. "What ship are you from?"

No one answered. What if these were Japanese rescuers?

Suddenly the patrol boat's huge searchlight was snapped on, and it began probing the rafts.

"Are you American?"

The answer came loud and clear from a hundred throats.

"Yes. Yes. We're Americans. *Gambier Bay!*" They could see the outline of the vessel against the moonlight and the big numbers 623 painted against the gray hull at the bow.

The patrol boat slowed and sailors began lowering nets over the side for the men to climb. The able began to swim toward the boat. Lieutenant Odum, one of the first to start swimming, was overrun and nearly drowned by his fellows as the boat pulled in toward the rafts and dozens of men began climbing over him as he clung to the net. Finally he was freed and made his way hand over hand to the deck. Sprawled face down on that cold steel, he wept and thanked God for his deliverance. His was an emotion shared by every one of the survivors of the *Gambier Bay*.

## CHAPTER THIRTY-THREE

# The Survivors

Admiral Barbey's rescue team spent the next ten hours picking up survivors. Some of the men, like Odum, were nearly drowned in the rush. Lieutenant Patterson and a chief were hanging onto the lines of a small raft that was completely filled with wounded and injured men. They crawled onto the raft and used their single paddle to move toward the patrol boat, following instructions from its bullhorn to head for the starboard ladder where there was a small landing platform. They got to within twenty feet of the boat, and the chief shouted, "Hallelujah!" and threw the paddle over his shoulder and swam for the ship. Without the paddle the raft drifted to the side of the ship near the stern, and then away. Patterson and his crew of wounded were not picked up for another two hours.

The rescued men were treated like kings. They soon had water and food and sleep. When they awakened they were fed and slept again. The wounded were treated by the medics and the doctors, and some amputations were performed aboard ship in a matter of hours. Lieutenant Odum discovered, as he pulled himself up the netting, that his lower body was paralyzed, but this wore off in a few hours. Oiler Lemirande had not recovered consciousness all during the last day of the ordeal. He came to aboard a rescue ship, with someone feeding him water from a teaspoon. Lieutenant Pyzdrowski nearly drowned when some-on stepped on his head as he began climbing the net. A sailor grabbed him and lifted him up to the deck.

"Do you need any help to walk?"

"No, thank you," said Pyzdrowski. He took a step and fell flat on his face. When Pyzdrowski came to in a bunk bed, it was twelve hours later.

At 10 o'clock on the morning of October 27, Commander Baxter decided that all the survivors in the area had been rescued, and set the course of the little fleet for San Pedro Bay on Leyte. The squadron had 1,150 survivors aboard the half dozen ships. But Baxter was wrong. Several groups of the *Gambier Bay* survivors had not been rescued, and the same must have been true of survivors of the *Hoel, Johnston,* and *Samuel B. Roberts.* Seaman DiSipio's group was still out there. On the night of October 27, several men died, including DiSipio's friend Jim Henderson. This group was finally rescued, by a PT boat, after seventy-two hours in the water.

By this time, Admiral Barbey's rescue group had reached port after several adventures. Around noon on that first day, a single Japanese aircraft had swooped down on the formation, looking them over. When the pilot saw decks crowded with survivors, he refrained from attack and flew away. It was a narrow escape, however, because Olaf Emblem and Potochniak had decided to help the crew out, and without orders they were training a .50-caliber machine-gun on the plane and tracking, ready to shoot. The gunnery officer of the LCI came rushing up and put a stop to that. He chewed them out; if they were so stupid as to fire that popgun at the plane, the whole formation might be bombed within an hour. The Japanese plane was just looking them over. He was not interested in cripples or survivors, but in bigger game. Now, if the brave sailors would just relax . . .

Potochniak and Emblem were first furious and then confused. What a way to fight a war, they told one another. Only later did they realize what enormous courage the men of the rescue force were showing in the entire operation, entering Japanese waters without protection and sailing in broad daylight in areas still under Japanese control.

Two hours later two more Japanese planes flew over the formation. These planes stayed around for several minutes as if deciding what to do. But in the end, they too flew away. By this time Commander Baxter was growing a bit nervous, so he put in a request by radio for air coverage to Admiral Barbey. But the request somehow got lost for no planes ever appeared.

As soon as Captain Vieweg and Commander Ballinger had regained strength, they began their first mournful task: assessment of the casualties their ship and the squadron had suffered. It would be many days before this task was completed. Commander Ballinger finally arrived at a figure of only twenty-three known dead, but a hundred missing. But the fact was that of the 950 men who remained on the ship after the squadron's planes had flown off, fewer than 800 had abandoned ship, and when the rescue was made, only about 700 men were rescued. Of these, nearly 150 were injured or wounded more or less seriously, and some later died of their wounds. That so many survived was in large part due to the heroic efforts of the men of Barbey's rescue group. Because not even the rescue group found all the men, the statistics concerning the survivors were a long time in preparation.

At midnight on October 27, the ships of the little flotilla approached Leyte and shortly after one o'clock in the morning they entered San Pedro Bay and the survivors were taken off, either to go aboard hospital ships or transports, for movement toward the United States.

Lieutenant Odum was sent aboard an LST with 115 men for transfer to Hollandia, where they would get a ship for the U.S. Their voyage was pleasant enough until they passed through a typhoon. When that unwelcome adventure ended, Lieutenant Odum occupied his time in taking statements from survivors about what they remembered, so that Captain Vieweg could write his action report as accurately as possible. Captain Vieweg rode south on the destroyer *Shaw*, working all the way. When they reached Hollandia, they found the big liner *Lurline* in the harbor to where it had been re-routed on direct orders of General MacArthur. Most of the survivors boarded her, and she sailed for Brisbane where they spent two days, before heading to San Francisco.

Within a matter of hours the news of the battle reached America and the story of the *Gambier Bay* was on the front pages of every newspaper in the land. Then, when the survivors appeared at Leyte, they were interviewed and more tales appeared in the press

* * *

Louise Bassett was living at her parents' home in Madison, Florida, at the time. She was pregnant and under the care of a doctor in Thomasville, Georgia, where she planned to have the baby. Late in October she went to Thomasville to stay with her cousin, in case the baby came early. She lived then very close to Flonnie Bell and saw her nearly every day.

Then, on the day of the battle, came the first fragmentary news that a tremendous sea fight had occurred off the Philippines and that several destroyers and an escort carrier had been sunk. Then came the news that it was the *Gambier Bay,* and nothing from Lieutenant Bassett or Lieutenant Bell. Finally, Louise Bassett received a strange letter written with pencil on tablet paper saying only that her husband was all right. Flonnie Bell was not so lucky. She had one of those telegrams from the Navy Department: "We regret to inform you. . . ." But it said missing. When Lieutenant Bassett (who had flown off the *Gambier Bay* that morning) called from Hawaii, he did not know that Vereen Bell was dead, so he gave them new hope. But by the time Lieutenant Bassett came home, he had found the other survivors, and knew the whole story. There was no hope.

The planes of VC-10 had continued to fight in the Battle of Leyte Gulf (as it came to be known to historians). Admiral Kurita hesitated, then turned back toward Leyte, but decided that the air attacks were too heavy. That day of the sinking of the *Gambier Bay* he learned of the destruction of Admiral Shima's force and of Admiral Nishimura's force, and he decided the SHO plan had no chance of success. Not being suicidal by nature, Kurita decided to go home, and headed back for the San Bernardino Strait. All the way he was harried by American planes and lost most of his force before he arrived back in Brunei Bay. In the north, Admiral Halsey caught up with Admiral Ozawa's decoy force and blasted it, putting an end to Japan's carrier power. By October 29, the last great naval battle of World War II was over. The ships that had sunk the *Gambier Bay* and so threatened the whole Leyte landing operation would never sink another vessel or threaten anyone again. Admiral Kurita was supposed to maintain a "fleet in being" at Brunei Bay, but the Americans paid it almost no heed.

As for the airmen of VC-10, one by one they began making their way homeward. Ensign Crocker's TBM went from Dulag to one carrier then another. The orders were cut and the crew went home. Lieutenant Stewart went to the *Marcus Island,* and then to the *Kitkun Bay,* which carried him to Pearl Harbor. He finally sailed for San Francisco aboard the *Belleau Wood,* which had taken a kamikaze plane in the flight deck and had to go home for repairs.

Fred DiSipio, whose group had become separated from the other survivors of the *Gambier Bay,* spent many months in army and naval hospitals, and never encountered another survivor of the ship until his discharge from the navy in November 1945.

When the *Lurline* reached San Francisco, the enlisted men were taken to Treasure Island, and herded into a fenced security area. Through the fence Chief Montgomery bought a San Francisco newspaper and saw a picture of some sailors on liberty in San Francisco.

"Survivors of the Leyte Gulf sea battle on leave," said the caption. Montgomery looked around him at the real survivors and laughed bitterly.

Finally, however, the chiefs and the officers were taken into San Francisco to be re-outfitted, and they did get leave. The men of VC-10 and of the *Gambier Bay* parted company here, subject to different treatment. In the next few days most of the enlisted men were given survivor's leave and started home.

Commander Huxtable arrived in San Francisco and set up VC-10 headquarters in room 521 of the Sir Francis Drake hotel near Union Square. Other members of the squadron were at first scattered in hotels all over town: Lieutenant Pyzdrowski was at the Maurice; Lieutenant McClendon was at the Sir Francis Drake; and some were at the Mark Hopkins and the Fairmont. The pilots drank, chased girls, and went to see friends. Pyzdrowski went out to the Mare Island hospital to see Lt. (jg) Jesse Holleman, who was recovering from the wounds he received in the battle of Saipan. Then he went back to room 521, which was more saloon than headquarters. In five days the pilots had lined the baseboards of the room with empty bottles.

Commander Huxtable was in charge. Each newcomer was given a "sobriety test." He was handed a paper bag filled with water and told to hit a car five floors below.

About thirty percent of the pilots passed, but it did not matter. Each test was accompanied by another drink.

On the fifth day, Pyzdrowski appeared. They had run out of waterbags, but Huxtable gave Pyzdrowski a telephone book, pushed him to the window and told him to aim at a big black limousine that was just driving up. Pyzdrowski aimed.

"Release," shouted Huxtable. Pyzdrowski released, and the big fat San Francisco telephone directory made a very satisfactory "thwunk" as it hit the top of the black limousine. A chauffeur dashed out one side, and an old lady out the other.

Fifteen minutes later the manager of the Sir Francis Drake appeared and handed VC-10 its eviction notice. Lieutenant McClendon went up to the Fairmont to bunk with Commander Borries. Pyzdrowski and the others mooched around among their pals to find places to doss down. They were waiting for the reformation of the squadron before they could go on leave.

Finally it was done. On December 7, 1944, VC-10 was reorganized and the pilots were given thirty-day leaves before reporting to Oxnard, California, to train again and be assigned to a new carrier.

For the men of the *Gambier Bay*, as distinguished from the aviation squadron, there could be no such continuity. A warship and its crew become an entity, with a personality that transcends all individuals, but once the ship is gone, the personality disappears and only a group of individuals is left. That was how it was with the men of the *Gambier Bay*. After their leave they were scattered east and west, north and south, to join new ships and other units. Some returned to the carrier service and some did not. Captain Goodwin already had a new post and the sinking of the *Gambier Bay*, although a wrench, could not affect his career. Captain Vieweg went on to higher posts; the loss of his ship under the circumstances was no cause for censure. The other professionals moved on, and a handful of the reserves continued in the navy to become professionals, and some of them enjoyed distinguished careers. Lieutenant McClendon, in particular, rose to flag command in naval aviation, before he retired.

When the war ended in 1945, most of the men of the ship and its squadron returned to civilian life to follow some of the multifarious pursuits offered in America. From time to time a few of the survivors got together, and some of them kept up correspondence. They had, after all, a unique experience that none but these several hundred men could share. As they grew older and the war receded in their memories, they reached back to the exciting times aboard the *Gambier Bay* for nostalgia and for inspiration. The searing experience of the Battle of Leyte Gulf had left on all of them an indelible mark greater than many had earlier realized. Out of this shared recall came the idea of perpetuating the name of their ship and the memory of its brief but hectic life with the tragic, heroic circumstances of the death of the ship and their comrades. They also wanted to leave a record of the valuable services performed by the small carriers whose exploits were almost always overshadowed by the tales of the big carriers of the fleet. The big carriers fought the big battles, by and large, and the men of the planes and ships of the small carriers were left "in support" of landing actions and supply lines. But whether in the Atlantic, where the small carriers were used mostly in anti-submarine warfare, or in the Pacific, where they participated in the major invasions, the small carriers performed a most valuable service. Several were lost: the *Liscome Bay* most tragically in terms of lives, and the *St. Lo,* and the *Bismarck Sea,* and the *Ommaney Bay,* and, of course, the *Gambier Bay,* the only U.S. carrier ever sunk by naval gunfire.

When the men of the *Gambier Bay* get together they still tell the stories of their first reactions to the sight of those tripod masts that meant Japanese battleships bearing down on them. But for their own part, these men need have nothing but pride, for it will never be forgotten that when Admiral Kurita came down on the Americans, he believed he was facing fleet carriers, so fiercely did the "Kaiser coffins" fight. And when the engagement was ended, and Admiral Kurita turned away to pass the men of the sunken American vessels struggling in the water, the crew of the cruiser *Tone* came to attention as their ship slid past—for the Japanese knew they had indeed faced stalwart American carriers of the fleet.

> There were many heroes of those days and nights, and most of them remain unknown.
>
> —*E. P. Hoyt*

# *Appendix*

THE SECRETARY OF THE NAVY

WASHINGTON

The President of the United States takes pleasure in presenting the PRESIDENTIAL UNIT CITATION to

TASK UNIT SEVENTY-SEVEN POINT FOUR POINT THREE, consisting of the U.S.S. FANSHAW BAY and VC-68; U.S.S. GAMBIER BAY and VC-10; U.S.S. KALININ BAY and VC-3; U.S.S. KITKUN BAY and VC-5; U.S.S. SAINT LO and VC-65; U.S.S. WHITE PLAINS and VC-4; U.S.S. HOEL, U.S.S. J^HNSTON, U.S.S. HEERMANN, U.S.S. SAMUEL B. ROBERTS, U.S.S. RAYMOND, U.S.S. DENNIS and U.S.S. JOHN C. BUTLER

for service as set forth in the following

CITATION:

"For extraordinary heroism in action against powerful units of the Japanese Fleet during the Battle off Samar, Philippines, October 25, 1944. Silhouetted against the dawn as the Central Japanese Force steamed through San Bernardino Strait toward Leyte Gulf, Task Unit 77.4.3 was suddenly taken under attack by hostile cruisers on its port hand, destroyers on the starboard and battleships from the rear. Quickly laying down a heavy smoke screen, the gallant ships of the Task Unit waged battle fiercely against the superior speed and fire power of the advancing enemy, swiftly launching and rearming aircraft and violently zigzagging in protection of vessels stricken by hostile armor-piercing shells, anti-personnel projectiles and suicide bombers. With one carrier of the group sunk, others badly damaged and squadron aircraft courageously coordinating in the attacks by making dry runs over the enemy Fleet as the Japanese relentlessly closed in for the kill, two of the Unit's valiant destroyers and one destroyer escort charged the battleships point-blank and, expending their last torpedoes in desperate defense of the entire group, went down under the enemy's heavy shells as a climax to two and one half hours of sustained and furious combat. The courageous determination and the superb teamwork of the officers and men who fought the embarked planes and who manned the ships of Task Unit 77.4.3 were instrumental in effecting the retirement of a hostile force threatening our Leyte invasion operations and were in keeping with the highest traditions of the United States Naval Service."

For the President,

James Forrestal.

Secretary of the Navy

# The Men of the *Gambier Bay*

*(Shipmates killed in line-of-duty noted in † italics)*

AAGARD Albert
ABERCROMBIE Bill
ABEYTA Gilbert
ADAMS Telfer
AKERS Patrick
AKIN Bobby
ALBERS Fred
ALBERS William
ALGAUKIS Edward
ALLEN James
*†ALLEN Robin*
ALLEN Thomas
ALLISON Charles
*†ALM Frederick*
ALTERHOFEN Eugene
*†ALTIMAN Charles*
ALVIS Ralph
AMMON John
AMOS Carl
AMUNDSON Carl
ANDERSEN Ronald
ANDERSON Clayton
ANDERSON Doyle
ANDERSON Lars
ANDERSON Perry
ANDERSON Walter
ANDREWS Andrew
ARCHANGELI Dante
ARENDALL Eugene
ARNHART John
ARNOLD Bruce
ARNOLD Eugene
ARNOLD George
ARNOLD Jeff
*†ARPIN Louis*
ASHBY James
ATKINS James
ATWELL Maynard
AUSBORNE James
AUSLEY Elbert
AUSTIN Lawrence
AUSTIN Orville
AUSTIN Wesley
*†AVERILL Donald*
AVILA Ygnacio

*†BACON Jack*
BADGERO William
BAGLEY Earl
BAHR Marcus
*†BAILEY Rollie*
BAILEY William
BAKER George
BAKER Harry
BALDACCI Harold
BALDWIN Ira
BALL James
BALLINGER Richard
BALLOU William
BANISTER Erwin
BARBER Verle
BARNHAM Ellis
*†BARNETT Mearl*
BAROK Frank
BARONA Samuel
BARR Robert
BARRETT Marshall
BARROWS Robert
BARRY Gerald
BARTHLOW James
BARTLEY James
BASHE Henry
BASSETT Henry
BATES Ivory
BATTISHILL William
BAUER George

BAUGHMAN Donald
BEAIRD William
BECK Joseph
BECKER Donald
BECKER Edward
BECKETT George
BECKETT Glen
BEHAN Robert
BEISANG Albert
BELCOURE Robert
BELL Hugh
BELL Richard
BELL Robert
†*BELL Vereen*
BENCE Hobert
BENDER Earl
BENDER Robert
BENNETT Darrell
BENNETT Frank
BENNETT Paul
BENOIT Artel
BEQUETTE Robert
†*BERDAHL Alfred*
BERGMAN Raymond
BERLANGA Salvador
†*BERNING Leslie*
†*BERRY John*
BERRYMAN Edwin
BERVEN Harold
BESAU Frank
BIANCO Dominick
BIANCONI Romeo
BILLER Rudolph
BILLINGSLEY Oscar
BISBEE George
†*BISHOP Floyd*
†*BLAKE Glenn*
BLAKER Edward
BLANEY Donald
BLANFORD Donald
BLOCKER Richard
BOLTINGHOUSE Leonard
BONANATA Aldo
BONNER Henry
BONNETT Kenneth
BORDT Robert
BOREN Edward
BORRIES Fred
BOSTONI Samuel
BOUNDS William
BOUVIA Frederick
†*BOWERS John*
BOYD William
BRADFORD Everett
BRADSHAW Perman
BRENNER Charles
BRETZ William
BRIDGES Edward
BRIDGES Roy
BRITT John
BROD Raymond
BROWN Garland
BROWN Herman
BROWN Joseph
†*BROWN Kenneth*
†*BROWN McLain*
BROWN Murray
†*BROWN Scott*
BRUNETTE Kenneth
BRUSCATTO Joseph
BRYAN James
BUCKNER Zenas
†*BUDERUS William*
BUEHLER George
†*BUFORD John*
BURGER Fletcher
BURGIN Hulin
BURNEY Ernest
BURNS Edgar
BURNS Roy
BURTSCHER John
BUTLER Jack
†*BUTTRY Robert*
BUTTS Leslie
BUTZ Walter
BYRNE Howard
CAIN Simpson
†*CAMBRA Edward*
CAMERON Daniel
CAMP William
CAMPBELL Melton
CAMPBELL Thomas
CAMPION Thomas
CANADY James
CANE Glenn
CANTEY Henry
CARITHERS William
CARLSEN Verner
CAROTHERS Lloyd
CARROUCHE Maurice
CARTER Emmitt
CARTER Nick
†*CASE Leonard*
CASE Phillip
CASSARO Joseph
CHAPMAN Lawrence
CHICK Clarence
†*CHOATE Howard*
†*CHRISTENSEN Julius*
CHRISTENSEN Vernon
CLANCY Thomas
CLARK Lawrence
CLARKE Donald
CLARKSON Charles
CLAVELL Thomas
CLAYTON Donald
CLEMENTS Harold
CLEMETSON Clair
CLOSSON Lester
COLE Marvin
†*COLE Norman*
COLEMAN Edward
†*COLLINS Paul*
COMBS Donald
CONE Herschel

CONKLIN Frank
CONNICK R. M.
CONRAD Carl
COOK Edward
COOK Frank
COOK Ira
CORBELLO Clyde
CORDNER William
COURTNEY Ernest
COVINGTON Elbert
COWAN Roy
*†COWLES Marion*
COX Virgil
CRANE Chester
CRANE Donald
CRANTRA Cesare
*†CRAWFORD George*
CRAWFORD John
*†CRAWFORD William*
CREAMER Donald
CRESS Nicholas
CRISWELL Louis
CROCKER Robert
CROOM Herman
CROSS Russell
CROSTICK Barnett
CROUCH Charles
CROUSE Glenn
CRUSE Keith
CUMING William
CUNNINGHAM Harry
CURTIN Murray
CURTIN Neale

*†DAHLEN Walter*
DAHLSTROM Birger
DALEY James
DALGARN Harlan
DALTON John
DANIELS Robert
DAVIS Floyd
*†DAVIS J. C.*
DAVIS Robert
DAVIS Robert
DAY Jesse
DeBERARDINIS James
DEDRICK Charles
DEEL Wallace
*†DEERY Robert*
DEFFENBAUGH Berman
DEHN Harold
DELACY Robert
DELGADO Charles
DENEEF William
DENNARD Hillard
DENNIN Thomas
DeSHAW Leonard
*†DEVINE Harold*
DEVOLL Robert
DICHARRY Verne
DICKERSON Cloyd
DILL Melvin
DILLARD Berham
DiPIETRO Raymond
DiSIPIO Alfred
DISTEL Edward
DITTENHAFER John
DITTMAN Charles
DOMAN John
DOMROES Elmer
DONNELLEY John
DOPSON Kenneth
DOSH James
DUCHENE Robert
DUDLEY Richard
DUGAN Charles
DUGAN William
DUGGIN William
DUNFORD Samuel
DUNHAM Bill
DUNN John
DUQUETTE Carl
DURKOP George
DZUIK Rodney

EALEY Emmitt
EARLE Ausbie
ECHARD Charles
ECKE James
*†EDMONDSON Joseph*
EDMUNDS William
EDWARDS Robert
EELMAN Fred
ELKINS Kenneth
ELLEDGE Elfred
ELLEDGE Ray
ELLIOTT Richard
ELLISON Paul
ELWOOD Charles
EMBLEM Olaf
EMERSON Harold
EMERSON John
EMERY Clarence
EMMENGGER Oscar
ENGEL Franklin
ENGLE James
EPPING Lawrence
ERICKSON Stanley
ERNCE Wilson
ERWIN Bernard
ERWIN John
EVENVOLD George
EVINS Thomas

FALK Fred
FANT Braxton
FANT John
FATHREE Charles
FAULS Gerald
*†FAUST Anthony*
FAUST Donald
FEATHER James
FELIZ George
FETKENHIER Earl
*†FINCH George*
FINLEY George
*†FISH Joe*
FITCH Virgil
FLANDERS Walter
FLATLEY William
FLEISCHER Harold
FLOOD Lorne

FLORIDA Reginald
FLYNN Myron
FOLEY Robert
†*FORAN Harvey*
†*FORSYTHE John*
†*FRANKLIN Edmund*
FRANKLIN Lamoyne
FREDENBURGH Vernon
FREEMAN George
FUDGE Harry

GAGNON Mark
GALEY Wayne
†*GALLAGHER William*
GALLAHER Harold
GALLOWAY William
GALPIN William
†*GARDNER Rudolph*
GARMAN Harold
GRAZA Rudy
GAUL Robert
GAUVAIN Joseph
GAWLIK John
GELLHORN George
GELUZ Ernesto
GENDRON Leo
GEORGE Daniel
†*GEPPELT Robert*
GETZENDANNER, J. W.
†*GIBSON Maurice*
GIGER Lee
GILLEYLEN Essie
GILLIAM Henry
†*GILLIATT Dean*
†*GIMAN Clinton*
GITLIN Allen
GJESTVANG Conrad
GOBBI Joseph
GOFF Gaydie
GOFORTH John
GONZALES James
GOODWIN Hugh
GORDON Homer
GORRELL Lee
GORRY Thomas
GRABOS Fred
GRAFF Julius
GRAHAM Jack
GRAMM Paul
GRANT Ralph
†*GRAY Frank*
GREEN Floyd
GREEN Joseph
GREGORY Harold
GREIST Richard
GREENFIELD Watson
GROSS John
GUELICH Robert
GUETZLAFF William
GUMANSKI Walter
GUNN Robert
GUNSALLUS Clyde
GUNTER Leslie
GUTZWEILER Jerome
GWINN Harry

HAAS Ernest
HAGERTY Edward
HALL Sam
HALL Travis
HAMLET Buck
HAMMOND James
†*HANNA John*
HARDERS Herman
HARRELL Morris
HARRINGTON Francis
HARRIS Lawrence
HART Eugene
HART Samuel
HARTER Leon
HARTIN Albert
HARTLEY Harold
†*HARTSOC James*
HARTUNG Robert
HASHEM Fred
HASS Ernest
HATFIELD Marvin
†*HATHEWAY Ivan*
HAWKINS Carlton
HAWKINS Jack
HAWLEY John
HEAD Max
HEALD Thomas
HEARELL James
HEATH Forrest
HECK William
HEGLAND Arnold
HEINL Charles
†*HENDERSON* James
†*HENRY Wilfred*
HERD Joseph
HERIC Edward
†*HERTENSTEIN Arthur*
HESS Stanley
HESSON Earl
HEUER Howard
HEWITT William
HIGHSMITH Claude
HILLMAN Hubert
HINES William
HOBBS Bishop
HODGSON W. F.
HOFFMAN Robert
HOFFPAUIR Cornelius
HOLLAND Charles
HOLLAND James
†*HOLLAND James*
HOLLAND John
HOLLEMAN Boyce
HOLLOWAY Gordon
†*HOLLY Leonard*
†*HOLT Leo*
HOLT Leslie
HOOD Robert
†*HOOKS Carson*
HOOVER Arthur

HOPE John
HOPKINS Edward
HOPKINSON Joseph
†*HORN William*
HORTON Charles
HOSEA David
HOULIHAN John
HOULIHAN Kingston
HOUSMAN Calvin
HOVELAND Walter
HOWALD Christensen
HOWARD George
HOWE Winthrop
HUGHES Frank
HUNT Edward
HUNTING Charles
HUNTLEY Donald
HUXTABLE Edward

INGRAM Clarence
IRICK Lyndle
IVERSON Nordeen
IVIE John

JACKSON James
JACKSON Jesse
†*JACKSON John*
JAGGERS Lincoln
JAGIELSKI Albert
JANZ Allen
JARCIK Emil
JAROSZ Silvester
†*JARRELL Harvey*
JENNINGS Arthur
JENNINGS Wilbert
JENSEN Donald
JENSEN Robert
†*JOHNS Otto*
JOHNSON Allen
JOHNSON Ernest
JOHNSON George
JOHNSON James
JOHNSON Marion
JOHNSON Sam
JOHNSON Seymour
JOHNSON Tim
†*JOHNSON William*
JOHNSTON Dwight
JONES Alfred
JONES Calvin
JONES Carl
JONES Darold
JONES Evan
JONES Hilton
JONES James
JONES John
†*JORDAN Robert*
JUDD Andrew
JURGENSEN Robert

†*KALBE Walter*
†*KAMATS Mike*
KAMINSKY Ernest
KAMMER Walter
KANASKI Adam
KAPPY Frank
†*KEENAN John*
KEHLENBECK Robert
KEITH Sanford
KELLER Fred
KELLY Moss
KELLY Ralph
KELLY Thomas
KENNEDY Leslie
KENYON Erwin
KERR James
KETCHAM William
KILLION Joseph
KIMBALL Joseph
†*KIMBALL Sidney*
†*KIRK Bob*
KLEIN Laverlin
†*KLOTKOWSKY Henry*
KLUCHAR George
KNIGHT Leroy
†*KNIGHT Robert*
KOFFLER Frank
KOHRT Forrest
KOLODY Peter
KOLTONIAK Robert
KOPECKY Joseph
KOPPALA Carl
KOSER Douglas
KOTKOWSKI Raymond
†*KOZLOWSKI George*
KRANTZ Randall
KREYMER Donald
KRIDA Robert
KRIEGER Charles
KROGER William
KRUMREY Donald
KRZEMECKI Alfons
KRZEMECKI Edward
KUBICHECK Albert
KUIKSTRA Henry
KUSTER Merrill
KYNE Vincent

LaBARBARA Joseph
LAMAR John
LAMB Russell
LAMBERT Mayron
LAMP Raymond
LANCHSWERDT Alphonse
LAND William
LANGLEY William
LARIZA Castor
LARA Manuel
†*LARKIN Joseph*
LaROCCO Paul
LARSON Robert
LASHLEY William
†*LAURN Alvin*
LEACH Richard
LEE Edro
LEE Homer
LEE Jesse
LeFERR Henry
LEGATH George

LEHNHERR William
†*LEMAIRE John*
LEMASTER Glenn
LEMIRANDE John
LEONGUERRERO Mario
LEVERTON Kenneth
LEWANDOWSKI John
†*LEWIS Angelo*
LEWIS Eugene
LEWIS Frank
LEWIS Lionel
LEWIS Ralph
LEY Frederick
LIGHTWINE Lee
LILLER Chester
LINDLEY Jack
LINDOW Andrew
LISCHER James
LITTLEFORD Elmer
LIVERLY Thomas
LLOYD Butler
LOATS Norman
LOCK Jack
LOFTHOUSE Richard
LONG Harry
LOONEY William
LOPEZ Alfredo
LOPEZ Freddie
LORENZ Theodore
LOUGHERY Edward
LOVETT John
LOVILL George
LOWE Claudius
LOWE James
LOZANDO Charles
†*LUCCHESI Louis*
LUCE Bob
LUDWIG Leonard
LUKER Frederick
LUSTER Carl
LYERLY William
LYNCH William
MacDONALD Kenneth
MacFADDEN Harold
MACKEY Walter
MADISON Charles
MAHER Wesley
MAKI Alvin
MALIN Douglas
MALLGRAVE Fred
MANISCALCO August
MANNING Ennis
MANTZ Joseph
MARSH Theodore
MARSHALL Leonard
†*MARSHALL Walter*
MARTIN Eugene
MARTIN Fred
†*MARTIN Leonard*
MARTIN Richard
MARTIN William
MARTINDALE Daniel
MATALAS William
MAY Raymond
MAYBERRY William
†*MAYES Morrison*
MAYRANT Lowell
McARDLE James
McCABE Bernard
McCASLIN Frank
McCLELLAND Henry
McCLENDON Donald
McCLENDON William
McCOLLUM Lee
McCORMICK Chester
McCOY Dale
McCOY Ernest
McCRORY John
McCUAN William
McDANIEL Lee
†*McDONOUGH Thomas*
McGRAW Joseph
McKNIGHT Earl
†*McLAUGHLIN Henry*
McLAUGHLIN Kenneth
McLENNAN Edward
McMILLAN Lee
McNAMEE Carlos
McQUADE Joseph
McWATERS Marlyn
MEACHAM Addis
MEADE Robert
†*MENTLICK William*
MERTENS Edmund
MESSENGER Orville
MEYER Delbert
MICANKO Edward
MICHAELS James
MICHELSON Gordon
MIDDLETON Delos
MILLER Charles
†*MILLER George*
MILLER George
MILLER Gerald
MILLER Lloyd
MILLER Wayne
MILNER Arthur
MINCEY Wyner
MINKIN Marcus
MITCHELL Marshall
MOEL Dean
MOESCHLER Harold
MOFFA Anthony
MONAHAN Robert
MONTGOMERY Morris
MOORE Carl
MOORE Robert

MORAN Edward
MORELAND William
MORGAN Benjamin
MORINGSTAR Richard
MORRIS John
†*MUDD Raymond*
†*MUNTZ Eugene*
†*MURRAY Eugene*
MURRAY Kenneth
MUSE William

NAPIER Joe
†*NASLUND Lage*
NATALE Daniel
NEELEY Leroy
NEIL Clifford
NELSON Phillip
NELSON Robert
NEUGART Kenneth
NEWTON James
NEWTON William
NIBLACK Arthur
NOLAN William
NORRIS Leslie
NUCCI Louis
NUSS Kenneth
NYSTROM Lowell

O'BRIEN Harvey
ODUM Rannie
OLIVER James
O'LOUGHLIN Kenneth
O'NEIL John
ORAM George
OREWYLER Jack
ORTIZ Jose
OSTERKORN Edwin
OSWALD George
OWEN Louis
OWRE Leslie

PADDOCK Robert
PARKER Artemas
PARKER Harold
PARKER Robert
†*PARMANTJE John*
PARR Arthur
PARRISH Monroe
PATE Jack
PATTERSON James
PATTERSON Joseph
PAULSON Roger
PAYER Francis
PAYNTER George
PEACORE Lawrence
PERON Darrel
PERONE Joseph
PERRY Harry
PERSON Richard
PESHINSKI Carl
PETERMAN Orval
PETERS John
PETERSON Arnold
PETERSON Clarence
PETERSON Oliver
PETERSON Robert
PETTIT Grover
PETROSINO Ernest
PETTIBONE Irving
PETTYS Myron
PEXA Raymond
PHILLIPS Grover
PHILLIPS Horace
PHILLIPS H. T.
PHILLIPS Rockford
PHILLIPS William
†*PHIPPS John*
PIA Louis
PICKERAL Acie
PIETRZAK Edmund
†*PILGRIM Edward*
PILGRIM Henry
PINCH Richard
PIPKIN William
†*PITTMAN Everett*
PITTS Albert
PLATNER Robert
PLEASANT James
POLANSKY Charles
POLITO Dominick
POLLOCK Preston
POMYKALSKI Frank
POOLE Ray
PORTER Ben
POTOCHNIAK Anthony
POTTER John
POWELL Robert
POWER Stewart
POWERS James
†*PRIBISKI Mike*
PRIHODKA Jack
PRIVETTE Herman
PROFITT David
†*PROKOP Edward*
PROPES Orville
PROSPER Vincent
PRUITT Charles
†*PRUITT Forrest*
PUGH James
PUSCHERT William
PYZDROWSKI Henry

QUINN Chenry
QUINN Thomas

RAAB Harry
RACINE Edward
RADER W. W.
RADTKE Floyd
RAE P. P.
RAGUSA Anthony
RANE Thomas
RANKIN William
†*RANSOME Larry*
†*RAWLINGS Cecil*
RAY Allen
RAY Romaine
RAYMAKER William
†*RAYMOND Ralph*

RAYMOND Arthur
REAMS Wayne
REED Eugene
REID J. A.
REYNDERS Donald
†*REYNOLDS Homer*
REYNOLDS Howard
RHINES Samuel
RHODA Joseph
RICCIARDI Vincent
RICE Louis
RICH Cecil
RICH David
†*RICHARDS James*
†*RICHARDSON Hubert*
RICHIE Chester
RING Cletus
RITCHEY Floyd
†*RIVERS Howard*
†*RIZZO Charles*
ROACH John
ROBERTS Martin
ROBERTSON Neal
ROBINSON Keith
ROBINSON Robert
ROBINSON Roy
ROBY Richard
ROCK Cortland
ROGGE Carlton
ROSE Keith
ROSE Thornton
ROSE Victor
ROSINSKY Henry
ROSS James
ROSS Robert
ROTH Albert
ROURKE John
ROUSE Harry
†*RUFFIN Reginald*
RUNNELS Fred
RUSSELL Joseph
RUTH Eugene
RYAN Donald
RYCHLAK John
†*SABOVIK John*
SACKS Murray
†*SAINTS George*
SANDERS James
SANDERS Klim
†*SANDERSON J. P.*
SANKEY August
SCHAEFFER Edward
SCHAERER Curtis
SCHAFFNER Harold
SCHEER Lawrence
SCHIELE Donald
SCHIFFER Vernon
SCHLICTER Charles
SCHMIDT Henry
SCHMITZ Bernard
†*SCHNEIDERJAN Dan*
SCHREURS Harvey
SEEVER Clarence
SEITZ Eugene
SELDERS Dan
SENDELBECK Paul
SEVCIK Frank
SEVESTRE Frank
†*SEYMOUR Hovey*
SHANNON Maxwell
SHARP William
SHARRER William
SHEFLIN Robert
SHEPHERD Robert
SHERROD James
†*SHIPLEY Roger*
SHIPP Raymond
SHIVELY Franklin
SHLESMAN Aaron
†*SHORT Edward*
SHOWERS Merle
SHRADER John
†*SHRIVER Warren*
SHROYER William
SICA Peter
†*SICKERMAN Burton*
SIGLER Robert
SILL Jacob
SINGER Laurel
†*SKAGGS Ralph*
SKOW Leslie
SLONE William
SLYCORD Jack
†*SMEHYL Charles*
SMITH Albert
SMITH Albert J.
SMITH Carroll
†*SMITH Ernest*
SMITH Frank
SMITH Harold
SMITH James
SMITH Leodia
SMITH Marvin
SMITH Robert
SMITH Thomas
SMITH Vernon
SMITH Warren
†*SMITH William*
†*SMURDA John*
SMYDEN Joseph
SORIANO Roy
SPANDLE Louis
SPARROW Weldon
SPAULDING George
SPEIRS Clarence
SPENCER Earl
SPIERS William
SROKA John
STAFFORD John
STAMPS Paul
STANTON Donald
STRAK Joseph
STEDMAN Robert
STEEVES Havelock
STEVENS Robert
STEWART Aaron
STEWART Jack
STEWART John
†*STEWART Wayne*
ST. GERMAIN Norman
STINSON Robert
STOCK Edward
STOCKS Charles

†*STONE Harold*
†*STONER Lyle*
STOW Walter
†*STRAITON James*
STRINGER Warren
STUCINSKI Florian
†*STURDY William*
SUBERS Jack
SULLIVAN Kenneth
SWEENEY E. J.
SWIECICKI Arthur
SYLVESTER George
SYVERTSEN Harry

TALLEY Richard
TANNEHILL Thomas
TARATKO Lester
TAYLOR A. Jr.
TAYLOR Donald
TAYLOR Joseph
TAYLOR Wilbur
†*TELLIER Leslie*
TERWILLIGER Edgar
TETZ John
TEULKER Alva
THERRY Arthur
†*THOMAS Harrell*
THOMPSON Bert
THOMPSON F. L.
THOMPSON Kenneth
THOMPSON Leonard
THOMPSON Paul
THORSELL Roland
THUMB Ward
TODD Edward
TOOMEY Andrew
TOPCZEWSKI Donald
TOVREA John
TOWSTIK Michael
TRAINOR Norbert
TRAPANI Eugene
TRAPP Harold
†*TREECE Otis*
TREMMELL Louis
TRIBBETT Raymond
TURNER John
TURNER Maurice
TURNER Robert
TUTCHTONE John

UBBINK James
ULBRIGHT Marvin

VAN PATTEN Clyde
VERICH Alexander
VESPY William
VEST William
VIEWIG Walter
VLACH Vincent
VOGAN James

WADE George
WADER Dave
WALKER Lowell
WALKER Stuart
†*WALL Theodore*
WALLACE Robert
WALLACE Wesley
WALTHER Virgil
WARING Elmer
WARN John
WARREN Aubrey
WATKINS Harry
WAUGH Roy
WAXLER Roscoe
WEATHERHOLT Robert
WEBB Wayne
WEIDENKELLER Bill
†*WEISS Freddie*
WELLS Waldo
WEST Robert
WESTBROOK Charles
WHEELER Owen
WHIPPLE James
†*WHITE Edgar*
WHITE Hugh
WHITE Robert
WHITNEY Kendall
†*WHITTED Raymond*
WICKERSHAM Charles
†*WILDER Paul*
WILDERMAN Ralph
WILDES Stanley
WILKINSON James
WILLIAMS Donald
WILLIAMS Harris
WILLIAMS Joe
†*WILLIAMS Junior*
WILLIAMS Roy
WILLIAMS Thomas
WILSON George
WINSHIP Donald
WINTER Delbert
WISE Myron
WITT Turman
WOOD Clifford
WOOD Joseph
WOOD Kenneth
†*WOLLAND Manuel*
WRIGHT Walter

YARBROUGH Cullen
YARNO Harvey
YOUNG Robert
YOUNG Winston

ZAHUMENSKY Frank
ZALEWSKI Charles
ZANETELL Lawrence
†*ZANON William*
ZEOLA Leo
ZIMMERMAN John
ZINK John
ZORN Calvin
ZUBE John
ZUBBRICK George
ZUCKERMAN Alex

# *Notes*

The author owes an enormous debt to Henry Pyzdrowski who "bird-dogged" the research for most of the survivor's tales that appear in the text. Rannie Odum's biographical notes were extremely valuable also, particularly for the early days at Astoria and in the shakedown cruises. Rear Adm. William McClendon, USN (ret.), was very helpful in answering questions and in giving time for an interview at Pearl Harbor. Admiral Thomas Moorer supplied official information from the navy files and copies of correspondence with the brother of Capt. Walter Vieweg. As always, Dr. Dean Allard, head of the navy's Operational Archives section at the Navy Historical Center in the Washington Navy Yard, was helpful in supplying action reports, war diaries, and interviews with survivors. J. V. Hammond's typed article on the "Life and Death of the U.S.S. *Gambier Bay*" was useful in several respects. His account of the sinking and the time in the water filled in several holes. Dean Baughman of Wenatchee, Washington, supplied an account of the activities of the sister ship, *Kitkun Bay*, which was useful, as were Bob Wallis's recollections that were published by him and the Natoma Bay CVE Association in the *Log Book* and the *Scuttlebutt* quarterly. Rear Adm. Richard Ballinger, USN (ret.), shared reminiscences in a telephone conversation with Henry Pyzdrowski who passed them to me. Tony Potochniak wrote a detailed biographical sketch of his life on the ship, as did Chief Walter Flanders. Charles Heinl's biography was useful for material about the ship and a number of the members of the crew. Assistant Air Officer Elmo Waring provided a study of his sphere of operations. Lt. Cdr. Leon Fletcher, USN (ret.), prepared for *Old Shipmates,* the *Gambier Bay* association magazine, a play-by-play account of the rescue of the survivors that was most useful.

Charles Westbrook, one of the air crewmen, gave a good account of life in VC-10 for the air crews. Captain Edward J. Huxtable, USN (ret.), prepared an account of his activities. So did John Stewart, leader of the fighter contingent. Henry Pyzdrowski wrote a complete study of his naval career. Captain Leo Zeola, USN (ret.), did the same. James Lischer made available his letters home, which were most revealing. From the U.S. Navy's files came Ballinger's report of the sinking of the *Gambier Bay,* which he wrote as executive officer.

William R. Cuming prepared an account of his life as a radar officer aboard the carrier. Al Beisang, the assistant navigator, did the same and so did Birger Dahlstrom, the helmsman. Quartermaster Hugh Bell's diary, written in the heat of the moment, recreates emotions and attitudes as well as giving facts. Louise Bassett prepared a paper she called "Memories," which told something of the lives of the women who stayed behind when their men went to war in the *Gambier Bay*. The Rev. Verner Carlsen wrote a reminiscence which was useful.

Attorney Edward Hagerty made available a term paper he had written on life aboard the ship for a college course shortly after the war. J. W. Patterson, Jr., sent a diary of the spring and summer months of 1944. Rannie Odum produced several records, one about his early days in the navy and those of the carrier, one about the various divisions of the ship, and one about the Leyte battle, the sinking, and the time in the water.

The official navy history of the *Gambier Bay* was helpful. Richard Dudley, an air crewman, also wrote a series of his impressions. Jesse Holleman provided a portion of a speech he made at a *Gambier Bay* reunion.

Captain Vieweg's narrative of the last battle is a part of the official navy record of the ship. Don Blaney, who was Commander Huxtable's air crewman, wrote his impressions of that last air battle. Berman Deffenbaugh prepared some interesting notes on his experiences as bugler.

Chenry C. Quinn contributed reminiscences, including the tale of his operation of the dice game in the potato locker. Al Johnson, a ship's photographer, wrote vivid accounts of the sinking.

Ship's Whaleboat Coxswain Jack Butler shared some reminiscences of his time aboard the carrier. Richard Elliott produced the commissioning issue of the *Gambier Bay*'s monthly tabloid. Fred Mallgrave provided a copy of the March 1944 issue of the monthly newspaper "FULL THROTTLE," which tells a good deal about various departments of the ship. Lawrence Barber of Portland, Oregon, provided many statistics and news clippings given him by the Kaiser Shipbuilding Company. Various copies of the *Gambier Bay* veterans association's magazine, *Old Shipmates,* published by its historian Tony Potochniak, produced tidbits and vignettes about the small carrier and life aboard her.

Vice Admiral Hugh H. Goodwin, USN (ret.), had a long tape-recorded conversation with Henry Pyzdrowski several years before this book was written, and it was extremely useful to the author. Admiral Goodwin once considered writing the book himself, as did Rannie Odum; both decided against it. This enthusiasm undoubtedly sparked the rest of the men of the *Gambier Bay* to foster the project at this time of their life.

> ". . . a spark in the great blue motion of the sunlit sea,
> yea, some of them do sparkle . . ."
>
> —*Camelot.*

# Bibliography

BOOKS

Morison, Samuel Eliot. *United States Naval Operations in World War II*. Vol. VIII, New Guinea and the Marianas. Boston: Little, Brown and Company, 1953. Vol. XII Leyte. 1958.

Millot, Bernard. *Divine Thunder*. New York: McCall Publishing Co., 1971.

Hoyt, Edwin P. *How They Won the War in the Pacific*, New York: Weybright and Talley, 1970.

*The Battle of Leyte Gulf*. New York: Weybright and Talley, 1972.

Jensen, Oliver. *Carrier War*. New York: Pocket Books, 1945.

Pratt, Fletcher. *Fleet Against Japan*. New York: Harper and Bros., 1943.

Gilbert, Price. *The Escort Carriers in Action*. Atlanta: Ruralist Press, 1945.

*The Kaiser Story*, published by the Kaiser Industries Corporation, Oakland.

MAGAZINES

United States Naval Institute Proceedings. "The Cinderella Carriers." August, 1976.

"Old Shipmates," various issues.

Bupers. "They Ran—But Won." January, 1945.

*Time,* October 26, 1959.
"Oak Leaf" (Naval Supply Depot Oakland) account of the *Gambier Bay.*

NEWSPAPERS

The *Chicago Tribune.* 1944.
The *Philadelphia Inquirer.* 1944.
The *San Francisco Chronicle.* December, 1944.
The *Vancouver Shipyard News* (undated). Account of the Battle of Leyte Gulf.
The *Southern Illinoisian.* October 1944.
*St. Louis Globe-Democrat.* October, 1944.

# Index

Note: The names of the men of the *Gambier Bay* are listed in this index in capital letters.